CW01091594

COLLABORATIVE COACHING
FOR DISCIPLINARY LITERACY

Also Available

The Common Core Coaching Book:
Strategies to Help Teachers Address the K–5 ELA Standards
Laurie Elish-Piper and Susan K. L'Allier

Collaborative Coaching for Disciplinary Literacy

STRATEGIES TO SUPPORT TEACHERS
IN GRADES 6–12

Laurie Elish-Piper
Susan K. L'Allier
Michael Manderino
Paula Di Domenico

THE GUILFORD PRESS
New York   London

Copyright © 2016 The Guilford Press
A Division of Guilford Publications, Inc.
370 Seventh Avenue, Suite 1200, New York, NY 10001
www.guilford.com

All rights reserved

Except as indicated, no part of this book may be reproduced, translated, stored in a retrieval system,
or transmitted, in any form or by any means, electronic, mechanical, photocopying, microfilming,
recording, or otherwise, without written permission from the publisher.

Printed in the United States of America

This book is printed on acid-free paper.

Last digit is print number: 9   8   7   6   5   4   3   2   1

LIMITED DUPLICATION LICENSE

These materials are intended for use only by qualified professionals.

The publisher grants to individual purchasers of this book nonassignable permission to reproduce
all materials for which permission is specifically granted in a footnote. This license is limited to
you, the individual purchaser, for personal use or use with individual students. This license does
not grant the right to reproduce these materials for resale, redistribution, electronic display, or
any other purposes (including but not limited to books, pamphlets, articles, video- or audiotapes,
blogs, file-sharing sites, Internet or intranet sites, and handouts or slides for lectures, workshops,
or webinars, whether or not a fee is charged). Permission to reproduce these materials for these
and any other purposes must be obtained in writing from the Permissions Department of Guilford
Publications.

Library of Congress Cataloging-in-Publication Data

Names: Elish-Piper, Laurie, author. | L'Allier, Susan K., author. |
    Manderino, Michael, author. | Domenico, Paula Di, author.
Title: Collaborative coaching for disciplinary literacy : strategies to
    support teachers in grades 6–12 / Laurie Elish-Piper, Susan K. L'Allier,
    Michael Manderino, Paula Di Domenico
Description: New York : The Guilford Press, a division of Guilford Publications,
    Inc., [2016] | Includes bibliographical references and index.
Identifiers: LCCN 2015032641 | ISBN 9781462524389 (acid-free paper)
Subjects: LCSH: Language arts teachers—In-service training—United States |
    Language arts (Middle school)—United States. | Language arts
    (Secondary)—United States. | Language arts—Correlation with content
    subjects—United States. | Content area reading—United States. | Reading
    (Middle school)—United States. | Reading (Secondary)—United States.
Classification: LCC LB2844.1.R4 E55 2016 | DDC 428.0071/2—dc23
LC record available at *http://lccn.loc.gov/2015041548*

About the Authors

Laurie Elish-Piper, PhD, is Acting Dean of the College of Education at Northern Illinois University, where she also holds the titles of Distinguished Teaching Professor and Presidential Engagement Professor in the Department of Literacy and Elementary Education. Her research and teaching focus on literacy leadership and coaching, and she has published and presented widely on literacy coaching at the elementary, middle, and high school levels. Dr. Elish-Piper has worked extensively with school districts to develop and implement literacy coaching programs, and she teaches graduate courses related to literacy coaching and leadership. She has coauthored eight books, including *The Common Core Coaching Book* (with Susan K. L'Allier). Formerly, she worked as a middle school reading and language arts teacher and as an educational therapist in a clinical setting.

Susan K. L'Allier, EdD, is Associate Professor and Coordinator of the Reading Program in the Department of Literacy and Elementary Education at Northern Illinois University. She and Laurie Elish-Piper have conducted multiple research studies to examine the relationship between literacy coaching and student literacy achievement. In addition to their journal articles, chapters, and presentations about literacy coaching, they have published a video "workshop in a box" titled *The Literacy Coaching Series,* which enables viewers to see and analyze interactions between literacy coaches and teachers. Formerly, Dr. L'Allier worked as an elementary teacher, a lead teacher, and a principal.

Michael Manderino, PhD, is Assistant Professor in the Department of Literacy and Elementary Education at Northern Illinois University. He has presented widely with Laurie Elish-Piper, Susan K. L'Allier, and Paula Di Domenico on disciplinary literacy coaching at the secondary level. He coauthored a book on content-area learning and has published articles on disciplinary literacy in leading journals. He received dissertation awards from the Literacy Research Association and the Association of Literacy Educators and Researchers. Dr. Manderino also works closely with school districts to implement disciplinary literacy in the curriculum and teaches undergraduate and graduate courses related to disciplinary literacy. Formerly, he was a high school history teacher and disciplinary literacy coach.

Paula Di Domenico, EdD, is a secondary disciplinary literacy coach at Leyden High School District 212 in Franklin Park, Illinois, and serves as an adjunct instructor of graduate courses in literacy education at Northern Illinois University and at Lewis University in Romeoville, Illinois. Her research focuses on teachers' disciplinary literacy knowledge and on secondary literacy coaching. Dr. Di Domenico has presented on the topic of disciplinary literacy coaching with the other authors of this volume. Formerly, she was a high school English and developmental reading teacher.

Preface

For the past several years, we have worked as a team with literacy coaches and teachers in secondary schools to address the teaching and learning demands associated with the discipline-specific literacy instruction that is integral to today's standards. In this work, we were often met with comments such as "You should put these ideas into a book" or "Is this all written down somewhere so I can refer back to it?" This book is our attempt to share the insights, best practices, strategies, and words of wisdom that we've learned in our work coaching teachers in the disciplines, supporting coaches in middle and high schools, and conducting research.

It's a well-known fact that today's teachers are faced with increased demands to make sure their students are "college and career ready." Traditional models of professional development simply are not sufficient to help these teachers update and enhance their practice. Although literacy coaching has been well documented in the professional literacy field and lots of "how-to" books are available for elementary literacy coaches, the notion of coaching teachers in the disciplines at the middle and high school levels is fairly new. Furthermore, disciplinary literacy coaching, although promising, is fraught with challenges that require new and different approaches to coaching that move beyond what has been done in elementary schools. This book is our attempt to address these issues and provide a readable research-based resource for literacy coaches and leaders in middle and high school settings. In addition, this book offers guidance for professionals who are studying or who aspire to take on literacy coaching responsibilities in middle and high schools.

In this book, we propose a model of coaching that foregrounds the disciplines and helps teachers leverage the reading, writing, listening, speaking, and thinking skills needed to learn in their content areas. Furthermore, we demonstrate how a three-layered approach allows coaches to work efficiently and effectively with teachers in the disciplines of science, social studies, and English language arts. We provide 17 practical coaching strategies that you can implement immediately with the teachers in your school. We offer step-by-step instructions, as well as examples of real coaches and teachers implementing each of the strategies. We also provide profiles of seven highly effective disciplinary literacy coaches to show how they have addressed (and overcome) some of the biggest and most common challenges they faced in their work.

It is our sincere hope that you will find this book to be a useful road map and toolbox of resources to draw on as you continue or begin your journey in disciplinary literacy coaching. We also hope it offers you reassurance and encouragement, and helps you find patience and perseverance as you engage in the types of heavy coaching necessary to make sure students (and teachers) are ready to meet learning standards designed to prepare students for college and career.

Acknowledgments

We would like to acknowledge the support of Dr. Mikkel Storaasli and Leyden District 212's administrative team for allowing us to study the coaching program over several years. Further, we extend our thanks to Leyden's teachers who participated in numerous coaching studies and whose collaboration with coaches allowed us to develop and test many of the coaching strategies shared in this book. We are also grateful to the exemplary doctoral students at Northern Illinois University who also serve as literacy coaches, especially Rachel Lesinski Roscoe and Mike Henry. We also acknowledge the support of the Center for the Interdisciplinary Study of Language and Literacy at Northern Illinois University.

We wish to thank the many reading specialist candidates we've worked with for many years at Northern Illinois University. We have learned so much from their questions and insights, and we have been inspired by their commitment, professionalism, and collegiality. We are proud to have contributed to the preparation of so many exemplary literacy coaches, reading specialists, and literacy leaders who make such a positive impact on the professional development of teachers and the literacy learning of students.

We also want to thank our mentors, colleagues, and families for their support and encouragement, which sustained us as we wrote this book. Finally, we extend our hearty thanks to Senior Editor Craig Thomas, Senior Production Editor Laura Specht Patchkofsky, and all the other fabulous professionals at The Guilford Press. We truly appreciate their guidance, efficiency, patience, gentle reminders, and attention to both the big ideas and the smallest of details.

Contents

Contents

Purchasers of this book can download and print the reproducible forms
at *www.guilford.com/elish-piper2-forms* for personal use
or use with individual students (see copyright page for details).

PART I

Disciplinary Literacy in a Standards-Based Era

If you walk into any middle or high school and ask the teachers, "What is disciplinary literacy?" you will likely get a wide variety of responses and possibly some confused looks. You may even be asked, "Why should we care about disciplinary literacy?" As a disciplinary literacy coach, you will be at the forefront of change in your school as you help teachers to understand, embrace, and update their instruction to address disciplinary literacy demands. To make sure you are ready for this important yet challenging role, let's start near the beginning of this new priority for middle and high school curriculum and instruction. A focus on disciplinary literacy instruction can be traced to the adoption of the Common Core State Standards (CCSS) in over 40 states (Zygouris-Coe, 2012). The CCSS have called for several significant shifts in teaching: close reading of complex fiction and informational texts, synthesis of multiple texts, increased literary nonfiction in English language arts (ELA), and literacy standards particularly identified for social studies, science, and other technical subjects (National Governors Association Center for Best Practices and Council of Chief State School Officers [NGA & CCSSO], 2010). Discipline-specific literacy practices have been targeted as a central means of learning disciplinary content in grades 6–12. The purpose of this part of the book is to define disciplinary literacy and identify the connections between disciplinary literacy and the CCSS, as well as the Next Generation Science Standards (NGSS; NGSS Lead States, 2013) and the College, Career, and Civic Life (C3) Framework for Social Studies State Standards (National Council for the Social Studies [NCSS], 2013). In addition, we outline the ways that you, as a disciplinary literacy coach, can support content-area teachers who do not feel they are "teachers of reading" with their instruction for disciplinary literacy.

What Is Disciplinary Literacy?

A major goal of standards such as CCSS, NGSS, and C3 is to improve students' reading and writing of literature, literary nonfiction, science, and history texts. These standards are a response to National Assessment of Educational Progress (NAEP) data that suggest that high school students have not improved in reading over the past several years (National Center for Education Statistics [NCES], 2010), nor are they prepared to tackle the rigorous demands of disciplinary texts in college (American College Testing [ACT], 2006). Additionally, a common frustration for middle and high school teachers is that, when using content-area reading strategies that focus on general comprehension skills such as summarization or prediction, they feel they are spending time "teaching reading" rather than teaching their content. And even when content-area reading strategies are implemented, they have been insufficient because they fail to account for the specific literacy demands of the disciplines (Conley, 2008).

Middle and high school students have to negotiate multiple literacy demands as they take a wide variety of classes in different subject areas. Those subject areas include required courses (English language arts, science, social studies) and electives (business education, music, technology). To help ameliorate these challenges, disciplinary literacy has been proposed as an approach to building the necessary knowledge in a content area using discipline-specific texts, tasks, writing, and talk (McConachie & Petrosky, 2010).

Several literacy researchers have argued that improving the literacy of adolescents means focusing on particular literacy practices that are unique to each discipline (Moje, 2008; Shanahan & Shanahan, 2008). Rather than teaching strategies for reading texts that can be applied across content areas, these researchers advocate the teaching of discipline-specific strategies (Lee & Spratley, 2010; Moje, 2008; Shanahan & Shanahan, 2008, 2012). At the core of the argument for disciplinary literacy instruction is the belief that literacy demands become increasingly specialized when learning disciplinary content. Literacy instruction in the lower-elementary grades is focused on literacy processes such as word identification. As students develop basic literacy skills and texts become more complex, teachers use intermediate-level strategies to support students. Often, literacy instruction remains at this intermediate level throughout middle and high school (see Figure I-1.). Unfortunately, use of these intermediate literacy strategies alone rarely leads to more complex disciplinary learning.

Examples of intermediate literacy strategies include activating prior knowledge, clarifying, making predictions, and summarizing. These strategic behaviors are embedded into what have been termed "content-area literacy strategies." They are typically taught as students begin to shift from "learning to read" to "reading to learn" (Chall, 1983). Examples include strategies that focus on comprehension (e.g., SQ3R; Generating Interactions between Schemata and Text [GIST]), vocabulary (e.g., Frayer models; concept circles), or writing (e.g., Role Audience Format Topic [RAFT]; marathon writing). Teaching for disciplinary literacy does not preclude

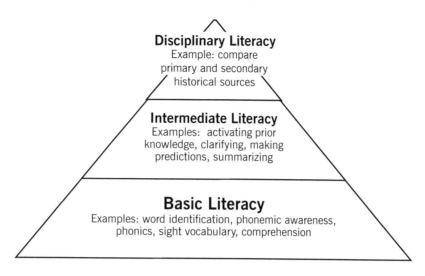

FIGURE I.1. Increasing specialization of literacy. Adapted from Shanahan and Shanahan (2008). Copyright 2008 by Harvard Education Publishing Group. Adapted by permission.

teachers from using intermediate literacy strategies. While the goal is to teach students to use disciplinary habits of reading and writing, students may still need support through the use of content-area strategies (Fang & Coatoam, 2013).

Content-area literacy strategies can serve as important scaffolds for disciplinary habits of reading, writing, talking, and thinking (Brozo, Moorman, Meyer, & Stewart, 2013). Unfortunately, the sole application of intermediate reading strategies, as mentioned earlier, is not sufficient to support students' reading of complex disciplinary texts. Although content-area reading strategies are well researched and have been shown to increase students' general comprehension of a text, they are insufficient to support students' use of those texts to construct, critique, and communicate disciplinary knowledge (Shanahan, 2009). That is, content-area reading strategies help to provide a baseline of comprehension but are less effective in supporting specific habits of disciplinary thinking. A disciplinary literacy approach acknowledges the complex literacy practices that are needed to learn in a discipline. "Literacy thus becomes an essential aspect of disciplinary practice, rather than a set of strategies or tools brought into the disciplines to improve reading and writing of subject-matter texts" (Moje, 2008, p. 99).

To identify the literacy demands in the disciplines, researchers have focused on the reading and writing practices of experts in the disciplines because experts possess unique ways of reading, writing, and thinking about disciplinary texts (Shanahan, Shanahan, & Misischia, 2011). For example, historians critically analyze the author(s) of a text, and they continuously compare and contrast primary and secondary sources to reconstruct the past (Wineburg, 1991). Scientists focus on information they do not know and information that may contradict what they have previously known about scientific phenomena (Bazerman, 1985). Although students may not become experts in all or any of the school-based disciplines, the ability to read and learn from complex disciplinary texts is necessary for their success in school. As stated in the CCSS (NGA & CCSSO, 2010, p. 60):

> Reading is critical to building knowledge in history/social studies as well as in science and technical subjects. College- and career-ready reading in these fields requires an appreciation of the norms and conventions of each discipline, such as the kinds of evidence used in history and science; an understanding of domain-specific words and phrases; an attention to precise details; and the capacity to evaluate intricate arguments, synthesize complex information, and follow detailed descriptions of events and concepts.

As such, students need opportunities to engage in the habits of thinking used in the disciplines. Some researchers have thus defined disciplinary literacy in the following way:

> Disciplinary literacy involves the use of reading, reasoning, investigating, speaking, and writing required to learn and form complex content knowledge appropriate to a particular discipline. (McConachie & Petrosky, 2010, p. 16)

Disciplinary literacy, then, is an approach to building disciplinary knowledge. Consequently, content teachers should use the primary disciplinary literacy habits of thinking as a cornerstone of their instruction if students are to acquire deep content knowledge. Disciplinary literacy entails the practices valued in the disciplines and comprises (1) the habits of thinking used to make meaning; (2) the full range of texts and language use that shape thinking and practice; (3) the habits of practice enacted within the disciplines; and (4) the beliefs about knowledge and knowledge production that constitute the disciplines (Fang, 2012; Manderino, 2012; Moje, 2007, 2009; Shanahan & Shanahan, 2008; Wilson, 2011). These elements of disciplinary literacy are an essential part of content instruction (see Figure I.2).

Teaching for Disciplinary Literacy

The challenge of a disciplinary literacy approach to instruction is making expert practices accessible to students who are most often novices in the disciplines. The dual focus of teaching content through disciplinary habits of reading, writing, and speaking may be unfamiliar to many middle and high school teachers. One way to conceptualize disciplinary literacy instruction, based on the work of Geisler (1994) and McConachie and Petrosky (2010), is "learning on the diagonal." Instruction is guided by the content or big ideas and driving questions of a discipline, through the processes (e.g., using disciplinary habits of thinking, examining beliefs about knowledge) that experts use to construct, critique, and communicate knowledge about that content (see Figure I.3).

	ELA	Science	Social Studies
Habits of thinking	Demonstrating a critical stance Interpreting Reflecting/responding	Questioning Hypothesizing Model building	Sourcing Contextualizing Corroborating Reconstructing the past
Valued texts	Novels Short stories Poems Essays	Informational texts Three-dimensional models Data tables Graphs	Primary sources Secondary sources Maps Political cartoons
Habits of practice	Identifying and using literary devices Rereading texts for different meanings	Building representational models Testing hypotheses	Reconciling competing accounts of the past Identifying causal relationships
Beliefs about knowledge	Literature and literary nonfiction can serve as a window and a mirror for human behavior.	Science is a constantly expanding field.	The past is approximated and contested.

FIGURE I.2. Expert disciplinary literacy practices in ELA, science, and social studies.

If students are to "learn on the diagonal," teachers need to "teach on the diagonal." "Teaching on the diagonal" means designing approximated activities that foster growth of knowledge while simultaneously using the habits of thinking in a discipline. The following section provides an example from research on disciplinary literacy in history.

Disciplinary Literacy in Action

Recent studies suggest that a disciplinary literacy approach garners increased achievement both in content acquisition and in literacy in history classes (Monte-Sano & De La Paz, 2012; Reisman, 2012a). One example of teaching on the diagonal comes from an intervention in which history teachers taught a series of historical inquiry tasks using authentic primary and secondary sources (Reisman, 2012b). The content aligned with the curriculum implemented at the high schools but also focused on teaching disciplinary ways of reading primary and secondary sources to investigate the historical questions posed (*https://sheg.stanford.edu/rlh*). For example, one inquiry asked students to read two primary sources about the Battle of Little Bighorn, as well as a textbook account of the event, in order to investigate the question "Who was responsible for the Battle of Little Bighorn?" Rather than directly telling students about the Battle of Little Bighorn or having students summarize

CONTENT

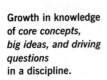

For students to become literate in a content area or discipline, they need to develop knowledge along two dimensions

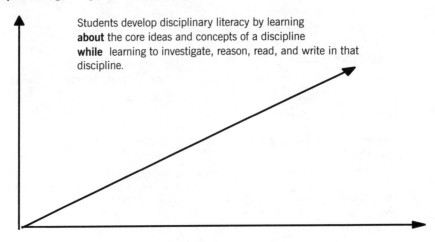

Students develop disciplinary literacy by learning **about** the core ideas and concepts of a discipline **while** learning to investigate, reason, read, and write in that discipline.

Growth in knowledge of *core concepts, big ideas, and driving questions* in a discipline.

Growth in habits of mind in a discipline. Development of ways of investigating, reasoning, reading, writing, talking, and problem solving in a discipline.

PROCESS

FIGURE I.3. Learning on the diagonal. Adapted from Geisler (1994) and from McConachie and Petrosky (2010), with permission from the Institute for Learning at the University of Pittsburgh.

each source, the instruction focused on historical analysis of authentic historical sources to create an interpretation of an event. The task, designed to support students' inquiry, both focused on building their content knowledge about relations between the Lakota and the United States *and* had students engage in the habits of thinking that are valued in history: sourcing, contextualization, and corroboration. That is, they questioned authentic historical sources by asking questions about bias and reliability (sourcing), when each source was written (contextualization), and reconciling differences across the primary sources and the textbook account (corroboration). After teachers implemented several of these types of lessons over the course of the year, students grew substantively not only in their content knowledge but also on measures of reading comprehension (Reisman, 2012b).

The preceding example demonstrates ways to enact disciplinary literacy instruction in history. Science courses may use science experiments and informational texts to have students build models of scientific processes. English classes may focus on particular literary devices, such as the use of an unreliable narrator, to critically examine a work of fiction. In all of these examples, the teachers are teaching on the diagonal by engaging students in learning the content while they are simultaneously learning the important processes and habits of thinking in the discipline. Many teachers have pushed back against content-area literacy strategies because they take time and attention away from the content valued in the disciplines. However, teaching on the diagonal allows teachers to be more efficient in their teaching by addressing both the content and the processes needed to access, understand, and use that content for meaningful learning.

Disciplinary Literacy: An Integral Aspect of Today's Standards

For the first time, literacy standards have been designed to treat reading, writing, talking, and thinking in the disciplines as distinct practices. These standards "are meant to complement the specific content demands of the disciplines, not replace them" (NGA & CCSSO, 2010, p. 60). The CCSS have also been aligned to standards in science and social studies. The NGSS contain an appendix that addresses these connections. The C3 Framework from the NCSS also contains parallels to the CCSS. It is important for you as a disciplinary literacy coach to examine these documents (see Figure I.4) and see the connections between the literacy standards set forth by the CCSS and the content standards designed for the disciplines of science and social studies.

Thus it is clear that the CCSS have placed disciplinary literacy as a focus within the grade bands 6–12 (NGA & CCSSO, 2010). As a result, all teachers need to consider disciplinary literacy as an avenue to helping their students learn discipline-specific content as well as to address the specific demands of the CCSS (Zygouris-Coe, 2012). As a disciplinary literacy coach, you are a key resource to help teachers incorporate the standards into their disciplinary instruction.

The Complexity of Disciplinary Literacy Instruction

As discussed earlier, Shanahan and Shanahan (2008) proposed a model for disciplinary literacy that represented increasing levels of specialization, from basic to intermediate and, finally, to disciplinary literacy practices. Our work with disciplinary literacy coaches has illuminated the complexities of what it means to teach

ELA	Science	Social Studies
www.corestandards.org/ ELA-Literacy	www.nextgenscience.org/sites/ngss/files/ Appendix%20M%20Connections%20to%20 the%20CCSS%20for%20Literacy_061213.pdf	www.socialstudies.org/system/ files/c3/C3-Framework-for- Social-Studies.pdf

FIGURE I.4. Standards documents in ELA, science, and social studies.

for disciplinary literacy. In order to teach for disciplinary literacy, teachers need to possess an interconnected set of knowledge domains that, when considered together, make up what is needed to teach for disciplinary literacy. Thus we have expanded the top part of Shanahan and Shanahan's model to depict those four knowledge domains (see Figure I.5).

Figure I.5 represents the different types of knowledge teachers need for disciplinary literacy instruction. Knowledge about students includes teachers' understandings of their students' sociocultural backgrounds, prior knowledge, and beliefs about learning in the discipline. Knowledge of the discipline comprises two subcategories: knowledge of disciplinary content and knowledge of disciplinary processes. Knowledge of disciplinary content refers to the scope of teachers' topic and content knowledge. Knowledge of disciplinary processes includes teachers' understanding of the means of knowledge construction, critique, and communication in their disciplines. Pedagogical knowledge represents the teachers' command of their instructional designs, including lesson and unit planning, assessment, and their classroom instruction. Finally, teachers' understanding of reading and writing processes, including reading and writing strategies, constitutes their knowledge of literacy.

When viewed in this way, disciplinary literacy instruction is a complex intersection of teachers' knowledge about their students, disciplinary knowledge, pedagogical knowledge, and literacy knowledge. These disciplinary literacy knowledge domains represent the knowledge that teachers need to embed disciplinary literacy into their instruction. Therefore, these knowledge domains are important to consider when you are working with teachers because they can guide your work toward shifting teacher practice to address disciplinary literacy instruction.

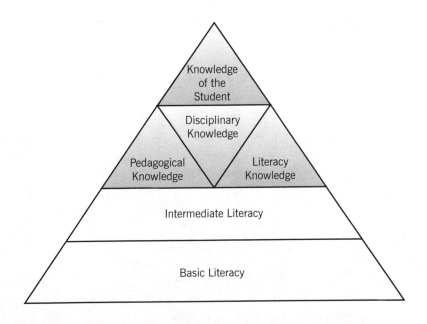

FIGURE I.5. Knowledge domains for disciplinary literacy instruction.

Why Disciplinary Literacy Matters for Secondary Literacy Coaches

In this book we propose that your role as a literacy coach is to support teachers' instruction of their content using disciplinary ways of reading, writing, speaking, thinking, and doing. In other words, your role is to support teachers' efforts to teach their content deeply and meaningfully. As a disciplinary literacy coach, an important role you will play is helping teachers bridge the content that undergirds their curriculum and the often tacit ways of reading, writing, speaking, thinking, and doing that are used to construct meaning in a discipline. For example, whereas traditional curriculum may have focused heavily on content, the new standards include specific treatment of the habits of thinking, using disciplinary texts to examine, construct, and critique disciplinary knowledge (Shanahan, 2009). As a disciplinary literacy coach, your role is not to become a content expert in each discipline. Rather, your support of teachers in identifying, planning, and assessing the reading, writing, speaking, and thinking activities that they use to make the content accessible to adolescents is a part of building teachers' pedagogical content knowledge (Shulman, 1986). That is, your support is critical to expanding teachers' knowledge of literacy pedagogy in relation to their knowledge of their content so that they may design instruction that builds students' disciplinary literacy (Manderino & Wickens, 2014).

To support teaching on the diagonal, the development and implementation of disciplinary literacy strategies are critical to support students' text-based learning. Disciplinary literacy coaches can leverage their knowledge of literacy to help teachers identify the discipline-specific literacy practices, as teachers may not readily recognize them in their own practice (Di Domenico, 2014). As a disciplinary literacy coach, you serve a vital role in helping teachers make sense of the complexity of teaching for disciplinary literacy. Specific strategies to provide that support are the heart of this book and can be found in Parts IV, V, and VI.

This part of the book has outlined key elements of disciplinary instruction to support teachers' use of disciplinary literacy as a core of content instruction. Parts II and III discuss key elements of the coaching process and different models for enacting disciplinary literacy coaching.

PART II

Disciplinary Literacy Coaching

What Is Literacy Coaching?

Literacy coaching is an approach to professional development that is ongoing and job embedded. Because literacy coaches are situated in schools, they are available on a day-to-day basis to help teachers grapple with the pressing challenges they face in their teaching (Toll, 2005). Literacy coaches may have many titles, including instructional coach, reading specialist, reading teacher, literacy specialist, team leader, or department chair. Although their titles may vary widely, there are typical literacy coaching activities in which they engage (Bean et al., 2015). Coaching activities include providing large-group professional development such as workshops, small-group support such as facilitating study groups and professional learning communities, and individual teacher support such as co-planning and co-teaching. Unlike traditional approaches to professional development that often rely on a single workshop and expect that teachers will "figure it out" on their own, literacy coaching provides ongoing support that aligns with teachers' daily work in their own classrooms with their own students.

What Is Disciplinary Literacy Coaching?

A great deal has been written about literacy coaching in general, especially at the early childhood and elementary levels. Coaching at the middle and high school levels, however, has unique considerations, features, and challenges (Snow, Ippolito, & Schwartz, 2006). In 2006, the International Reading Association (IRA) published the *Standards for Middle and High School Literacy Coaches* that outlined expectations for coaches in the areas of leadership and content areas. More specifically, the leadership standards focus on being a skillful (1) collaborator, (2) job-embedded coach, and (3) evaluator of literacy needs. In addition, middle and high school literacy coaches are expected to be skillful instructional strategists in the areas of ELA, mathematics, science, and social studies. Furthermore, coaches are expected to know and understand the content and curriculum in the disciplines in which they coach, as well as how literacy is valued and used within each discipline. Taken as a whole, these standards can be overwhelming, suggesting that a literacy coach must be expert in all of the core disciplines. Beyond the IRA standards, there are also expectations for teachers (and therefore for coaches) regarding disciplinary literacy in the CCSS, NGSS, and C3 Framework. When considering all of these expectations for both coaches and teachers, the notion of coaching at the middle and high school levels becomes increasingly complex and daunting. How can we expect a single literacy coach to have expertise and experience in all of these areas? Is that even a realistic or aspirational model for middle and high schools?

In recent years, additional investigation has been done in the field of disciplinary literacy coaching has resulted in a more realistic model for disciplinary literacy coaching wherein the coach must be an expert collaborator and learner who positions the teacher as the expert regarding the discipline (Elish-Piper, Manderino, Di Domenico, & L'Allier, 2014). By working collaboratively as partners with teachers in the disciplines, the literacy coach can be an expert listener, questioner, and facilitator who helps teachers examine, enhance, and reflect on their teaching practices. It is this collaborative model of disciplinary literacy coaching that we describe and develop in this book.

A Note on the Use of the Term "Disciplinary Literacy Coach" in This Book

For the purposes of this book, we use the terms "disciplinary literacy coach," "literacy coach," and "coach" interchangeably to refer to any professional who delivers job-embedded professional development for teachers in the core disciplines of ELA, science, and social studies, regardless of that professional's official job title or the amount of time he or she spends coaching.

Coaching Adults

Many professionals charged with disciplinary literacy coaching responsibilities have not had any professional development or coursework in how to work with adults. Most often, disciplinary literacy coaches were trained as teachers in their disciplines, with a strong emphasis on content knowledge and teaching pedagogy. When they begin to take on coaching responsibilities, they may find that they are uncomfortable, underprepared, and nervous about working with adults—especially their own colleagues! Obviously, working with adults is different from teaching adolescents, but what are those differences? And how can you, as a disciplinary literacy coach, prepare to work effectively with adults? You have likely seen and used the term "pedagogy," which is the art and science of teaching children, but you may not be familiar with the term "andragogy," which is the art and science of helping adults learn. The theory of andragogy was developed by Knowles (1970), who described adult learners as being self-directed, motivated, experienced, ready to learn, and oriented toward application. The following six principles provide insight and guidance about how adults learn (Knowles, Holton, & Swanson, 2005).

1. Adults want to know why they need to learn something.
2. Adults are most interested in learning when it has immediate relevance to their jobs or personal lives.
3. Adult learning tends to be problem-centered rather than content-oriented.
4. Adults need to be involved in the planning, evaluation, and implementation of their learning.
5. Experience, including mistakes, provides the basis for learning activities.
6. Adults respond best to internal rather than external motivators.

Disciplinary Literacy Coaching and Adult Learning Theory in Action

After reading the characteristics of adult learners and the six principles, you might wonder "What does this look like in disciplinary literacy coaching?" Marilyn Ramirez, a disciplinary literacy coach at Middletown High School, has been coaching for 3 years. She was a social studies teacher, and she also earned an English as a Second Language (ESL) endorsement to help her meet the needs of the many English learners in her school. Marilyn spends four periods per day coaching, and the rest of the day she teaches two sections of global studies for freshman ESL students. During her coaching times, Marilyn attends department meetings, co-plans and co-teaches lessons, and facilitates professional learning community (PLC) meetings related to issues of disciplinary literacy.

When we asked Marilyn to reflect on her transition to disciplinary literacy coaching and to share what she has found to be effective for her coaching, she responded, "I loved and still love teaching social studies. I was excited to take on disciplinary literacy coaching, but I was nervous because I had no formal training or experience coaching or teaching adults. There are a lot of experienced teachers in our school, so I was worried about how I would be able to work with and support them."

Marilyn went on to explain, "During the summer before I started coaching, I read some useful resources [see Figure II.1], and I reached out to other disciplinary literacy coaches who worked in local high schools. Talking to them was a great help because they were able to show me what worked for them and what did not. They were also willing to answer my questions. For someone just going into disciplinary literacy coaching, I recommend finding a support network either within or beyond your own school."

Marilyn also explained, "I started working with my colleagues in social studies, and that was very helpful. I already knew them and the curriculum so I was able

Resource	Description
Knight, J. (2007). *Instructional coaching: A partnership approach to improving instruction.* Thousand Oaks, CA: Corwin Press.	This book provides a clear picture of instructional coaching, and it is an ideal resource to read if you are just getting into coaching.
International Reading Association. (2006). *Standards for middle and high school literacy coaches.* Newark, DE: Author.	This set of standards clarifies what literacy coaches need to know and be able to do. It also contains useful background information about coaching in middle and high schools.
Lesinski, R. A. (2011). "Experience is the best sculptor": From high school reading specialist to literacy coach. *Illinois Reading Council Journal, 39*(4), 15–23.	This article focuses on lessons learned by a new high school literacy coach. The practical suggestions are very useful for focusing your coaching work.
Sturtevant, E. G. (2003). *The literacy coach: A key to improving teaching and learning in secondary schools.* Report presented at the annual American High School Policy Conference of the Alliance for Excellent Education, Washington, DC.	This report provides an overview of coaching in high schools, but the part I found most useful was the program examples so I could see different models of coaching.
Stevens, N. L. (2010/2011). The high school literacy coach: Searching for an identity. *Journal of Education, 191*(3), 19–25.	This case study of a practicing high school literacy coach helped me understand the roles, responsibilities, and challenges of coaching.

FIGURE II.1. Literacy coaching resources.

to work with them and build my confidence as a coach. I also reflected on when I had attended professional development workshops or had questions about my own teaching. I thought about what helped me and what frustrated me, too. Beyond thinking about my own experiences, I talked with several teachers at my school, and I asked them what they hoped to get from coaching. They shared insights such as, 'I want to resolve the big challenges I have in my teaching' and 'I want someone to work with me in a nonjudgmental way to help me improve my teaching and my students' learning.'"

As you can see, many of the insights Marilyn developed in her early work as a disciplinary literacy coach align directly with the six principles of adult learning (Knowles, 1970). Marilyn also said, "Once I relaxed, took on the role of collaborator and listened carefully to what the teachers wanted and needed from me, I could really dig into coaching. This is my third year as a coach, and while I'm much more knowledgeable and confident, I sometimes still remind myself to think about the adults I'm coaching and how they learn."

Disciplinary Literacy Coaching and Change

Disciplinary literacy coaches are at the leading edge of change due to expectations in new learning standards. Teachers are being asked to teach in ways that are very different from how they were trained and how they may have taught previously. Teachers in the disciplines are now being asked to consider how literacy is valued and used and to incorporate these uses into their teaching. Although some middle and high school teachers may embrace these changes with open arms, others may be fearful, anxious, or even angry. Therefore, it is essential that disciplinary literacy coaches keep two key ideas in mind as they lead toward change. First, they must understand the change process itself; second, they must work as part of a literacy leadership team so that change is supported by a team of professionals, not just by a lone literacy coach.

Understanding the Change Process

Change is a staple in education. With new standards, initiatives, and assessments, educators are consistently faced with changing expectations for their teaching and their students' learning. Because disciplinary literacy coaches are charged with supporting teachers as they enact new instructional practices, they need to understand the change process. Although the notion of being a change agent may feel overwhelming, it's important to realize that the change process is fairly predictable.

As we've worked with teachers and coaches in schools, we have found that the concerns-based adoption model (CBAM) is a helpful tool to guide literacy coaching (Hall & Hord, 1987). CBAM is a developmental model composed of seven stages that teachers generally go through as they learn about, struggle with, and implement a new curriculum or instructional approach. Although each teacher may not progress step by step through the stages of CBAM, most teachers do move through the stages in a fairly predictable way that begins with an emphasis on "self," moves to "implementation," and ends with a focus on "results." CBAM is grounded in the idea that the concerns that educators experience at different stages of adopting an innovation offer coaches insights about the types of support teachers may need at certain points in time. To get a better idea of the CBAM, let's look at Figure II.2.

The change process usually begins with a focus on oneself. Teachers typically start at the bottom step with the Awareness phase when they wonder "What is this new initiative?" For example, teachers at the Awareness stage may be asking questions such as "What is disciplinary literacy?" Teachers generally progress to the Information stage as they want more details about the initiative. Teachers at the Information stage may ask "What are the standards for disciplinary literacy in my subject area?" Teachers who are at the Personal stage are most interested in how the initiative will affect them and will ask questions such as "How am I going to address disciplinary literacy instruction in my classroom?"

Once teachers begin to shift their focus to task considerations and are concerned with the logistics of implementing the initiative, they are at the Management stage. Teachers at this stage are concerned with issues such as "How can I use disciplinary literacy instruction in meaningful ways that help me teach my content?" When teachers begin to focus on results, they are at the Consequence stage. At

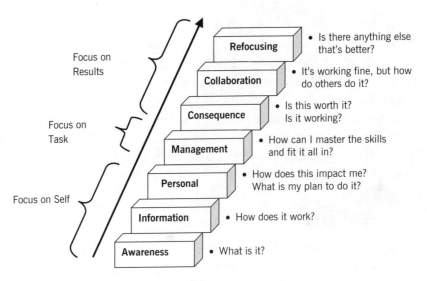

FIGURE II.2. Hall and Hord's (1987) concerns-based adoption model (CBAM). From Elish-Piper and L'Allier (2014). Copyright 2014 by The Guilford Press. Reprinted by permission.

this point, they grapple with the impact and efficacy of the initiative. They tend to ask questions such as "How effective is my disciplinary literacy instruction?" and "How well are my students doing with developing their abilities to read and write arguments in my discipline?" At the Collaboration stage, teachers start to wonder how other educators are implementing the initiative because they want to enhance their own use of it. Teachers may ask questions such as "Who is further along with disciplinary literacy instruction, and what can I learn from them?" The last stage of the change process is Refocusing. During this stage, teachers start to ask questions such as "What else can we do to enhance teaching and learning beyond just implementing disciplinary literacy instruction?" An understanding of CBAM can help disciplinary literacy coaches plan and structure their coaching efforts to make certain that teachers receive the type of coaching support they need when they need it (Hall & Hord, 2006).

Guidelines for Effective Disciplinary Literacy Coaching

Coaching in general, and disciplinary literacy coaching specifically, can feel overwhelming and open-ended. Knowing that you are working with teachers in multiple disciplines and that there are so many different coaching activities you could do, it's essential to set priorities so you can focus your coaching in meaningful and effective ways. Based on our research in schools, we've developed a set of guidelines to help you target your coaching efforts. These guidelines reflect the current state of knowledge regarding effective literacy coaching and provide direction about priorities for literacy coaching (Elish-Piper & L'Allier, 2014; Elish-Piper et al., 2014).

1. *Build capacity.* The main purpose of literacy coaching is to build the instructional capacity of teachers so that all students are taught by highly skilled and effective teachers. Furthermore, by building the capacity of teacher leaders or liaisons, you can also establish a strong literacy leadership team to support professional development efforts across your school.

2. *Consider teacher knowledge.* As discussed in Part I, teachers bring different kinds and levels of knowledge to disciplinary literacy instruction. Namely, they bring their knowledge of their students and how they learn, knowledge of teaching pedagogy and instructional methods, knowledge of both the content and processes of the discipline, and knowledge of literacy. Different teachers will be at different points in terms of what they know and how much they know in each of these areas. If the coach considers teacher knowledge in planning and providing coaching support, he or she can tailor the coaching more closely to teacher needs and goals.

3. *Create sustainability.* If you select and use predictable structures and protocols for meetings, PLCs, and teacher leader meetings, you can make these processes part of the operation of your school so the focus is on disciplinary literacy rather than on deciding how to run a meeting, discuss an article, or examine student work. As your school builds a cadre of teacher leaders, these teachers can begin to take on the role of facilitating some meetings, such as article study groups (Strategy 2). In this way you can build a team to ensure that all teachers have the coaching support they need and want.

4. *Spend as much time as possible working directly with teachers and teacher leaders.* Because they do not teach every period of the day, literacy coaches may be asked to do managerial or administrative tasks, such as inputting assessment data, ordering instructional resources, or "covering" classes for absent teachers. Although those tasks are certainly important and helpful, they do not directly contribute to the quality of teaching or learning in the school. If the tasks you are asked to complete as a coach do not support building capacity or sustainability, work with your administrators to reassign those tasks to others, such as paraprofessionals, clerical staff, student interns, or school volunteers so that you can devote your coaching time to activities that directly support teachers and teacher leaders.

5. *Situate the coach as a collaborator, not an expert.* Given the complexity of coaching at the middle and high school levels and in multiple disciplines, it is not realistic or effective to expect a disciplinary literacy coach to be an expert in each of these areas. Therefore, it is essential that the literacy coach present him- or herself as a collaborator, relying on teacher expertise in the discipline, as well as with the curriculum. Although the coach should strive to gain as much expertise as possible in the disciplines in which he or she coaches, taking a collaborative approach will be most effective in working with the wide variety of teachers and disciplines in middle or high school settings.

6. *Let collaboration develop.* Collaboration is generative, and like any relationship a coaching collaboration takes time. Be patient, listen carefully, and follow

through so your collaborations with teachers can deepen and extend to address more complex and important goals and challenges over time.

7. *Leverage coaching strategies.* Carefully select coaching strategies that will build capacity and address and leverage teacher knowledge. Match coaching strategies carefully to teacher goals and needs. As you consider the coaching strategies presented in this book, make sure you are selecting the best coaching strategy for the teacher and situation based on the available data, as well as your professional judgment.

8. *Focus on student learning.* If you focus your coaching on student learning and student work, you and your colleagues can concentrate on what is actually happening (or not happening) in classrooms. Even the most hesitant teachers tend to take notice and engage in professional development discussions and coaching when they compare their students' work or assessment data with standards or with the work of other teachers' students.

If you remember these eight guidelines, you can make sure that your literacy coaching will be focused, purposeful, and effective.

Three Layers of Coaching

Disciplinary literacy coaching is not a single activity but a range of job-embedded professional development opportunities and supports for classroom teachers. Because disciplinary literacy coaches tend to coach a large number of teachers due to the size of most middle and high schools, it is imperative that they use their time wisely and efficiently. Due to the complexity of teaching and learning, as well as the many changes needed in instructional practice to incorporate disciplinary literacy in meaningful ways, we advocate a layered literacy coaching model (Allen, 2007). We envision the three layers of literacy coaching as the professional development support provided for (1) large groups of teachers, (2) small groups such as teams, departments, or PLCs, and (3) individual teachers (see Figure II.3).

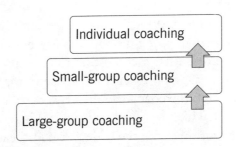

FIGURE II.3. Layers of literacy coaching. From Elish-Piper and L'Allier (2014). Copyright 2014 by The Guilford Press. Reprinted by permission.

To lay the groundwork for disciplinary literacy coaching, we recommend starting with large groups of teachers, such as all of the sixth-grade teachers in a middle school or the entire science department in a high school. Large-group coaching activities focus on building the "big picture" related to disciplinary literacy. Three main benefits of large-group coaching activities are (1) they use coaching time efficiently; (2) they build a common focus, purpose, or goal across many teachers in the school; and (3) they help to create a collaborative climate and shared knowledge base that will be a foundation for coaching that goes more deeply into enhancing teacher practice and improving student literacy learning. Although large-group coaching activities are valuable and a key component of a disciplinary literacy coaching program, they are not sufficient to support teachers in their work to embrace and enact disciplinary literacy instruction.

Small-group coaching activities are an essential layer of coaching because these types of coaching activities are tailored specifically to the needs of small groups of teachers, such as teachers of a specific course, for example, seventh-grade science or high school chemistry. Small-group coaching activities may be facilitated by the literacy coach, but they may also be facilitated by teacher leaders who work with the literacy coach. When teacher leaders are able to facilitate small-group meetings and article study groups, the responsibility for literacy coaching (and leadership) is shared across professionals in the school, which is a critical step toward creating a sustainable coaching model that is not dependent on a single person. Small-group coaching activities focus on supporting teachers in working collaboratively to dig down into disciplinary literacy that is directly relevant to the curriculum and student learning outcomes in the courses they teach.

In some situations, two layers of coaching may be sufficient. This is especially true in schools with strong teacher leaders and a climate of collaboration that supports professional development. However, there are often situations in which teachers require or request individual coaching support to address their specific concerns, goals, or challenges. Newer teachers, those who have recently changed levels or courses, and those who lack confidence or struggle with how to implement disciplinary literacy instruction in their own classrooms are excellent candidates for individual coaching. Ideally, individual coaching flows directly from small-group coaching activities so that the teacher can layer and deepen his or her understanding of what disciplinary literacy is and how to enact some aspect of it in instruction and then actually apply that approach in his or her teaching. Although individual coaching can be quite time-consuming, it can lead to powerful outcomes.

Coaching Stances and Coaching Language

Disciplinary literacy coaches will engage in a wide variety of coaching activities, but there are two important factors that contribute to the coach's effectiveness: coaching stance and coaching language. If coaches listen carefully to what teachers say and how they say it, coaches are able to adjust the coaching stance they use to support teachers and the language they use to communicate with them (Lipton & Wellman, 2007). A coaching stance is defined as the way that a literacy coach positions him- or herself in terms of the type of support he or she provides and whether the coach or the teacher takes the lead in providing information and problem solving. The three literacy coaching stances are facilitating, collaborating, and consulting (L'Allier & Elish-Piper, 2012a; Lipton & Wellman, 2007). The coaching stances are described in Figure II.4.

The three coaching stances are presented separately, but literacy coaches typically shift from one stance to another within a single coaching conversation. As teachers share their challenges and ask questions, the literacy coach listens carefully to determine the appropriate stance. By listening carefully and considering what teachers say (and how they say it), the literacy coach can determine the most appropriate stance to take and the types of language to use. Figure II.5 demonstrates how teacher language cues can be used to determine the appropriate coaching stance and coaching language for that teacher and situation.

Making the Most of Coaching Time

Many of the middle and high school literacy coaches we know tell us that there are more things to do than there is time. A coach we have worked with, Kim Dauber,

Stance	Description of support	Who provides information and leads problem solving
Facilitating	The literacy coach serves as someone for teachers to "think and problem solve with." The coach asks open-ended questions and paraphrases what teachers say. This stance is most appropriate when teachers have a good deal of knowledge about the issue and just want to have someone with whom to share ideas and discuss options.	The teacher
Collaborating	The literacy coach serves as a partner for teachers in this stance. Both the teacher and the literacy coach bring knowledge to the coaching conversation and share in the problem-solving process. In this stance, the coach often uses inclusive language such as "we," "us," and "our" to show that she or he is working as a partner with the teacher.	The teacher and the literacy coach
Consulting	The literacy coach takes the lead because teachers are frustrated, overwhelmed, or extremely unfamiliar with the topic or issue. In this stance, the literacy coach brings most of the information to the coaching activity and takes the responsibility for leading the problem-solving process.	The literacy coach

FIGURE II.4. Literacy coaching stances. From Elish-Piper and L'Allier (2014). Copyright 2014 by The Guilford Press. Reprinted by permission.

confided that she often wondered, "What did I accomplish today?" Although she could tick off a long list of "random acts of coaching" that had kept her incredibly busy, she couldn't identify how any of these activities could contribute to building capacity, enhancing teacher practice, or improving student learning. In collaboration with Kim and other veteran coaches, we developed two useful tools to help coaches determine how to spend their time in the most effective ways possible: the job description and the purpose statement (Elish-Piper & L'Allier, 2014).

Coaching stance	Teacher cues	Coaching language
Facilitating	[The coach knows that the teacher has knowledge and experience with the topic.] [The teacher appears to be seeking confirmation or a chance to talk through what he or she is already doing or thinking.] "I have been working on this, and I'd like to talk through with you how it has been going."	"What did you notice [about the data, the lesson, the students' reading behaviors]?" "What do you think helped the students make progress?" "In light of what you know about your students and have already done in the area of _____, what are you planning to do next?"
Collaborating	"I was thinking that I'd do [insert name of strategy]. What do you think?" "Can I bounce some ideas around with you for a lesson I'm planning?" "I just got the data from my students' assessments. Can I talk through some of the data with you?"	"Let's think about this together." "Let's brainstorm some ideas." "That's a great idea. I was also thinking of. . . ." "How about if we work through this together?"
Consulting	"I just don't know what else to try [to help my students . . .]." "What did you do about this when you were teaching?" "I've heard about this strategy, but I don't really know how to implement it [or if it is appropriate for my students or situation]. Can you give me some advice?" "Don't give me lots of choices. Please just tell me which one you think is the best option for my students."	"What has worked for me with students was. . . ." "Some of our colleagues have found this worked well with their students. . . ." "Here is a research-based practice that I think might work well with your students."

FIGURE II.5. Coaching stances, teacher cues, and coaching language. From Elish-Piper and L'Allier (2014; adapted from L'Allier & Elish-Piper, 2012b). Copyright 2014 by The Guilford Press. Reprinted by permission.

What Is Your Purpose as a Disciplinary Literacy Coach?

Ideally, disciplinary literacy coaches will have a clear job description that outlines literacy coaching responsibilities. However, many of the literacy coaches we have worked with report that they do not have job descriptions, which makes their jobs fuzzy and frustrating (Elish-Piper, L'Allier, & Zwart, 2009). If you don't have a job description that specifies your duties as a literacy coach, we urge you to sit down with your administrator or supervisor to develop one as soon as possible. Having a clear job description is the first step in determining the focus of your disciplinary literacy coaching work. Then we suggest that you develop and share your purpose statement for disciplinary literacy coaching so that the teachers, support personnel, and administrators you work with will understand the focus of your coaching work. We have provided two sample purpose statements in Figure II.6.

If you share your purpose statement with the administrators and teachers at your school, you can begin to establish a common understanding about the type of work you will be doing (and not doing) as a disciplinary literacy coach. We have also learned from coaches that this purpose statement is very helpful in another important way. It can be your personal "sounding board" about how to spend your time. Jamie Nichols, the literacy coach who wrote the first statement in Figure II.6, explained that she often looks back at her purpose statement to decide whether a task is something she should spend her limited coaching time doing or whether it is a task that someone else, such as a secretary, paraprofessional, or student intern, could do. As Jamie explained, "I had become the go-to person if a teacher's class needed to be covered, if in-school suspension needed to be supervised, or if the librarian needed help cataloging new inventory. While I'm definitely a team player who likes to help others, I realized that spending so much time doing these helpful tasks was actually limiting what I could do as a coach. I spoke about this with the assistant principal, who is my direct supervisor. She agreed, and we were able to come up with a plan

---

Sample Statement 1: Jamie Nichols

The purpose of my literacy coaching work is to build teacher instructional capacity related to disciplinary literacy; to improve student literacy learning; and to build a collaborative professional learning climate for teachers at my school.

Sample Statement 2: David Nuñez

The three goals that define my purpose for disciplinary literacy coaching at Hilltop High School are:

1. *To help teachers enhance their practice.*
2. *To improve student learning outcomes.*
3. *To build a strong literacy leadership team that will contribute to accomplishing purposes 1 and 2.*

FIGURE II.6. Literacy coaching purpose statements. Adapted from Elish-Piper and L'Allier (2014). Copyright 2014 by The Guilford Press. Adapted by permission.

to limit these other duties so I could make sure that I was spending my time in ways that directly address my purpose statement."

We suggest that you review your coaching purpose statement at least two times per year to make sure it aligns with district and school priorities, as well as with your literacy coaching job description. We also recommend that you share your coaching purpose statement often, display it prominently on your planning book or in your electronic calendar, and refer to it regularly so that you don't end up frittering away your time caught up in the "random acts of coaching" that can fill your day but do not contribute directly to meaningful outcomes.

Summary

In this chapter, we've defined literacy coaching as well as disciplinary literacy coaching and discussed working with adults, understanding the change process, and building a literacy leadership team. We've also shared eight guidelines to keep your coaching focused, presented a three-layered model of disciplinary literacy coaching, discussed coaching stances and language, and shared two strategies for making the most of coaching time. If you consider and apply these ideas, you can ensure that your disciplinary literacy coaching will be more focused and effective.

PART III

Models of Disciplinary Literacy Coaching

Laying a strong foundation for a disciplinary literacy coaching program is critical to its success. This foundation must include developing a vision statement for the program (Kral, 2007), determining an appropriate model for the coaching program (Bean, 2009; Vogt & Shearer, 2011), and selecting coaches who can operationalize that vision within the selected model (Sturtevant, 2003). In addition, before any coaching begins, the administrative team needs to show strong support for the program when introducing the vision statement and coaching model to the entire teaching staff (Matsumura, Sartoris, Bickel, & Garnier, 2009)

In our work with coaches at the middle and high school levels, we have seen a wide variety of coaching approaches. These approaches can generally be classified into one of four models: the teacher-initiated model, the co-teaching model, the department/team model, and the liaison model. In this part we describe each model, sharing its main characteristics, as well its strengths and constraints. Careful attention to the details of each model can be helpful if your school is in the planning stage of its disciplinary literacy coaching programs. On the other hand, if your school has already adopted one of these models, you might read this section to find ways to strengthen that model or to consider changing to a model that more closely aligns with your program's vision statement and/or the needs of your school.

Regardless of the model selected, it is imperative that an administrator and disciplinary literacy coach introduce the model at a faculty meeting so that all faculty members gain a shared understanding of the model and observe that school administrators support the model. Oftentimes, the administrator gives a brief overview of the model and the rationale concerning the selection of the particular coaching model. The disciplinary literacy coach then explains the model in more detail, providing examples of how the teacher and the coach might collaborate to improve student learning. In addition, for some models, the coach may explain how teachers can volunteer to be part of the initial phase of the coaching program.

Teacher-Initiated Model

What Is It?

In the teacher-initiated model, the disciplinary literacy coach works with individual teachers to help them build their knowledge and implementation of disciplinary literacy practices (Bean, 2009; Lassonde & Tucker, 2014). Teachers initiate the coaching process; coaches are not assigned to work with specific teachers or teams or departments. When internal motivation by teachers is the impetus for collaborations with the coach, teachers are demonstrating a belief that such interactions will help them meet a need or solve a problem related to their students' learning. In this way, the teacher-initiated model is aligned with several of the adult learning principles discussed in Part II and thus is likely to produce positive results. In connection with the layered approach to coaching described in Part II, the teacher-initiated model is strongly aligned with the individual coaching layer.

What Are the Typical Coaching Activities within This Model?

As shown in Figure III.1, the teacher-initiated model usually begins with a meeting between the teacher and the coach to discuss the teacher's concerns about his or her students' learning and to set a goal for their work together. The coach often takes on a facilitating stance during this initial meeting, acknowledging the content expertise of the teacher and developing a clearer understanding of the course content, current disciplinary literacy practices, and students. After this initial meeting, it is common for the coach to observe in the classroom in order to gain additional information about the curriculum, instruction, and students. The postobservation discussion between the coach and the teacher often results in a clarification of the goal and a plan for beginning their collaborative work. As seen in Figure III.1, the collaborative work can involve a variety of activities including but not limited to (1) co-planning lessons to teach specific disciplinary literacy strategies; (2) selecting texts appropriate for the content and disciplinary literacy strategies; (3) teaching of the lesson by the coach, the teacher, or both; and (4) reflecting on the lesson's outcomes in order to determine next steps. Although the cycle of activities shown in Figure III.1 may be ideal, it is a flexible cycle in which considerations such as the nature of the goal, the teacher's prior experiences with the coach, and the teacher's and coach's schedules may determine which activities are most appropriate. After a teacher and coach have completed the work related to the teacher's goal, the teacher can decide whether or not to collaborate with the coach on a new goal.

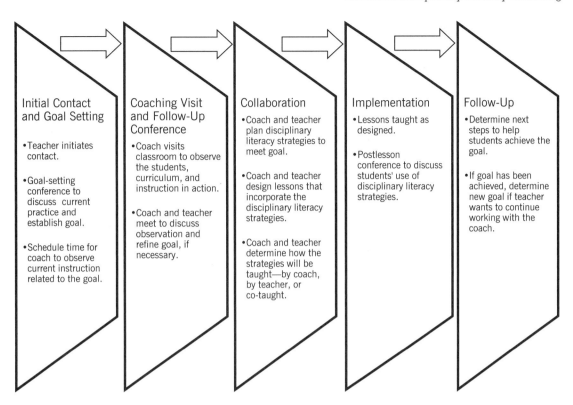

Initial Contact and Goal Setting

- Teacher initiates contact.
- Goal-setting conference to discuss current practice and establish goal.
- Schedule time for coach to observe current instruction related to the goal.

Coaching Visit and Follow-Up Conference

- Coach visits classroom to observe the students, curriculum, and instruction in action.
- Coach and teacher meet to discuss observation and refine goal, if necessary.

Collaboration

- Coach and teacher plan disciplinary literacy strategies to meet goal.
- Coach and teacher design lessons that incorporate the disciplinary literacy strategies.
- Coach and teacher determine how the strategies will be taught—by coach, by teacher, or co-taught.

Implementation

- Lessons taught as designed.
- Postlesson conference to discuss students' use of disciplinary literacy strategies.

Follow-Up

- Determine next steps to help students achieve the goal.
- If goal has been achieved, determine new goal if teacher wants to continue working with the coach.

FIGURE III.1. The teacher-initiated model.

What Is the Time Commitment for This Model?

Because the teacher-initiated model involves numerous conversations about a series of classroom activities, there is generally a large time commitment on the part of both the coach and the teacher. However, depending on the nature of the goal, the length of this commitment can vary from just a few weeks to several months. Coaches should be careful not to commit to several long-term collaborations at the beginning of the year. When this happens, there is room in their schedules to work with only seven or eight teachers, which could reduce the chance to build the disciplinary teacher practices of other teachers who tire of waiting for their turn to collaborate. Coaches can interact with a larger number of teachers if they work with some teachers on goals that will take a short amount of time (e.g., 2–3 weeks), with some teachers on medium-length goals (e.g., 4–8 weeks), and with a few teachers on goals that will take a longer period of time (e.g., a semester). In addition, it may be possible for two or three teachers who teach the same course and have the same concerns about their students' learning to work as a group with the coach. By using these approaches, coaches will consistently have openings in their schedules to work with additional teachers.

What Are This Model's Strengths and Constraints?

As shown in Figure III.2, the strength of the teacher-initiated model lies in its teacher-driven aspects. Teachers volunteer for and take the lead in the development of the goals for the collaborative work. Thus teachers see the model as flexible—designed to meet their individual needs. In addition, because teachers initiate the collaborations, it is likely that the teacher–coach relationship will be a positive one.

As the teacher-initiated model is time-consuming, it may not be the best model if a person has only 1 or 2 hours per day to devote to coaching. Furthermore, because the model builds the disciplinary literacy practices of a small group of teachers each semester or each year, it may not be the best model if a school is trying to build capacity of a large number of teachers in a relatively short time. To partially address these concerns, coaches involved in the teacher-initiated model are often also expected to give large-group professional development presentations to help build capacity on a schoolwide or departmental basis.

Perhaps the most frustrating constraint for coaches is that, because teachers volunteer for coaching, the start-up phase may be slow. Coaches can encourage volunteers in a variety of ways. For example, at the beginning of the year, coaches can send out a one-page flyer that reminds the teachers about the coaching program, briefly describes some examples of past collaborations, and explains how teachers can contact the coach if they would like to discuss opportunities for collaborative work. In addition, when giving large-group professional development workshops around some aspect of disciplinary literacy, coaches can encourage teachers who want to know more about implementing the ideas from the workshop to contact them.

Co-Teaching Model

What Is It?

In the co-teaching model, a literacy coach and a teacher work together to teach a group of students (Casey, 2006; Little & Dieker, 2009; Moran, 2007). Depending on the structure of the school and the needs of the teacher, they might work together for a quarter, a semester, or a year. For example, a literacy coach and a second-year biology teacher might be assigned to teach the second-period ninth-grade biology

Strengths	Constraints
• Organic. • Teacher driven. Builds teacher capacity. • Creates positive teacher–coach relationships. • Flexible.	• Start-up phase may be slow. • Time-consuming. • May not build capacity beyond the teacher level.

FIGURE III.2. Strengths and constraints of the teacher-initiated model.

class for the fall semester. With this model, coaches develop a strong understanding of the content and processes within a discipline so that they can better ascertain which disciplinary literacy practices will enable the students to engage in the types of thinking, reading, and writing done by experts in that discipline. In addition, teachers are provided with ongoing support from the coach as teacher and coach work together to plan and incorporate some of these disciplinary literacy practices into their daily instruction. As was true of the teacher-initiated model, the co-teaching model fits into the individual layer of coaching described in Part II.

What Are the Typical Coaching Activities within This Model?

In the co-teaching model, represented in Figure III.3, the literacy coach and the teacher merge their expertise on a daily basis to develop effective disciplinary instruction for their students. As they set the curricular goals for each unit of study, the teacher shares his or her knowledge about the content, as well as the instructional methods and materials that have been used in previous years to deliver this content to the students. The coach asks questions to build her or his understanding of the content and to clarify the types of thinking, reading, writing, and speaking expected of the students. Then the coach offers suggestions for refining existing disciplinary literacy practices and for incorporating new disciplinary literacy practices as the two work together to finalize the overall plan for the unit.

In addition to co-planning, the teacher and the coach share the responsibility for co-teaching the individual lessons of the unit. The coach often takes the responsibility for teaching any new disciplinary literacy strategies, serving as a model for the teacher. They meet together on a daily basis to debrief the day's work, with a

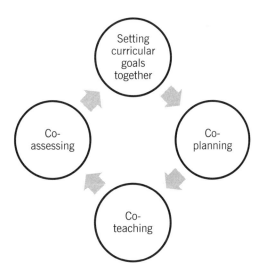

FIGURE III.3. The co-teaching model.

focus on how the disciplinary literacy practices are helping the students to build the requisite knowledge of the discipline. They use their reflections to adjust plans for the following day. They co-assess students throughout the unit, not just at the end of the unit, in order to ensure that their ongoing instruction is systematic and meets student needs. At the end of the unit, they document which disciplinary literacy practices were effective for students and what, if any, revisions would enhance the effectiveness the next time those strategies are used—in future units or when this unit is taught to another group of students.

What Is the Time Commitment for This Model?

As was the case with the teacher-initiated model, the co-teaching model requires a large time commitment on the part of both the coach and the teacher. In addition to teaching together on a daily basis over the course of a quarter or a semester or a year, the coach and the teacher spend time co-planning the unit as a whole, as well as planning and debriefing daily lessons. Analysis of student work and assessments may be completed during those debriefing/co-planning sessions, although, if those sessions are relatively short, additional meetings may need to be held for that analysis.

What Are This Model's Strengths and Constraints?

The strength of the co-teaching model comes from the ongoing collaborations between the coach and the teacher (see Figure III.4). The idea that "two heads are better than one" is certainly the cornerstone of this model, as the content expertise of the teacher and the literacy expertise of the coach are combined to design and implement effective disciplinary literacy instruction. As a result of the co-planning, co-teaching, and co-assessing, the teacher will build his or her capacity to create units of study that enable the students to engage in the habits of thinking, reading, writing, and speaking that are representative of those used by disciplinary experts.

Time is the major constraint of the co-teaching model. First, the decision to co-teach must be made before the master schedule is developed in order to ensure that the coach and teacher are both free to teach the designated class. Second, it is

Strengths	Constraints
• Combines subject-area and literacy knowledge. • Coach gains "insider" perspective of the discipline and student needs. • Immediate application of ideas. • Opportunities for modeling new strategies. • Builds teacher capacity.	• Scheduling constraints. • Consistent co-teaching time. • Planning and reflection time. • Incompatibility of personalities. • May not build capacity beyond the teacher level.

FIGURE III.4. Strengths and constraints of the co-teaching model.

optimal that the coach and the teacher have a common planning time so they can engage in the planning and debriefing activities previously described. When teachers and coaches do not have a common planning time, they need to fit their discussions into their already busy schedules. Thus, without a common planning time, discussions may not be possible on a daily basis or may be so short that they result in incomplete planning and/or surface reflection, leading to poorly taught lessons that do not facilitate student learning.

Because they spend so much time together, it is important that the teacher and the coach have established a collegial relationship before beginning their co-teaching adventures. Acknowledging each other's expertise, being willing to consider each other's ideas, and being willing to take instructional risks while co-teaching are three critical elements of a collegial co-teaching team.

Department/Team Model

What Is It?

In the department/team model, hereafter referred to as the team model, the coach works with teachers representing a specific department or team (Bean & Eisenberg, 2009; McKenna & Walpole, 2008). Thus a middle school coach might work with all of the social studies teachers, whereas a high school coach might work with all of the faculty from the science department or perhaps just with the faculty who teach biology. At the middle school, another approach to the team model is for the coach to work with a set of teachers from different disciplines who all teach the same group of students. For example, a coach might work with the ELA teacher, the science teacher, the social studies teacher, and the math teacher who all teach the same group of 27 sixth-grade students. Finally, a PLC is a team that could benefit from the coach's expertise in disciplinary literacy instruction. Often, PLCs are composed of teachers who want to focus on a particular topic or specific group of students. For instance, a coach could easily work with a PLC that is examining assessment data and current practices to make improvements to their instruction of English learners. Depending on the size of the department, team, or PLC, this model could fit into the large-group or small-group layer of coaching discussed in Part II.

What Are the Typical Coaching Activities within This Model?

Coaching in the team model (see Figure III.5) generally begins with the coach's active participation in department or team meetings. Whenever the team is discussing curriculum, instruction, or assessment, there are opportunities for the coach to address the importance of disciplinary literacy practices. Think about a team that is reviewing a common assessment and determining whether the proposed instructional activities for the unit will enable the students to achieve the unit's goals and perform well on the assessment. This discussion provides an opportunity for the

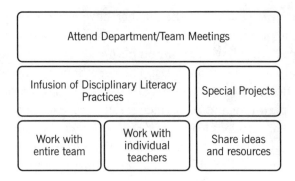

FIGURE III.5. The department/team model.

coach to talk about how specific disciplinary literacy practices might help the students achieve those goals. For example, the coach who has examined the texts that the students will be expected to read could suggest and demonstrate to the group a disciplinary literacy strategy that would guide the students in organizing and discussing the text's content so students could gain a firm understanding of the requisite knowledge of the unit. After hearing the coach's ideas, one or more individual members of the team might then ask the coach to help them incorporate the strategy into their instruction, thus providing opportunities for coaching at the individual level.

Sometimes a coach is invited to work with a team on a special project, such as creating curriculum maps or developing instructional activities for a new unit of study or to enhance an existing unit of study. These invitations open the door for discussions about disciplinary literacy practices. However, to provide appropriate suggestions, the coach must prepare carefully for these meetings. Depending on the nature of the project, the coach will spend time doing one or more of the following: becoming familiar with the goals and essential questions of the unit of study, examining texts that students are expected to read, asking questions about the instructional activities that are currently used during instruction, making observations in classrooms, and researching literacy practices applicable to the discipline. With this careful preparation, the coach will be ready to actively participate in the discussion, asking clarifying questions and making relevant, feasible suggestions for infusing disciplinary literacy practices into the project.

What Is the Time Commitment for This Model?

Working closely with a department or team requires coaches to attend the team's regular meetings, as well as to prepare for these meetings. In addition, because one or more members of the team often request individual assistance with implementing the ideas discussed at the team meetings, coaches must have some room in their schedules for working with individual teachers. Thus coaches must carefully consider how many teams they can work with at any one time. If coaches commit to working with too many teams, they may find it difficult to engage in the preparation necessary to make good suggestions regarding disciplinary literacy instruction.

What Are This Model's Strengths and Constraints?

Schools choose to use the team model of coaching because it provides the promise of building capacity and sustainability in a relatively efficient manner (see Figure III.6). In terms of capacity, groups of teachers learn about and begin to implement disciplinary literacy practices. Coaching may be especially effective in building capacity when working with teachers of a discipline in which large numbers of students are struggling to succeed. The team model is more efficient than the teacher-initiated or co-teaching models, in which capacity generally is built one teacher at a time. In addition, when coaches work with teams on special projects, such as curriculum mapping or infusing disciplinary literacy practices into a new unit of study, they are helping the team develop a process for approaching such projects. Thus, as the team moves on to the curricular mapping of different courses or designing additional units, they should need less support from the coach. Ultimately, the team may be able to approach these projects independently, resulting in the sustainability of the processes that will ensure the ongoing incorporation of disciplinary literacy practices into the curriculum.

Working with teams does not always run smoothly. If the team has already formed a close working relationship, it is often difficult for a coach to be fully accepted into the group. Even if the coach is welcomed onto the team, it may be difficult to make meaningful contributions if one or more members of the group consistently find reasons not to incorporate any of the coach's suggestions into the project being discussed. Coaches may avoid this obstacle by starting their participation with a "listening more/talking less" and "asking more/suggesting less" approach. This acknowledges the team's expertise and shows the coach's willingness to learn more about the discipline. In addition, when a coach thoughtfully selects and clearly explains appropriate strategies for the project at hand, the team will gain confidence that the coach can provide strategies that will help the students gain the knowledge and skills that the team has designated as critical to understanding the content of the discipline.

Strengths	Constraints
• Builds capacity at the department/team level. • Creates sustainability. • Can tackle departmentwide/teamwide projects. • Efficient in terms of coach's time.	• All members of the department/team may not be supportive of the model. • Departments/teams can be difficult to join; coach may feel like an outsider or bystander. • Time constraints within department/team meeting structure.

FIGURE III.6. Strengths and constraints of the department/team model.

Liaison Model

What Is It?

The liaison model (Elish-Piper et al., 2012; Ippolito & Lieberman, 2012) offers a three-pronged approach to coaching: professional development workshops, individual disciplinary literacy coaching, and sharing of ideas with departments or teams. The program begins with coaches recruiting a small set of teachers in specific disciplines to be literacy liaisons. This is most effective when, after the coaching program has been introduced by the administrators and coach, the teachers complete an application to become liaisons. Completing an application makes it more likely that the teacher understands and is committed to full participation in the program. The selected liaisons then participate in a series of professional development workshops that are offered over the course of the year and that are led by the literacy coach or coaches. Professional development topics typically include theoretical underpinnings of disciplinary literacy, developing disciplinary literacy objectives that are matched to the curriculum, and analyzing current instructional practices in terms of disciplinary literacy. Throughout the year, coaches also work individually with the liaisons on a weekly or biweekly basis. The individual coaching sessions provide opportunities for the coach and liaison to co-plan and perhaps co-teach instruction that incorporates disciplinary literacy practices. Literacy liaisons are not only expected to enact disciplinary literacy practices in their classrooms but are also expected to share information about and examples of disciplinary literacy instruction with colleagues in their departments.

The liaison model encompasses all three layers of coaching described in Part II. Depending on the number of coaches in the building, the professional development sessions for the liaisons may fall within the large-group layer (e.g., three coaches and 20–25 liaisons) or the small-group layer (e.g., one coach and 8–10 liaisons). Coaches also collaborate with liaisons on an individual basis, representative of the individual layer of coaching. Finally, when coaches collaborate with liaisons to share at department meetings (e.g., science or social studies) or specific team meetings (e.g., biology teachers or history I teachers), they are operating within the large-group or small-group layer of coaching, respectively.

What Are the Typical Coaching Activities within This Model?

The three components of the liaison model described above are shown in Figure III.7. The coach takes on several roles: provider of large-group professional development, collaborator during individual coaching sessions, and facilitator in helping the liaison share information and strategies with his or her department.

Typically in the liaison model, a new set of liaisons is selected each year. Often, the liaisons from the previous year continue to participate in professional development workshops and are given the opportunity to continue with their individual

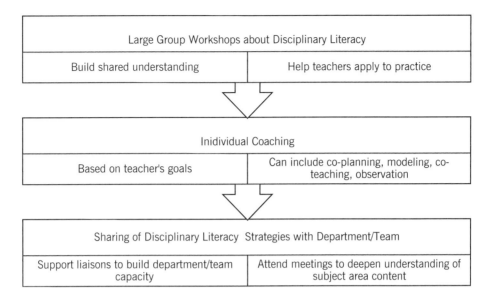

FIGURE III.7. The liaison model.

coaching sessions. Thus, over the course of several years, multiple teachers from each discipline will have become liaisons—building capacity in and sustainability of disciplinary literacy instruction.

What Is the Time Commitment for This Model?

The liaison model works best when the literacy coach is a full-time coach. This allows time to plan and deliver the professional development workshops, to work with the liaisons on a weekly basis, and to attend department meetings as needed. The number of liaisons selected for the program may depend on the number of literacy coaches in the building. A single literacy coach might be able to accommodate 10–12 liaisons in her or his schedule, whereas a larger number of liaisons could be selected if there were two or even three literacy coaches in the building.

What Are This Model's Strengths and Constraints?

The liaison model has the potential to build capacity at the individual and department levels, thereby resulting in creating sustainability within and across departments. When implemented as designed with teachers who are committed to the program, this model can lead to the use of discipline-specific literacy practices across an entire school. To achieve its potential, the liaison coaching model needs to have a strong commitment from the administration. They need to understand that the liaison model is most effective when conducted over the course of several years. To sustain such a model will require a financial commitment in terms of hiring full-time literacy coaches and providing substitutes so the liaisons can attend the professional development sessions. It also requires that the administration show ongoing support of the program at faculty and department meetings.

Although there are several constraints (see Figure III.8), perhaps the most difficult aspect of the liaison model is the sharing of information by the liaison with other department members. Our work with liaisons has shown that it takes at least 2 years of professional development and individual coaching for them to feel confident about incorporating disciplinary literacy practices into their own instruction. Until they develop this confidence, they are hesitant to share their ideas with other members of their departments. Even when they are confident about their own practice and the coach assists them to design the sharing session, liaisons still may find it challenging to discuss their ideas. Their colleagues may appear reticent to change their current practice or, because there are several different disciplines within the department, the liaison may not be sure that what worked for her discipline (e.g., biology) would be appropriate for another discipline (e.g., chemistry). However, as multiple liaisons from the same department go through the program, they can work together to share with their departmental colleagues, which will make the process easier and will likely lead to building capacity across the department.

Selecting a Disciplinary Literacy Coaching Model

In Part III, we have described four disciplinary literacy coaching models: the teacher-initiated model, the co-teaching model, the department/team model, and the liaison model. To determine which one is best for your school, several factors should be considered.

- How many coaches are working in the school? Is each coach full time or part time?
- Do the coaches have a good understanding of disciplinary literacy instruction? If not, perhaps they need to participate in professional development (e.g., attending workshops, reading professional articles and books, visiting other schools with disciplinary coaching models) before a model of coaching is selected.

Strengths	Constraints
• Voluntary. • Builds capacity at the department/team level. • Creates sustainability. • Large-group professional development is efficient in terms of coach's time.	• Individual coaching component is time-consuming. • Teachers may volunteer for the wrong reasons. • Transfer to departments can be slow.

FIGURE III.8. Strengths and constraints of the liaison model.

- Which model fits better with the current master schedule? If the fit for a preferred model is not a good one, could changes to the master schedule be made?
- In terms of disciplinary literacy instruction, where do the teachers fall on the concerns-based adoption model described in Part II? Perhaps there is a need for large-group professional development before any of these models is selected.
- Is there strong administrative support for one model over another?

Finally, we would like to note that it is not uncommon for a school to begin with one model and move to another after a year or two. Neither is it unusual for a coach to combine two models to fit the needs of the teachers and students. For example, Jonas Streeter, a former social studies teacher with a reading teacher endorsement, started his coaching work at Hill High School using the teacher-initiated model. After a successful year and a half of working with individual teachers, two teachers requested that he spend more time in their classrooms. Jonas approached the principal to see if he could be assigned to co-teach with each of these teachers for one period of the second semester. In addition to his co-teaching during the spring semester, Jonas continued to coach individual teachers—thus effectively merging the teacher-initiated coaching and co-teaching models.

Summary

The first three parts of this book have provided an overview of disciplinary literacy, disciplinary literacy coaching, and models of disciplinary literacy coaching. In the next parts, you will be introduced to a variety of large-group, small-group, and individual disciplinary literacy coaching strategies that have been used successfully by coaches who work in middle and high school settings.

PART IV

Large-Group Coaching Strategies to Build a Foundation for Disciplinary Literacy Instruction

If you are just getting started with disciplinary literacy coaching, the whole process might seem so complex and enormous that you don't even know where to begin. You may only have a small amount of time in your schedule designated for coaching, or the teachers in your school may not be familiar or comfortable with the idea of disciplinary literacy. Or you may work with many veteran teachers who tend to dismiss new approaches because they are likely to "go away," as previous initiatives did. As you consider your coaching context, what can you do to get started? How can you use your coaching time efficiently and effectively? Using the three layers of literacy coaching model discussed in Part II, we suggest beginning with large groups of teachers to build a foundation for both disciplinary literacy and coaching. Depending on the size and structure of your school, large groups might include the whole staff, all eighth-grade teachers, the entire English department, or all of the U.S. history teachers.

Working with large groups of teachers is definitely the most efficient approach to coaching because you are able to connect with and support many teachers at the same time. Furthermore, when you coach large groups of teachers, you are able to make sure that all of the teachers understand the concept of disciplinary literacy and the demands of the relevant learning standards such as the CCSS, NGSS, and the C3 Framework. Because disciplinary literacy and coaching may be new ideas for many teachers at your school, it will be important to build a shared understanding and common goals across your whole school. For example, if your school targets writing arguments as an important goal, all of the teachers in the large group will be learning about, thinking about, and exploring ways to teach students to write arguments in their disciplines. Once you begin implementing large-group coaching activities, you will likely hear teachers talking during lunch, meetings, and hallway conversations about writing arguments, even sharing ideas and resources they have found online or in other sources. Because you and the teachers will all be working toward the same disciplinary literacy goal, you can begin to establish a collaborative climate and shared knowledge base that will support and encourage teachers to update and enhance their instructional practices.

Part IV contains five literacy coaching strategies you can use with large groups of teachers. Strategy 1 focuses on how you can establish a climate in your school that is conducive to coaching. In addition, Strategy 1 provides useful suggestions to ensure that you are ready for disciplinary literacy coaching. Strategy 2 shows you how to conduct article study groups so teachers can read, respond to, and reflect on professional articles related to disciplinary literacy. In Strategy 3, you'll learn how to use your limited coaching time efficiently by embedding coaching activities and support into already scheduled faculty and department meetings.

To ensure that you are ready and confident to facilitate large-group professional development sessions, Strategy 4 offers useful information about how you can plan, deliver, and evaluate sessions with large groups of teachers. Finally, Strategy 5 provides practical ideas about how to use technology to connect with and support large groups of teachers. Suggestions for specific tools are also included to ensure that you are ready and able to harness the power of technology to support disciplinary literacy coaching at your school.

By implementing some or all of the strategies in Part IV, you will be able to build a solid foundation of teacher knowledge about and engagement with disciplinary literacy instruction. Then, by layering on appropriate small-group and individual coaching activities that are presented in Parts V and VI, you can help teachers update their instruction to incorporate important disciplinary literacy practices that will enhance student learning.

Establishing a Climate for Disciplinary Literacy Coaching

What Is It?

Disciplinary literacy coaching is most effective when a school has already established a collaborative climate that values professional development (Sweeney, 2013). Creating this type of climate takes time as administrators, teachers, and specialized professionals work together to develop a common vision that focuses on high expectations for student learning and a shared responsibility for helping all students meet those expectations (Gross, 2010). A school's administrative team (e.g., principal, assistant principals, department chairs, team leaders) plays a key role in establishing and sustaining a school climate that encourages collaboration and provides ongoing opportunities for professional development (Leithwood, Seashore-Louis, Anderson, & Wahlstrom, 2004).

The real success of disciplinary literacy coaching depends on what the coach brings to the job in terms of knowledge, skills, and dispositions. More specifically, coaches must have a strong knowledge base about literacy instruction and assessment, as well as the disciplines being coached. Furthermore, coaches must understand the discipline-specific uses of literacy in the content areas in which they will be coaching. Coaches must also be skillful collaborators who can work effectively with teachers in a variety of disciplines (IRA, 2006). Additionally, coaches must understand how adults learn and how to support teachers through the change process (Hord & Tobia, 2012). Finally, coaches must also have strong communication and interpersonal skills so they can effectively work with large groups, small groups, and individual teachers. Being a disciplinary literacy coach is a challenging and complex role; therefore, you may find that you do not already possess all of the knowledge, skills, and dispositions necessary to be a successful literacy coach. You can, however, reflect on your strengths, identify your needs, and take actions to get yourself ready for disciplinary literacy coaching in your school.

The two questionnaires in this strategy (see Forms 1.1 and 1.2) will help you determine how prepared your school and you are for disciplinary literacy coaching. By completing these questionnaires and analyzing and reflecting on the responses, you will be able to identify areas of strength and also areas in which more development is needed. You can then use that information to develop an action plan to ensure that your school is ready for disciplinary literacy coaching and to enhance your own preparedness for disciplinary literacy coaching.

Evaluating the School Climate for Disciplinary Literacy Coaching

The questionnaire in Form 1.1 is designed to help you examine how prepared your school is for disciplinary literacy coaching.

How Do I Do It?

1. Read the questions in the left column of the "How Ready Is My School for Disciplinary Literacy Coaching?" questionnaire (see Form 1.1).

2. Do your best to write an example or two for each indicator of readiness.

3. Mark an X in the box that describes your school's readiness regarding each question.

   a. *We are ready!* If you are able to list at least one specific example for each indicator, your school is ready for literacy coaching.

   b. *We are almost ready.* If you are able to list an example for most of the indicators, your school has made progress but still has work to do to get ready for coaching.

   c. *We have a long way to go to be ready.* If you are unable to provide examples for most of the indicators, your school still needs to make significant progress to be ready for coaching.

4. Review the results of the questionnaire and develop an action plan for enhancing your school's readiness for disciplinary literacy coaching. Write your action plan in the box at the bottom of Form 1.1.

   a. For "Short-Term Goals," focus on those areas you marked as "We are almost ready." Think of how you can work with others at your school to address these indicators. Record your ideas on Form 1.1.

   b. For the areas you marked as "We have a long way to go to be ready," you will need to develop a long-term action plan. You will want to meet with the administrative team and teacher leaders such as department chairs to discuss those areas that need improvement and to determine a plan to move your school toward readiness for disciplinary literacy coaching.

The Strategy in Action

Oscar Jimenez recently accepted a position as a disciplinary literacy coach at Middlebury High School, where he has worked for 7 years as an English teacher. Because coaching and disciplinary literacy are new concepts for most of the teachers and administrators at his school, he completed the "How Ready Is My School for Disciplinary Literacy Coaching?" questionnaire. He identified several foundational areas in which his school was well prepared: climate for professional development (item 1), administrators as curricular leaders (item 2), open communication (item 3), teachers observing each other (item 6), and time for coaching (item 7). When he reviewed items 4 and 5, he found that his school was not prepared in relation to understanding disciplinary literacy (item 4) and the norms and conventions of the disciplines (item 5). He scheduled a meeting with his assistant principal and the department chairs in science, social studies, and English, which were the disciplines in which he would be coaching. They discussed where they felt the teachers' (and their own) knowledge about disciplinary literacy was, and they determined that this needed to be a focus of an upcoming professional development session. They also created a plan for Oscar to visit the science, social studies, and English departments following that professional development session to collaborate with the teachers to develop a plan that would help them get ready to embrace this disciplinary literacy approach in their teaching.

As Oscar reflected on this process, as well as his school's readiness for disciplinary literacy coaching, he commented, "It's a little overwhelming to think about how much work we have to do to get ready for disciplinary literacy coaching. At least we now have a plan so I know how to spend my time to help our school move toward this goal."

Establishing Your Readiness for Disciplinary Literacy Coaching

Whether you are new to coaching or bring years of experience to your work, analyzing and reflecting on your strengths and areas for improvement can help ensure that you are ready for disciplinary literacy coaching. The questionnaire in Form 1.2 will guide you through this process.

How Do I Do It?

1. Read each question in the left column on the "How Ready Am I for Disciplinary Literacy Coaching?" questionnaire (see Form 1.2).

2. For each question, mark an X in the box that describes your own readiness

for disciplinary coaching: *Yes*, *Somewhat*, or *No*. Be honest with your self-assessments so that you can get a true understanding of your readiness for disciplinary literacy coaching.

3. For the questions you marked *Somewhat* or *No*, read the suggestions in the right column for improving your readiness.

4. Create an action plan by circling the suggestions you believe will be most useful to improve your readiness. If you have other ideas for improving your readiness in a specific area, write them in the section labeled "Additional action(s) you might take."

5. Prioritize the circled items and develop a timeline for completing the activities.

The Strategy in Action

Rachel Cosby has been a reading specialist at Buffalo Ridge Middle School for 3 years. Before that, she taught seventh- and eighth-grade ELA and social studies. She is in her 1st year as a middle school literacy coach, and she has been asked to work most closely with the science teachers in grades 6–8 to build their disciplinary literacy as required by the NGSS. At first, Rachel reported feeling like "a fish out of water" when talking with the six science teachers at her school. After completing the "How Ready Am I for Literacy Coaching?" questionnaire (see Form 1.2), Rachel realized she had two major areas to address in her own professional preparation for disciplinary literacy coaching. First, she identified a need to learn more about

Action Plan	
List, in priority order, the most important activities you plan to complete to improve your readiness for disciplinary literacy coaching.	Date for completion
Build my knowledge of the norms and conventions of earth science, life science, and physical science. • Review the Next Generation Science Standards for grades 6–8 (middle school), as well as the Common Core State Standards for science and technical subjects. Identify standards that I find confusing or unclear so I can investigate these further. • Meet with Alan Chang, Ashley O'Dowd, and Caroline Miller, veteran science teachers, to discuss how they (and their students) use reading, writing, listening, speaking, viewing, and visually representing. Reflect on what I learn to determine areas where I need to build my knowledge. • Read at least one article, chapter, or resource about disciplinary literacy instruction at the middle school level.	October 12
Build my understanding of adult learning, change theory, and coaching. • Read at least one article, chapter, or resource for each area. Select from the recommended readings under item 7 of Form 1.2.	October 26

FIGURE 1.1. Action plan for Rachel Cosby.

the norms and conventions of science in the areas of earth science, life science, and physical science. Second, she realized she needed to enhance her knowledge about adult learning, change, and coaching. Rachel then created an action plan (see Figure 1.1) to address these two areas.

Rachel also initiated a meeting with Sherri Anderson and Karlissa Jones, the coaches at the two other middle schools in her district. They discussed Rachel's action plan and how they could work together as they all enhanced their readiness to be effective disciplinary literacy coaches at their middle schools. Rachel reported, "Meeting with Sherri and Karlissa each month has been a lifesaver! We share ideas, discuss challenges, and most of all, encourage each other. It's great to have other people who understand this exciting and complex role so we can support each other."

How Ready Is My School for Disciplinary Literacy Coaching?

Questions	Indicators of Readiness	Examples from My School
1. Is there a climate of professional development in departments, teams, and across the entire school? ☐ We are ready! ☐ We are almost ready. ☐ We have a long way to go to be ready.	a. Professional development efforts are directed at enhancing teacher knowledge and practice. b. Professional development efforts are directed at improving student achievement. c. Professional development efforts involve teachers in the planning, implementation, and evaluation stages.	a. b. c.
2. Do members of the administrative team operate as curricular leaders? ☐ We are ready! ☐ We are almost ready. ☐ We have a long way to go to be ready.	a. Administrative team members are knowledgeable about the school's curriculum. b. Administrative team members provide the time and resources necessary for professional development. c. Administrative team members attend and, when possible, actively participate in meetings and workshops related to curricular issues.	a. b. c.
3. Is there open, productive communication among teachers? ☐ We are ready! ☐ We are almost ready. ☐ We have a long way to go to be ready.	a. There are multiple opportunities for teachers to talk during professional development sessions, department or team meetings, and professional learning communities. b. In informal settings, teachers talk openly to each other about strategies and resources. c. Good lines of communication have been established among teachers and other staff members such as speech–language pathologists, counselors, psychologists, and social workers.	a. b. c.

(continued)

From *Collaborative Coaching for Disciplinary Literacy: Strategies to Support Teachers in Grades 6–12* by Laurie Elish-Piper, Susan K. L'Allier, Michael Manderino, and Paula Di Domenico. Copyright © 2016 The Guilford Press. Permission to photocopy this form is granted to purchasers of this book for personal use only (see copyright page for details). Purchasers can download additional copies of this form (see the box at the end of the table of contents).

Questions	Indicators of Readiness	Examples from My School
4. Is there a shared definition and understanding of disciplinary literacy held by administrators and teachers? ☐ We are ready! ☐ We are almost ready. ☐ We have a long way to go to be ready.	a. Teachers and administrators have engaged in multiple discussions about the meaning of disciplinary literacy. b. Teachers and administrators regularly talk about disciplinary literacy as they discuss lessons, curriculum, and assessments. c. If asked, "What is disciplinary literacy?" teachers' and administrators' responses would be consistent.	a. b. c.
5. Teachers know the norms and conventions of their disciplines. ☐ We are ready! ☐ We are almost ready. ☐ We have a long way to go to be ready.	a. Teachers are able to identify and discuss the norms and conventions of their disciplines. b. Teachers model the norms and conventions of their disciplines in their instruction. c. Teachers provide opportunities for students to use disciplinary literacy practices.	a. b. c.
6. Are teachers open to having others in their classrooms? ☐ We are ready! ☐ We are almost ready. ☐ We have a long way to go to be ready.	a. Teachers regularly observe one another teaching. b. Teachers leave their doors open and welcome others into their classrooms. c. A push-in model for supporting students who struggle is being used when appropriate.	a. b. c.
7. Does the schedule allow for literacy coaching? ☐ We are ready! ☐ We are almost ready. ☐ We have a long way to go to be ready.	a. There are common planning times for departments and teams so the coach can meet with them on a regular basis. b. The coach has several periods or more per day designated for coaching. c. The coach's schedule is free of duties right before and after school to provide convenient times to meet with teachers.	a. b. c.

(continued)

Action Plan for Enhancing the School's Readiness for Disciplinary Literacy Coaching			
Short-term goals	*Tasks*	*People who need to be involved*	*Date for task completion*
Long-term goals	*Tasks*	*People who need to be involved*	*Date for task completion*

How Ready Am I for Disciplinary Literacy Coaching?

Questions	What Can You Do to Increase Your Readiness for Disciplinary Literacy Coaching?
1. Do I understand the curriculum (in the disciplines in which I coach) and how it is aligned with the Common Core and other relevant standards? ☐ Yes ☐ Somewhat ☐ No	a. Carefully read the curriculum and review available curriculum maps and common assessments. Develop a list of questions you want to discuss with others to enhance your knowledge of the curriculum. b. Read the standards that are expected to be met by students. Write down questions you have about the standards. Identify people at your school or in your district who will be able to help you get answers to your questions. c. Determine whether the curriculum includes explicit alignment with the required standards. If it does not, think about the steps that might be necessary to create alignment between the curriculum and the required standards. How might you, as the literacy coach, be involved in that process? d. Additional action(s) you might take:
2. Do I understand what instruction looks like in my school in the disciplines in which I am coaching? ☐ Yes ☐ Somewhat ☐ No	a. Determine the disciplines, grade levels, and specific settings in which your understanding of instruction could be enhanced. b. To enhance your understanding of instruction in those settings, make multiple observations and engage in collegial conversations with those teachers. c. Reflect on your observations and conversations. • Is the instruction aligned with the literacy curriculum? • What differences are there across settings? Which differences seem appropriate and why? Which differences may warrant discussion with teachers? • Does the instruction address disciplinary-specific literacy practices? • Additional action(s) you might take:
3. Do I understand the makeup and demographics of my school community? ☐ Yes ☐ Somewhat ☐ No	a. If your state or school district provides a school report card for each school, carefully examine it. These report cards typically provide information about student diversity in terms of gender, race/ethnicity, language, and socioeconomic status. In addition, student performance on state assessments is generally included. If your state or school district does not provide a school report card, work with your administrative team to collect this type of information. b. Create a list of teachers and the disciplines, grade levels, and classes they teach. Add the other professionals and paraprofessionals in your school. What role does each of these people play in the school? With which students do they interact and for what purposes? c. Make a list of how parents and community members are involved with the school (e.g., volunteering, working in after-school programs, supporting extracurricular activities, participating in the PTO or PTA, attending parent conferences, providing resources to support programs).

(continued)

From *Collaborative Coaching for Disciplinary Literacy: Strategies to Support Teachers in Grades 6–12* by Laurie Elish-Piper, Susan K. L'Allier, Michael Manderino, and Paula Di Domenico. Copyright © 2016 The Guilford Press. Permission to photocopy this form is granted to purchasers of this book for personal use only (see copyright page for details). Purchasers can download additional copies of this form (see the box at the end of the table of contents).

Questions	What Can You Do to Increase Your Readiness for Disciplinary Literacy Coaching?
	d. Additional action(s) you might take:
4. Have I worked with the school's administrative team to establish a foundation for literacy coaching? ☐ Yes ☐ Somewhat ☐ No	a. Work with your school's administrative team to develop a job description and purpose statement for the disciplinary literacy coaching aspect of your position. b. At a faculty meeting, department meetings, or team meetings, ask a member of the school's administrative team to share the job description, and you can share your purpose statement. You can also provide a list of ways that you can support teachers as they work to improve student learning through disciplinary literacy instruction. c. After these meetings, send an email to the teachers and invite them to contact you if they are interested in collaborating with you. d. Additional action(s) you might take:
5. Do I know who the "experts" are in my school? ☐ Yes ☐ Somewhat ☐ No	a. Make a list of the teachers who you know from personal observation are expert or highly skilled at various aspects of teaching (e.g., classroom management, student relationships, instructional methods, discipline-specific literacy practices, technology use). b. Add to your list as you make classroom observations and as you talk with teachers individually and at meetings and professional development sessions. c. Additional action(s) you might take:
6. Am I knowledgeable about the norms and conventions of the disciplines in which I coach? ☐ Yes ☐ Somewhat ☐ No	a. Meet with teachers in the disciplines in which you coach. Ask them how they (and their students) use reading, writing, listening, speaking, viewing, and visually representing in their disciplines. Identify areas in which you need to deepen your knowledge. b. Review the relevant standards and identify those that address disciplinary literacy instruction. c. Start with two or three areas about which you want to know more. Locate articles and resources related to those areas. As you read these articles and resources, consider how they connect with classroom instruction at your school. d. Additional action(s) you might take:

7. Do I understand key ideas related to adult learning, change theory, and coaching?
 	
☐ Yes
 	
☐ Somewhat
 	
☐ No
	a. For more information about adult learning, read:
	  • Terehoff, I. I. (2002). Elements of adult learning in teacher professional development. *NASSP Bulletin, 86*(232), 65–77.
	  • Trotter, Y. D. (2006). Adult learning theories: Impacting professional development programs. *Delta Kappa Gamma Bulletin, 72*(2), 8–13.
	b. For more information about change theory, read:
	  • Reeves, D. B. (2009). *Leading change in your school.* Alexandria, VA: ASCD.
	  • Chapter 1 of Hall, G. E., & Hord, S. M. (2006). *Implementing change: Patterns, principles, and potholes* (2nd ed.). Boston: Allyn & Bacon.

(continued)

Questions	What Can You Do to Increase Your Readiness for Disciplinary Literacy Coaching?
	c. There are several recently published professional books about literacy coaching in middle and high schools. Go to *www.amazon.com* and type "secondary literacy coaching" in the search box. Browse the tables of contents and purchase one or two that include chapters related to your specific needs. d. Attend workshops related to literacy coaching. e. Meet regularly with other coaches to discuss literacy coaching issues, challenges, and strategies. This group may also want to participate in a book study that focuses on a professional book about literacy coaching. You can also join online groups for Twitter chats or enroll in a MOOC (massive open online course) related to your professional development needs. A great resource for MOOCs for educators is *www.mooc-ed.org*. f. Additional action(s) you might take:

8. Have I established my credibility as a teacher?
 	
☐ Yes
 	
☐ Somewhat
 	
☐ No
	a. If you have been a teacher in the school where you coach, you probably have established a certain level of credibility. For example, if you taught 9th- and 10th-grade English, your credibility may extend to all English teachers.
	b. To establish credibility with teachers in disciplines and grade levels in which you have not taught, try some of these ideas:
	  • Offer to do demonstration lessons related to a standard with which the teachers are grappling.
	  • Offer to teach a short lesson on vocabulary to show new ways to help students learn academic vocabulary.
	  • Offer to come in and assist teachers with small-group activities, special projects, or writing-intensive activities so teachers can see you interacting with their students.
	c. Additional action(s) you might take:

9. Am I a good listener? ☐ Yes ☐ Somewhat ☐ No	a. As you have conversations with teachers, consider whether you are listening at least as much as you are talking. b. Use active listening strategies such as restating what you've heard, asking questions, making eye contact, leaning in, and nodding. Using a prompt such as "tell me more" can signal to teachers that you are there to listen. c. Additional action(s) you might take:
10. Have I reflected on previous curricular initiatives in my school? ☐ Yes ☐ Somewhat ☐ No	a. Make a list of things that contributed to the success of those initiatives. b. Make a list of things that impeded the success of those initiatives. c. Consider how you can incorporate the successful things and avoid the unsuccessful ones as you work with teachers and your school's administrative team to incorporate disciplinary literacy instruction. d. Additional action(s) you might take:

(continued)

How Ready Am I for Disciplinary Literacy Coaching? *(page 4 of 4)*

Action Plan	
List, in priority order, the most important activities you plan to complete to improve your readiness for disciplinary literacy coaching.	Date for completion

Facilitating an Article Study Group

What Is It?

A study group of teachers can come together with a literacy coach to read and discuss a professional journal article or book chapter related to some aspect of their teaching practice. Such study groups offer a safe, supportive setting for teachers to discuss professional literature by sharing their reactions, insights, questions, and concerns through small-group discussion (Burbank, Kauchak, & Bates, 2010). When teachers participate in an article study group, they can be part of a community of learners that supports the enhancement of their own professional development and teaching practice (Commeyras, Bisplinghoff, & Olson, 2003). Facilitating an article study group is an easy and effective coaching strategy, especially for coaches who have limited coaching time in their schedules.

Articles or book chapters are excellent texts to use for study groups because they are focused, can be read fairly quickly, and can be discussed in a single face-to-face meeting or in an online format. To ensure that the articles or chapters selected for study groups are relevant, applicable, and accessible in terms of length, complexity, and amount of background knowledge needed, the literacy coach, department chair, or team leader typically chooses them. The literacy coach serves as the facilitator to get the discussion going, to make sure that all members participate, and to help the group stay focused on key ideas and important application ideas. After the literacy coach has modeled the process, others, including the department chair or team leader, can facilitate future article study groups.

When teachers participate in article study groups, they can build a common language and understanding of educational issues and instructional practices as they read, discuss, and apply ideas from the article. Article study groups can contribute to building a school climate that values and fosters ongoing professional development and collaboration. In addition, article study groups can serve as an entry point for other coaching activities, as teachers often contact the literacy coach for support in implementing in their teaching practice the new strategies they've read about and discussed in article study groups.

How Do I Do It?

To implement article study groups, there are three processes you'll complete: preparing, facilitating, and following up. The steps for preparing, facilitating, and following up for article study groups are detailed next.

Preparing for an Article Study Group

1. Determine which teachers will be in the article study group. Article study groups work best when the groups are fairly small (i.e., fewer than 10 people) and the text is directly applicable to the participants' teaching. For example, high school biology teachers or eighth-grade ELA teachers might make up an article study group. At times, teachers may choose to be part of an article study group based on professional interests or goals, such as incorporating technology into teaching, supporting English learners in the disciplines, or using problem-based learning.

2. Confer with the group members to determine the purpose for the article study group. You may find it useful to ask the teachers directly, "What do you hope to learn or accomplish as a result of participating in this article study group?"

3. Locate at least one article or book chapter that addresses the specific purpose the group has set. A list of sample articles and book chapters related to disciplinary literacy instruction is provided in Figure 2.1, and many more can be located in professional journals, books, and online sources. If two or more articles or chapters are available, briefly share an overview of the article or chapter so the teachers can choose which one they want to read and discuss. If you are only able to locate one appropriate article or chapter, provide a quick overview to the teachers to ensure that it meets their purpose.

4. Select a format that the article study group members can use to record their reactions and refer to during the discussion. A standard article discussion group format is provided in Form 2.1, and three additional formats are offered in Figure 2.2.

5. Determine the time, place, and location for the article study group to meet. Depending on the length of the article and the complexity of the ideas presented, a group meeting may be as short as 20 minutes or as long as 1 hour. In some middle and high schools, teachers' schedules and extracurricular obligations make online discussions an appealing and manageable option. Two easy-to-use, free online options are Google Groups, which allow for threaded discussions, and Google Hangouts, which offer video discussions.

Articles

Cervetti, G., & Pearson, P. D. (2012). Reading, writing, and thinking like a scientist. *Journal of Adolescent and Adult Literacy, 55*(7), 580–586.

Gillis, V. (2014). Disciplinary literacy: Adapt or adopt. *Journal of Adolescent and Adult Literacy, 57*(8), 614–623.

Gillis, V. (2014). Talking the talk: Vocabulary instruction across the disciplines (or what to do instead). *Journal of Adolescent and Adult Literacy, 58*(4), 281–287.

Hynd-Shanahan, C. (2013). What does it take?: The challenge of disciplinary literacy. *Journal of Adolescent and Adult Literacy, 57*(2), 93–98.

Lawrence, J. F., Galloway, E. P., Yim, S., & Lin, A. (2013). Learning to write in middle school? Insights into adolescent writers' instructional experiences across content areas. *Journal of Adolescent and Adult Literacy, 57*(2), 151–161.

Book Chapters

McConaghie, S. M., & Petrosky, A. R. (Eds.). (2009). *Content matters: A disciplinary literacy approach to improving student learning.* San Francisco: Jossey-Bass.
- Chapter 3: Disciplinary literacy in the history classroom (by A. K. Ravi)
- Chapter 5: Disciplinary literacy in the science classroom (by S. A. Spiegel, J. Bintz, J. A. Taylor, N. M. Landes, & D. L. Jordan)
- Chapter 6: Disciplinary literacy in the English language arts classroom (by A. R. Petrosky, S. M. McConachie, & V. Mihalakis)

Jetton, T. L., & Shanahan, C. (Eds.). (2012). *Adolescent literacy in the academic disciplines: General principles and practical strategies.* New York: Guilford Press.
- Chapter 6: Learning with texts in the English language arts (by T. Hicks & S. Steffel)
- Chapter 7: Learning with texts in science (by C. Shanahan)
- Chapter 8: Learning with texts in history: Protocols for reading and practical strategies (by B. Van Sledright)

FIGURE 2.1. Sample professional articles and book chapters for study groups

Discussion format	Description	Implementation considerations
Golden nuggets	Teachers either highlight or use sticky notes to mark passages that they found important, interesting, or applicable to their own teaching. They also mark passages that they found confusing or with which they disagreed.	Golden nuggets offer a flexible approach to having a text-based discussion. Teachers can each be invited to share a golden nugget to get the discussion started or to keep it moving forward.
Annotating	Teachers write comments, questions, and application ideas in the margins of the article.	Annotations allow teachers to record the things that are most important and meaningful to them about the article. To begin the discussion, each teacher can share one thing he or she annotated.
Double-entry journal	Teachers identify quotes from the article that they find important, relevant, or provocative. They record each **quote** and then record a **note** to show their thinking about the quote.	The double-entry journal focuses the discussion directly on the text. During the discussion, teachers take turns sharing a quote and note, and then other teachers can respond by inviting additional teachers to share their ideas and insights.

FIGURE 2.2. Article study group discussion formats

6. Clarify the expectations for the article study group. A sample set of expectations for a face-to-face article study group is shown in Figure 2.3.

7. Prepare to facilitate the meeting (whether face-to-face or online) by reading the article or chapter carefully, recording your own comments using the same discussion format as the teachers, and developing open-ended questions to move the discussion forward, if needed. Two sample questions are:

   a. "What ideas from the article can you use in your classroom?"

   b. "What ideas are you struggling with from this article?"

Facilitating an Article Study Group

1. Begin and end the meeting on time.

2. For the standard article group discussion format, start by asking each teacher to share his or her rating of the article, as well as the reasons for that rating. Share your rating last so you don't influence the responses of the teachers in the group.

3. Continue through the discussion prompts, asking the teachers to volunteer to share their responses.

4. Use open-ended prompts as needed to keep the discussion moving. Sample prompts include: "Can you share an example?" "What do the rest of you think?" and "Who has an idea to share?"

5. Reserve time near the end of the meeting for teachers to share application ideas associated with the article.

6. Ask teachers how you or other group members can help them move forward with their application ideas.

7. Determine the next steps for the article study group.

   a. Is the group meeting again?

   b. If so, when and where?

   c. What topic or focus does the group want to address in the next meeting?

   d. If the group is not meeting again, how will members share their application experiences related to the article?

- Read the article or chapter completely and carefully before the meeting.
- Note your reactions to the article or chapter using the discussion format provided by the facilitator.
- Be on time for the meeting and be sure to have the article or chapter and your responses handy.
- Stay and participate in the entire meeting.
- Participate fully by sharing your responses, listening carefully, and keeping an open mind.
- Focus on your own professional learning. Consider new knowledge and applications to your practice.

FIGURE 2.3. Article study group expectations.

Following Up after an Article Study Group

1. Send an email or put a note in the participating teachers' mailboxes thanking them for participating in the article study group. Include a recap of one or two of the main ideas from the discussion. Remind the teachers about whether the group is meeting again. If the group is not meeting again, specify how the teachers will share their experiences with applying ideas from the article. Conclude with an offer to provide individual coaching support or share resources with the teachers. A sample email message is shown in Figure 2.4.

2. Follow up with the teachers individually to discuss application ideas and how you can help.

3. If the group is meeting again, begin preparing for the next article study group discussion.

The Strategy in Action

Carolyn Walters is a middle school reading specialist who spends about 20% of her time on literacy coaching. Most of her day is spent teaching strategic reading courses to small groups of students who are reading below grade level. She is assigned to coach the two seventh-grade teams at her school. Each of the teams has five teachers: one each for math, science, and social studies and two ELA teachers. At recent team meetings, the teachers have been discussing concerns about academic vocabulary,

---

To: Emily Anderson, Meaghan Collins, David Johansen, Emma Kim, Maria Oros, Brian Palmer, Anita Rogers, and Joel Stanowski

From: Carolyn Walters

Hi Everyone!

Thanks for participating in our article study group yesterday. The group shared many great insights and challenges about teaching academic vocabulary in your classrooms. The group will be meeting again on November 3 at 1:15–1:45 in the team center. We decided to keep focusing on academic vocabulary. Our first agenda item will be to share experiences with applying ideas from the article. If I can help as you work on applying ideas from the article, just let me know. I'm here and happy to co-plan, co-teach, model, share resources, or just be someone to bounce ideas around with.

Our second task at the November 3 meeting will be to discuss the new article which I will share with you by the end of the week.

Thanks,

Carolyn

FIGURE 2.4. Sample email message following first meeting.

so Carolyn suggested that they consider doing an article study group. Carolyn then carefully reviewed possible articles and finally selected a short, informative article about academic vocabulary ("Talking the Talk"; Gillis, 2014a) to recommend to the teachers. After she did a short article talk at each team's next meeting, the teachers agreed that the article was a good choice for them to read and discuss.

When Carolyn started to plan for the article study group meeting, she realized that there was no time when all of the teachers could meet together with her. Because the teams are small and her coaching time is very limited, Carolyn suggested that they do an online article discussion. The teachers readily agreed, and Carolyn created a discussion forum by setting up a Google Group. She decided to have both teams participate in the same Google Group to allow for increased opportunities to share ideas, insights, and questions. Using the prompts on the Article Study Group Note Sheet (Form 2.1), she posted the first three prompts to get the teacher's individual ideas about the article. Carolyn then invited all of the teachers to join the group using their school gmail account. She asked the teachers to post their responses to the questions as well as to read and comment on the other teachers' posts. Carolyn then added the remaining three prompts from Form 2.1 and asked the teachers to post their responses. Carolyn was pleased with the quality and quantity of postings the teachers shared. She also posted several comments in order to participate in the online discussion without controlling it. After a week had passed, Carolyn posted the final question, "What do you think we should do next to work toward the goal of teaching academic vocabulary in all of our classes?" Two of the teachers posted requests for Carolyn to co-plan with them using ideas from the article, and several other teachers noted that they wanted to set aside time at future team meetings to discuss how the strategies were working in their classrooms. With her limited time for coaching, Carolyn has found that article study groups are an effective and efficient way to support the teachers on the teams she coaches. She was pleased with her first experience with the online discussion format, but she also wants to try Google Hangout for video chats as well as face-to-face discussions when schedules allow.

Article Study Group Note Sheet

Name: _____

Article Title: _____

AS YOU READ THE ARTICLE . . .

1. How you would rate the text on a scale of 1 (low) to 10 (high). Support your rating.

_____

_____

_____

_____

2. Describe how the article relates to your teaching. (Mark specific passages or pages to share with the group.)

_____

_____

_____

_____

3. What questions are you still considering related to the article?

_____

_____

_____

_____

DURING THE GROUP DISCUSSION . . .

4. Some new ideas and insights I gained from the group discussion are:

_____

_____

_____

_____

_____

_____

(continued)

From *Collaborative Coaching for Disciplinary Literacy: Strategies to Support Teachers in Grades 6–12* by Laurie Elish-Piper, Susan K. L'Allier, Michael Manderino, and Paula Di Domenico. Copyright © 2016 The Guilford Press. Permission to photocopy this form is granted to purchasers of this book for personal use only (see copyright page for details). Purchasers can download additional copies of this form (see the box at the end of the table of contents).

AFTER THE GROUP DISCUSSION . . .

5. What ideas from the article do you plan to apply to your teaching? Be as specific as you can.

_____

_____

_____

_____

_____

_____

6. What can the other teachers in the article study group and/or the literacy coach do to support your application of these ideas?

_____

_____

_____

_____

_____

_____

Providing Professional Development Golden Nuggets at Faculty, Department, and Team Meetings

What Is It?

Disciplinary literacy coaches who work in middle and high schools are often called upon to provide professional development to large groups of teachers (McKenna & Walpole, 2008; Sweeney, 2013). The number of participants will depend on the size of the school and the topic of the session. In some cases, all disciplinary teachers will be invited to the session; in other cases, the participants will consist of the teachers from one department. Sessions for all disciplinary teachers are typically held after school or on days designated for professional development, whereas those for specific departments or teams can be provided at their regularly scheduled meetings.

Although literacy coaches may be allocated an hour or more on those days that are specifically designated for professional development, they are seldom given that amount of time when presenting at after-school faculty or department meetings. Although these meetings often run for an hour, administrators generally want to address a number of items during that time period—resulting in a time frame of about 20 minutes for professional development. Even though this seems like a short amount of time, these professional development opportunities send the message to the participants that professional development is valued by the administrators (Matsumura et al., 2009). Within this time frame, coaches can share "golden nuggets" of information that often lead to more in-depth professional development efforts at the department, team, or individual level (McKenna & Walpole, 2008).

How Do I Do It?

Embedding professional development within faculty and department meetings enables you to discuss aspects of disciplinary literacy that are most relevant to participants. For example, if your school is in the early stages of incorporating disciplinary literacy into the curriculum, all teachers may benefit from an overview of disciplinary literacy and how it is closely aligned with the learning standards they are expected to help their students achieve. If teachers already have this understanding, they may want to meet as a department to focus on disciplinary literacy strategies within their discipline. Regardless of the group or the topic, the keys to successful short professional development sessions are careful preparation, thoughtful implementation, and timely follow-up. The following guidelines have helped us and the coaches we work with deliver powerful, engaging professional development golden nuggets. We think they will work for you, too.

1. Meet with the administrator responsible for the faculty or department meeting. Bring a concise list of items that need to be addressed during that meeting so that you can move forward with planning the professional development session.

   a. *Topics to be covered.* At a large-group session with all disciplinary teachers, the focus should be on some aspect of disciplinary literacy that would be relevant to all. The focus of your session should be based on such factors as the teachers' understanding of disciplinary literacy and related standards, the school's current initiatives, requests from the teachers, and past professional development sessions. The following list is illustrative of possible topics, but certainly not exhaustive.

   • Overview of disciplinary literacy and its alignment to standards adopted by the school/district (e.g., CCSS, C3, NGSS)
   • Reviewing general district data to determine areas in which disciplinary literacy instruction could be beneficial in meeting district goals
   • Ways in which disciplinary literacy instruction can promote student engagement

   When working with a department, your focus will generally be narrower. Teachers typically want to learn about strategies specific to their discipline that will help their students develop the requisite content knowledge. Some possible topics for professional development at department meetings might include the following:

   • Habits of thinking and habits of practice in the discipline
   • Helping students access the required text(s)
   • Creating text sets for units of study
   • Analyzing common assessments to determine ways that disciplinary literacy instruction could address common problem areas
   • Selecting vocabulary for in-depth instruction
   • Modeling a specific strategy that helps students to think, read, write, and speak like practitioners of the discipline (e.g., historians, scientists, authors)

b. *Time for professional development.* As noted previously, you generally will have only part of the faculty or department meeting for your professional development, so you should have selected your topic with that in mind. However, once you have determined the topic, you should confirm the date(s) and amount of time being allotted for professional development. If, for example, the administrator running the monthly faculty meetings understands the importance of the topic to the improvement of teacher practice and student achievement, he or she may decide to share some of the agenda via an email memo in order to give you more than 20 minutes. In terms of professional development at the department level, you and the department chair may determine that the selected topic will require 20 minutes at each of the next three weekly department meetings. For example, if you plan to model a specific strategy at the first department meeting, you may—at the second meeting—help teachers determine how they could incorporate that strategy into their instruction before the next department meeting. Then, at the third department meeting, teachers could share how the strategy worked, how they might adapt the strategy in the future, and what questions they would like to discuss with the group.

c. *Role of the administrator during the professional development session.*
   - Invite the administrator to introduce the professional development topic and its importance to the faculty. Research results indicate that administrators who support and attend professional development sessions contribute to teacher participation (Bredeson & Johansson, 2000; Matsumura et al., 2009).
   - Request that the professional development be the first item on the agenda. Our coaching colleagues have consistently noted that, when the professional development is scheduled for the end of the meeting, earlier agenda items may take longer than expected, and they are left with almost no time for their professional development segment.

2. Prepare for the professional development session.
   a. Begin by expanding on the administrator's introduction. As noted in Part II, adults want to know why the topic is one they need to understand, how it is relevant to their work as teachers, and what problem it might help solve. Your introduction should address one or more of these adult learning principles.
   b. Prepare an overview that can be shown or distributed to the teachers. Examples of overview formats can be found in Figures 3.1, 3.2, 3.3, and 3.4.
      - Figure 3.1 displays a format that you could use at a monthly faculty meeting to present an overview of disciplinary literacy instruction and to start the discussion about what constitutes disciplinary knowledge within each discipline. This format, which outlines key concepts and incorporates teacher participation, could easily be used when presenting other topics of schoolwide interest at monthly faculty meetings.
      - You could use the format in Figure 3.2 to discuss recent research about disciplinary literacy instruction. The article summarized in Figure 3.2 describes

"Disciplinary literacy is based on the premise that students can develop deep conceptual knowledge in a discipline only by using the habits of reading, writing, talking, and thinking which that discipline values and uses" (McConachie et al., 2006).

Domain Knowledge	Topic Knowledge
• History	• World War II
• Science	• Wave behavior
• Mathematics	• Quadratic equations
• English language arts	• Literary criticism

Disciplinary Knowledge

• Ways knowledge is created
• Ways knowledge is shared
• Texts that are used by the discipline
• Practices and discourses used in the discipline

Small-Group Discussion: Meet with a small group of colleagues from your department to begin a discussion of the specific ways that knowledge is created and shared in your discipline and the texts, practices, and discourses that are used in your discipline. Record your thoughts so they can be examined in more depth at an upcoming department meeting.

FIGURE 3.1. Developing a shared understanding of disciplinary literacy

disciplinary literacy instruction in the area of social studies that could be presented at a social studies department meeting. Teachers want to read and hear about how disciplinary literacy instruction works within their discipline and with students who are similar in age to their own students, so be sure to take these factors into consideration when selecting the research you plan to share.

• The format in Figure 3.3 will work well when the professional development focuses on an aspect of disciplinary literacy about which teachers have requested more information. When the English teachers at Davenport High School wanted to learn more about text selection, their literacy coach, Stella Tonks, used a format similar to the one in Figure 3.3 to present information that would encourage teachers to understand the complexity of text selection and to begin thinking about the texts they are currently using and those that they could use in the future.

• The format in Figure 3.4 could be used by a coach to introduce a disciplinary strategy or by a teacher to show how a disciplinary literacy strategy worked with his or her students. Teachers like to hear "success stories" from their own colleagues, but they are sometimes reticent to share those stories in a large venue. Teachers may be more willing to share if you help them create a visual that could be discussed with others at a department meeting. Stella Tonks worked with Mrs. Helen Morales, one of the science teachers at Davenport High School, to develop Figure 3.4 so Helen could share her disciplinary literacy "success story."

Purpose of Research
- To examine how ninth-grade students were able to identify and evaluate claims and evidence from two Web-based articles.
- To determine how students' personal and cultural knowledge influenced their analysis of the claims and evidence.

Findings from the Research
- Most students found the same text to be more convincing in terms of its claims and evidence.
- Students judged claims to be convincing when those claims were supported by facts, statistics, examples, and use of quotes.
- Students judged claims to be unconvincing if students felt they had strong personal knowledge about the issue that was in contrast to the claim.
- When asked, "What affects the way I read this site?", students' most frequent responses included "my opinions/values," "my background/culture," and "my parents/family."

Conclusions from the Research
- Students use both cultural and contextual knowledge when analyzing and evaluating issues.
- Scaffolding through written prompts and explicit explanation from teachers helps students think more like historians.
- Consider author intentionality/credibility
- Detect bias
- Evaluate and corroborate claims and evidence

Small-Group Discussion: Talk with a colleague about the texts and activities you use to help your students make claims and analyze evidence. In your discussion, consider how your students' cultural backgrounds and prior knowledge might be influencing their analysis.

FIGURE 3.2. Sharing research about disciplinary literacy. Ideas from Damico, Baildon, Exter, and Guo (2009/2010).

c. Determine how the teachers can be active participants during the session. Ideas for active participation can be found at the bottom of Figures 3.1, 3.2, 3.3, and 3.4. You could adapt these peer discussion ideas to fit your own presentation. In addition, you might find the following general questions helpful as you consider ways to stimulate participant discussion.

- How did this discussion move your thinking about the topic forward? What questions do you still have?
- How might the results of this research be applied to your teaching?
- Is this a disciplinary literacy strategy that would work with your students? If so, into what unit(s) could you incorporate strategy? What modifications would you need to make?

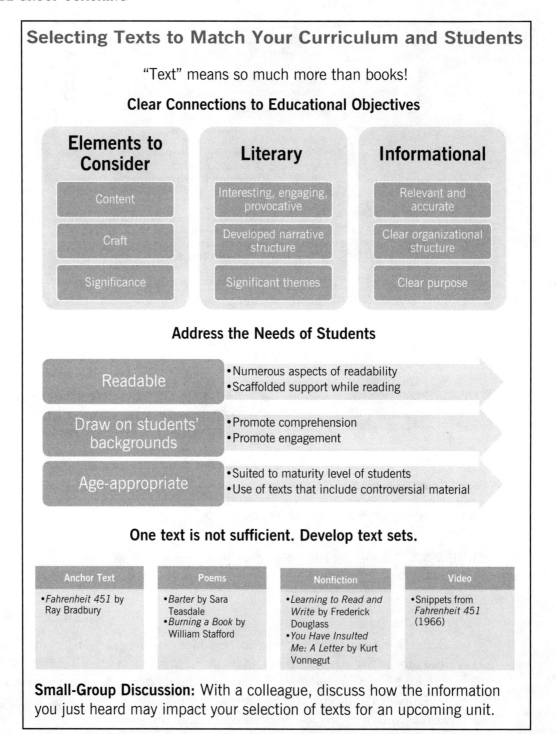

Selecting Texts to Match Your Curriculum and Students

"Text" means so much more than books!

Clear Connections to Educational Objectives

Elements to Consider	Literary	Informational
Content	Interesting, engaging, provocative	Relevant and accurate
Craft	Developed narrative structure	Clear organizational structure
Significance	Significant themes	Clear purpose

Address the Needs of Students

Readable	• Numerous aspects of readability • Scaffolded support while reading
Draw on students' backgrounds	• Promote comprehension • Promote engagement
Age-appropriate	• Suited to maturity level of students • Use of texts that include controversial material

One text is not sufficient. Develop text sets.

Anchor Text	Poems	Nonfiction	Video
• *Fahrenheit 451* by Ray Bradbury	• *Barter* by Sara Teasdale • *Burning a Book* by William Stafford	• *Learning to Read and Write* by Frederick Douglass • *You Have Insulted Me: A Letter* by Kurt Vonnegut	• Snippets from *Fahrenheit 451* (1966)

Small-Group Discussion: With a colleague, discuss how the information you just heard may impact your selection of texts for an upcoming unit.

FIGURE 3.3. Professional development for planning instruction.

3. Deliver the professional development session. Adhere to the time allocated for the session.

4. Follow-up after the professional development session.

    a. Post a copy of the overview form on your web page or on the school's shared computer drive. If your session included a discussion of a professional article, you may want to include an electronic version of the text.

    b. Determine whether additional professional development on the same topic is needed. For example, if you presented a session at the monthly faculty meeting,

---

Helping Students Synthesize from Multiple Sources

The Students: Helen Morales's 10th-grade science class

The Unit: Ecosystems

The Next Generation Science Standard: HS-LS2-8: Evaluate the evidence for the role of group behavior on individual and species' chances to survive and reproduce.

The Inquiry Question: How does group behavior affect individual and species' chances for survival and reproduction?

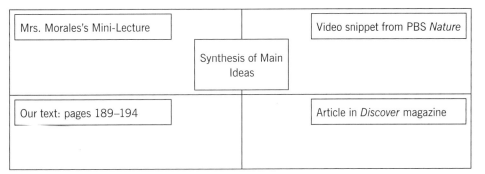

The Process

1. *Mini-lecture.* I gave the mini-lecture and modeled how to document the main ideas regarding the inquiry question.
2. *Video.* Students took notes as they watched the video snippet and met in small groups to discuss the main ideas they had written on their charts.
3. *Text.* Most students read and documented main ideas in small groups. I worked through the text with six students who had difficulty accessing the text independently.
4. *Article.* Reading and documentation completed as homework.
5. *Synthesis chart.* I used my chart to model how to synthesize the main ideas from the four sources, and then students worked as partners to support each other as they synthesized the information from their own charts.

Small-Group Discussion: Discuss with a partner how you might use a synthesis chart with your students. With what unit might it be used? What texts might you use? Would you be asking students to synthesize main ideas, assertions, or claims and evidence?

FIGURE 3.4. Disciplinary literacy in our school.

it might be appropriate to meet with specific departments so teachers could apply the ideas to their disciplines. Or, if you delivered a session at a department meeting, there might be individual teachers who would like to work with you to implement the ideas or strategies into their own classrooms. These examples align with the layered approach to coaching described in Part II. In the first example, you would be engaged in two large-group coaching situations, but the department session would involve a smaller number of teachers than the cross-disciplinary faculty session. In the second case, you are moving from coaching at the department level to individual coaching.

Presenting Powerful
Professional Development

What Is It?

Student success has always been an important goal for secondary (i.e., middle and high school) educators. However, the recent focus on disciplinary literacy has fostered an even wider view of student success, promoting an environment in which all teachers within the school are expected to take collective responsibility for the learning of their students (Bryk, Sebring, Allensworth, Luppescu, & Easton, 2010). Because disciplinary literacy instruction cuts across most departments and because it includes some new instructional aspects (e.g., selecting appropriate texts, helping students access texts, teaching academic vocabulary), large-group professional development sessions that include teachers from all content areas can be used to establish a firm understanding of disciplinary literacy within the school. In addition to schoolwide sessions, departments in many schools are composed of large numbers of teachers. In these schools, large-group professional development sessions at the department level can help teachers examine more deeply how disciplinary literacy instruction will enhance student learning within their specific disciplines.

Effective large-group professional development sessions have a number of features in common (American Education Research Association, 2005; Desimone, 2009; Learning Forward, 2010). Many of these features are aligned with the adult learning principles discussed in Part II of this book. They include the selection of a relevant needs-based focus, thoughtful preparation, active engagement of all participants, and a plan for moving the work from one session forward into further professional development and/or practice.

As a secondary literacy coach, you may feel overwhelmed by the idea of planning and presenting professional development sessions to large groups of teachers. It may seem that there is no end to the details that need attention—such as developing an agenda, preparing materials, and finding co-facilitators. However, you may be most concerned about presenting to teachers who come from different departments and who are likely to have different beliefs, knowledge, and experiences related to disciplinary literacy. To help you with these concerns, we offer a set of guidelines that we and our coaching colleagues have found helpful in planning and facilitating professional development in large-group settings.

How Do I Do It?

Throughout your years as an educator, you have undoubtedly attended numerous large- group professional development workshops. You remember the excellent ones in which you expanded your knowledge base, talked through possible solutions to instructional conundrums, or learned new strategies that were highly likely to enhance your students' learning. You also remember those that were difficult to sit through because the topic was not relevant, the presenter was not prepared, or you were not asked to be an active participant in the session. We suggest that the key to high-quality professional development sessions is careful preparation. With careful preparation, the implementation should go smoothly—resulting in enhanced teacher knowledge and practice and, ultimately, increased student learning.

The Four A's of Planning Powerful Professional Development

When working with students, you know that thoughtful, thorough planning is critical to the success of your teaching. The same is true of your work as a coach, except that you are now working with adults. By attending to the four A's of planning— aims, audience, agenda, and active participation—you will feel confident that you have carefully considered the details of your professional development sessions.

Aims and Audience

When planning large-group professional development in the area of disciplinary literacy, it's important to remember the adult learning principle that adults want to be involved in the planning of their professional development. You could work with your school's leadership team or department chairs to come up with a list of possible topics that would strengthen teachers' knowledge and practice related to disciplinary literacy. Then, to determine the final purpose, you can gather wider input from the proposed audience by asking them which of the suggested topics they feel would be of most benefit to them. When teachers are involved in selecting a topic that they feel will enhance their knowledge and practice, they are more likely to be engaged participants during the session.

When determining aims and audience for disciplinary literacy professional development, it is also important to consider the audience's knowledge and use of disciplinary literacy. For example, if the majority of teachers are at the awareness or knowledge stage of the CBAM discussed in Part II, an introductory session about disciplinary literacy might be appropriate for all content teachers in your building. On the other hand, if the teachers in the social studies department have a basic understanding of disciplinary literacy and are interested in examining how they could focus more on strategies for writing in their discipline (the personal and management stages of the CBAM), you might want to facilitate a professional development session restricted to social studies teachers, which, in many secondary schools, would still constitute a large group of educators. Both of these professional development session topics are aligned with one or more of the adult learning principles discussed in Part II. More specifically, each topic would be relevant to the audience and, in the case of the social studies teachers, the professional development addresses an instructional problem—how to help students write like historians.

Setting an *Agenda* That Includes *Active* Participation

Setting the agenda includes three important steps: (1) determining the time and place for the session, (2) thinking through a logical sequence of activities that focuses on the aims of the session and includes active participation from the audience, and (3) preparing the materials for the session.

TIME AND PLACE

Secondary school teachers are busy. In addition to their teaching, many are involved in after-school extracurricular activities. Thus setting a date and time for professional development is often a daunting task. Times that have already been set aside for professional development, such as districtwide teacher development days, late-start or early-dismissal days, or PLC times generally work well. It is important to confirm the date and time with the appropriate administrator(s) (e.g., principal, department chairs, team leaders) as early as possible, so other professional development efforts don't fill the available slots.

Once you have confirmed the date and time, you will want to select an appropriate location for the session. Consider the following when selecting the location.

- Select a space and seating arrangement that allows all participants to see the facilitator and that encourages discussion. A room with tables, rather than desks, may be a better choice, as this arrangement provides a writing space for each participant and divides the audience into small groups so they can hold in-depth discussions about session topics and/or work together to complete activities.
- Be sure the location has the technology you need or could accommodate whatever technology you plan to bring to the session. Make sure the visual media you plan to use (e.g., PowerPoint or Prezi presentations, videos, websites) can be easily viewed by all participants.
- While this may seem to be a minor point, it is important to select a location

where the temperature will be at a comfortable level. Participants often comment about uncomfortable conditions on their professional development session feedback forms; it may be that teachers who are too hot or too cold find it difficult to maintain their focus on the content of the session.

SEQUENCE OF ACTIVITIES

Planning a sequence of activities that will enable the participants to achieve the aims of the session takes careful thought. Consider the following items as you plan your session.

- Plan to start your session with a clear explanation of the aims or purposes for the session. Be sure to note that the participants provided input concerning the topic and specifically state how the session will enhance their knowledge and/or their practice, with a subsequent impact on student learning.
- Plan to include a variety of activities during the session. Typical activities include short presentations by you, large- and small-group discussions, and small-group activities. Keep in mind that most of the activities should involve active participation on the part of teachers. Consider how teacher liaisons as described in Part III or teachers with whom you are currently working can assist you—either as co-presenters or as facilitators of the small-group activities.
- Carefully plan how you will end the session.
  o Review how the aims of the session have been addressed and what the next steps will be in terms of integrating the ideas into practice and/or further professional development sessions.
  o Have the participants complete a feedback form about the session. If your school has an established method, such as using Google Forms, for providing feedback about professional development sessions, use that method. If there is not an established method, giving them time to complete the feedback form at the end of the session will ensure a high return rate.
- Develop a schedule for the session that includes all of the activities you've planned. If the session is a long one, be sure to include time for one or more breaks. Providing snacks also contributes to a positive learning environment.

PREPARING THE MATERIALS

Once you have developed your schedule, it's time to prepare the materials. Be sure to give yourself sufficient time to develop high-quality materials.

- Develop a written agenda that includes the aim(s) of the session and the list of planned activities.
- If your session includes one or more short presentations by you or a co-presenter, develop those presentation materials.
  o When creating PowerPoint presentations, keep text to a minimum by relying

on tables, charts, diagrams, and photographs to support your main ideas. Using SmartArt is a great way to convey your main ideas and capture the attention of the participants. The coaches we work with have found that participants generally appreciate receiving a handout version of the Power-Point slides so they can write notes as the coach presents.

   o When creating other types of presentation handouts, include just the main ideas and leave sufficient space for the participants to add their own notes.

• Prepare the materials for the small-group activities. Experience has taught us that it is important to include written instructions for these activities or to project the instructions on a screen that all participants can see.

• Develop a feedback form for the session. For short sessions, you may want to have participants share their feedback on index cards on which you ask them to write a response to two items, using one side for the first item and the other side for the second item. For example, you may have them respond to the following two items: (1) What were the two most important ideas you took away from this session? (2) Describe one way you plan to use the ideas from this session in your teaching. For longer sessions, you may want to use the feedback form shown in Form 4.1 or develop a similar feedback form on which the first and second items more specifically describe the focus of your session.

• Send out a reminder about the session's date, time, and location to the participants and appropriate administrators.

In addition to preparing the materials, you should check that the materials you've developed work with the technology that is available in the room or that will be brought to the room on the day of the session. Technology that does not work as expected is frustrating for both the coach and the participants, and the time spent troubleshooting the problem can disrupt your carefully planned schedule.

As you can see, when planning for the four As of professional development—aims, audience, agenda, and active participation—there are many details to consider. Using the template shown in Form 4.2 will help you address all of those details so you feel well prepared on the day of the session.

Four Final Suggestions about Implementing Powerful Professional Development

You've completed all of the items on the professional development planning template (Form 4.2). Now it's time for the professional development session! Our coaching partners have shared the following five suggestions that will help ensure that your session runs smoothly.

1. *Establish a collaborative learning environment.* Because you have developed activities that require active participation on the part of the teachers, you want to be sure that you quickly establish a collaborative learning environment. Adhering to a

set of working rules is one way to accomplish this. In most schools, working rules have been developed for use at department or PLC meetings. If this is the case in your school, you can simply remind the participants of these rules at the beginning of the session. If necessary, you can develop and present a set of working rules to the group. A possible set of working rules is:

- "We will maintain our focus on the topic/tasks throughout the entire session."
- "We will share ideas and insights that are directly related to the topics/tasks."
- "We will listen respectfully when others are talking and encourage others to share their ideas."
- "We will actively participate in all large- and small-group activities."

Be sure to model the behaviors set forth in the working rules. In terms of maintaining focus, think about ways you would draw the attention of the group back to the topic being discussed if one or more participants offer tangential comments. For example, you might be able to pose a question, or you may decide that those tangential comments are indications that it is time to move on to the next activity. Listen respectfully throughout the session. Be an active listener during whole-group discussions, thinking carefully about how you could move the discussion forward in light of what the participant is saying. During small-group activities, join some of the groups for short periods of time. Listening to their comments will help you determine how much debriefing of the small-group activity is needed and which participants' comments would be valuable to share with the whole group. When participants see you modeling the behaviors described in the working rules, they will be more likely to exhibit those behaviors as well.

2. *Clearly explain the aim of the session and how each activity is related to that aim.* Begin the session by explaining the aim/purpose of the session and how that purpose was determined. For example, if your professional development session is aimed at exploring disciplinary writing strategies with secondary social studies teachers, you might begin by saying, "As you can see from the agenda, today's session will focus on the types of writing used in your discipline and how we can help our students understand and use these types of writing. The impetus for this session came from last month's department meeting where many of you requested a session that would help you incorporate more discipline-specific writing activities into your instruction."

Then, as the session progresses, be sure that you connect each activity back to the overall aim of the session. At the end of the session, you could ask some of the teachers to summarize how each activity helped them achieve the aim of the session.

3. *Stick to your schedule.* You spent time carefully selecting, planning, and scheduling activities that would help you achieve the goals of the session, so it is important that your participants complete those planned activities. To do so, you will need to stick to the time you allotted for each activity. One way you can stick to

your schedule is to practice your own short presentations beforehand to be sure you do not talk longer than you should. Another tip for staying on schedule is related to the small-group activities. After describing the small-group work, remind the participants how much time they have to complete the task. In addition, give them a 2-minute reminder so they can finish the task on time. Of course, some activities may take a little more time than anticipated and others may take less, but keeping a close eye on the schedule and making small adjustments as needed should enable your participants to complete all of the activities that are critical for accomplishing the purpose of the session.

4. *Discuss the "next steps" related to this professional development session.* Most large-group professional development sessions end with a discussion about what teachers will do next in relation to what they have learned. The layered approach to literacy coaching described in Part II suggests three possible avenues. First, the group may decide that another large-group session is needed, suggesting specific ideas about what should be covered during the next session. Second, the group may decide to further explore the topic within a smaller group setting. For example, the social studies teachers may decide to continue their work on disciplinary writing by forming small groups of teachers who teach the same course. Third, some participants may feel that that they would benefit from additional individual coaching related to the session's topic. You, as the coach, could present this opportunity at the end of the sessions by saying something like, "If you'd like me to work with you to implement one of these strategies with your students, just stop by my office or drop me an email." You could also send out a follow-up email in which you thank everyone for attending the session, remind them of the "next steps" they agreed upon, and offer to engage in individual coaching with interested participants to follow up on the content of the professional development session.

Feedback Form for Large-Group Professional Development Sessions

Session Topic: _____

Please circle the title that describes your position:

Teacher: Content Area: _____   Administrator

Paraprofessional   Other: _____

Please rate the session based on the following scale:

SA   Strongly agree

A   Agree

D   Disagree

SD   Strongly disagree

NA   Not applicable to this session

The topic of the session strengthened my understanding of disciplinary literacy.	SA	A	D	SD	NA

What key ideas will you remember from the session?

The topic will help me incorporate specific disciplinary literacy strategies into my instruction.	SA	A	D	SD	NA

What ideas do you plan to try?

The purposes were clearly stated and addressed.	SA	A	D	SD	NA
The information was presented in a clear and organized manner.	SA	A	D	SD	NA
The pace and length of the session were appropriate.	SA	A	D	SD	NA
The session provided me with opportunities to be an active participant.	SA	A	D	SD	NA

Please write additional comments about the session and/or questions you may still have about the topic.

From *Collaborative Coaching for Disciplinary Literacy: Strategies to Support Teachers in Grades 6–12* by Laurie Elish-Piper, Susan K. L'Allier, Michael Manderino, and Paula Di Domenico. Copyright © 2016 The Guilford Press. Permission to photocopy this form is granted to purchasers of this book for personal use only (see copyright page for details). Purchasers can download additional copies of this form (see the box at the end of the table of contents).

Planning Template for Large-Group Professional Development Sessions

Aim	
Aim/purpose of the session	
Rationale for selecting the aim	

Audience	
Teachers	
Others	

Setting the Agenda

Date, time, and place	Date	Time	Place	
Set-up of room				✓ when done
List of co-presenters or co-facilitators				
List of activities, approximate time needed for each activity, and who will facilitate each activity *Asterisk activities that involve **active participation** by teachers				
Develop a schedule for the session				
List of materials that need to be developed for whole-group presentations and small-group work and who will develop each one				
Snacks				
List technology needed; confirm that technology works				
Send out reminder to participants and administrator(s)				

From *Collaborative Coaching for Disciplinary Literacy: Strategies to Support Teachers in Grades 6–12* by Laurie Elish-Piper, Susan K. L'Allier, Michael Manderino, and Paula Di Domenico. Copyright © 2016 The Guilford Press. Permission to photocopy this form is granted to purchasers of this book for personal use only (see copyright page for details). Purchasers can download additional copies of this form (see the box at the end of the table of contents).

Using Technology to Connect Coaches and Teachers

What Is It?

As a disciplinary literacy coach, you have opportunities to work with teachers within and across disciplines. Your collaborations may inspire you to share the innovative work those teachers design and implement. Working with a variety of teachers also puts you in a role that can lead to more teacher-to-teacher connections within and across schools. Technology platforms such as Twitter, Google, and blogs (e.g., WordPress, Blogger) provide multiple opportunities for educators to connect, share resources, and discuss teaching and learning. The power of these technology platforms is that they connect individuals across geographic regions, that they can be synchronous or asynchronous, and that they can curate resources quickly and efficiently. Literacy coaches can effectively leverage these technology platforms to provide flexible large-group coaching beyond time and location constraints. The purpose of technology integration in your coaching should be to amplify the robust practices you engage in face-to-face. Four reasons to use technology platforms to increase large-group professional learning and connect teachers and coaches in powerful ways are described below and summarized in Figure 5.1.

Sharing Content, Sharing Your Vision

One key benefit of using technology as a literacy coach is the ability to share the vast amount of information about literacy you possess. Maintaining a blog is one way to share valuable resources with teachers. Blogs are websites maintained by individual users and are typically "hosted" by larger websites such as Google or WordPress.

Purpose	Tool	Site
Sharing content	Blog	*www.blogger.com* *www.wordpress.com*
	Content curation	*www.smore.com* *www.livebinder.com* *www.blender.com*
Connecting	Twitter	*www.twitter.com*
Virtual PLC	Website	*www.weebly.com* *www.wix.com*
	Social network	Google Communities: *www.google.com/edu/resources/communities* *www.ning.com*
	Learning management system	*www.edmodo.com* *www.schoology.com*
Communicating	Video chats	Google Hangout: *www.google.com/+/learnmore/hangouts* Skype: *www.skype.com/en*
	Video recording	*www.jing.com* *www.screenr.com* Explain Everything (iPad): *www.screencast-o-matic.com*

FIGURE 5.1. Sample technology tools for coaching integration.

Users create blog entries or posts that are titled by topic, use more informal writing, and often include hyperlinks to websites. Bloggers can also embed images or video into their blogs. By blogging once a week or twice per month, you can provide a consistent flow of information, research, strategies, and successes. Examples of well-known literacy blogs include Literacy Beat (*www.literacybeat.com*) and Shanahan on Literacy (*www.shanahanonliteracy.com*).

Blogging is also a vehicle for sharing your voice as a literacy coach. As a literacy leader, you have knowledge, skills, and experiences that can benefit others. It provides opportunities to share your vision for literacy instruction for adolescents and to support teachers in that endeavor. A blog can be a place to cultivate ideas about topics in literacy that are most pressing in your coaching context. It can also be a place to highlight exemplary literacy instruction for teachers to view. In addition, maintaining a blog is a way to feed your own professional growth as a literacy coach because it provides a reflective outlet for your coaching experiences. Examples of these types of blogs include Coaches Coaching (*https://coachescoaching.wordpress.com*) and Gwerica on Literacy (*http://d96literacylink.blogspot.com*).

Connecting with People Outside of Your School

Literacy coaching can sometimes be isolating, especially if you are the only coach in the building. A key means of support is connecting with literacy coaches in other schools. Twitter is one such community through which you can connect with literacy coaches, as well as literacy leaders and researchers. Twitter is a microblogging platform that is limited to 140 characters per post (i.e., tweet). Users create a Twitter "handle" (e.g., @litleader) and follow other individuals by their "handle." Members of Twitter can then follow you in return. Twitter users then create their own personal learning network (PLN) based on the people that they follow. Users can tweet ideas, share resources, link to their blogs, and retweet what others in the literacy community are saying.

Twitter users can also participate in a plethora of weekly chats with other teachers and coaches around shared interests. Participating in Twitter chats helps you to build your PLN. Chats are organized around hashtags. A hashtag (e.g., #educoach) is a mechanism for organizing the tweets of users who have similar interests. If a literacy coach wants to share information with others, she might add #educoach to her tweet so that others who follow the hashtag #educoach will see her tweet. There are several established chats, such as #ILAchat (International Literacy Association), #engchat (English teachers), #sschat (social studies teachers), and #edchat (K–12 teachers), to name a few. You can also start your own hashtag and share with your school or district. Many school districts are forming their own Twitter chats this way.

Creating a Virtual PLC

Most people think of social networks such as Facebook as a means for connecting with friends and family. Social networks can also make use of groups that can be created by users. Coaches can create a Facebook group for other literacy coaches or for teachers in their buildings. Because Facebook is often more personal, other sites, such as Google Communities or Ning (*www.ning*), can be used to create groups that are separate from people's personal social networks. Google Communities and Google Groups are free to any Google user. Ning networks cost money to be maintained by the host but allow the creation of a social network specific to the area of interest. The advantage of a social network is that you can share information with users who have common interests. You can also share linked documents, photos, and videos. A social network can be used to create a more closed setting for sharing content and ideas that are only viewed by the members of the network.

Communicating Virtually

Skype and Google Hangouts are video hosting platforms that allow multiple users to video chat with one another. A user can initiate a chat and invite others to communicate via webcam. One additional feature of Google Hangouts is that they can be recorded and then uploaded to YouTube so that others may watch the conversation later. Web chats can allow teachers to meet across sites without traveling and to overcome the constraints of the school day. Recorded web chats can also be shared on your blog, via Twitter, or in a social network.

Other video recording software can be used to demonstrate a strategy or text analysis. Screen recording software on your personal computer (e.g., Jing, Quicktime, Screenr, Screencast-o-matic) or on your iPad (e.g., Explain Everything) allow you to record your voice, as well as what is on your screen. Possibilities include conducting a text analysis, sharing a PowerPoint from a professional development session, or explaining how to implement a literacy strategy. The videos can be converted to a number of digital formats, such as mp4 or WMV files or uploaded to YouTube and then shared on a blog, Twitter, or in your social network.

How Do I Do It?

With most technology, it takes some time to learn to use the tools that you choose. However, before choosing a tool, it is important to first determine your purpose for using technology—a purpose that supports your coaching. When you make that purpose clear to the teachers, they will want to engage with the technology. In addition to a purpose, teachers may need technical guidance. It is helpful to enlist the support of your technology department to be sure that the hardware that teachers have access to will support the platforms you intend to use. The upfront work you do will make recruiting early adopters easier. Once you have an emerging audience, being a consistent presence with quality content will grow your network. See Form 5.1 to help guide your process for selecting and evaluating technology tools.

Set a Purpose

Determine how you wish to use technology to support your coaching. What are your primary objectives? What type of approach will be most feasible? Have the most impact? What types of technology are supported in your district or school? What level of comfort do your colleagues have with technology platforms? Spending time carefully crafting technology integration into your coaching will yield more engagement from your colleagues, as they have limited time to invest in additional professional development related solely to technology.

Investigate the Technology

Once you have set a purpose, consider the type of content you will want to provide and what technology might best convey that content. This will mean also investing the time in learning the technology. Be sure to carve time into your schedule to learn and practice using the technology. Get feedback from others who have tried different software or technology platforms. YouTube also provides helpful tutorials for setting up a blog, Twitter account, or video recording. The technology will be the vehicle to drive your purpose and your coaching messages. Just like buying a car, you may want to test drive a few sites before settling on your final one. Form 5.1 is a template that can guide your evaluation of the myriad of technology resources available.

Bring People on Board

It is critical to get some early adopters on board who are digitally savvy or have influence. Holding a professional development session or using professional learning time to support individuals as they sign up and create accounts is essential to getting people to participate. If participants feel supported, they will be more likely to agree to collaborate. Sharing sign-up tutorials, assisting teachers in their navigation of unfamiliar technology features, and giving individuals time to practice are vital for successful implementation. You can model your own technology use and be a source of support by sharing your digital footprint publicly and coaching teachers as they begin to implement different digital tools.

Stay Consistent

It will also take time to develop your PLN on Twitter, to gain blog followers, or to become comfortable using screen recording software. It might be best to start with one tool and increase your use over time as you build knowledge and an audience. Over time, use multiple platforms. Blogging is a good place to start, and you can easily share the link to your blog via an email sent to the teachers. Then they can share with their professional networks. However, Twitter also allows you to spread your ideas to a wider audience so that you can link your blog in a Tweet and share with others. Later, the content you create through video recording can be embedded in your blog and shared via Twitter.

The Strategy in Action

Randy Watson is in his 4th year as a literacy coach at Twin Valley High School. As an experienced full-time literacy coach, Randy decided he should share his coaching resources. He decided to begin a blog called Watson on Disciplinary Literacy. He blogs every Friday about some practical classroom suggestions, such as vocabulary strategies or ideas to improve comprehension. Some of his colleagues have shared his blog with their colleagues and have wanted to discuss ideas further. Randy decided to begin linking his blogs to his Twitter account. Next, he decided to create a Twitter chat for his district. Teachers share their classroom ideas and questions at #SD13learns. Teachers have been sharing their own resources with each other.

One thing Randy has noticed is that while many of the teachers have benefited from talking across disciplines, they also want to share things that are relevant to their own discipline. Creating multiple hashtags would be too much to manage, so Randy decided to create a Google Community with multiple groups representing each teaching department. Social studies has its own space, as do science, English, and so on. Teachers can connect within and across disciplines in this closed social network hosted by Google. Although participating in the Google Community is voluntary, it is a place where the teachers can drop in and out for resources or to make connections.

After talking to his friend from another district, Randy also plans to try a Google Hangout with coaches from other local districts. Four have agreed to participate and share their struggles and successes. They hope that these virtual sessions will provide an opportunity to grow their coaching repertoire and improve their coaching efficacy.

Technology Tool Evaluation Template

Purpose:			

Web address:			

Features	Yes	Maybe	No
User friendly			
Technology support			
Free			
Compatible with district software			

Advantages	Limitations

Final Evaluation:

From *Collaborative Coaching for Disciplinary Literacy: Strategies to Support Teachers in Grades 6–12* by Laurie Elish-Piper, Susan K. L'Allier, Michael Manderino, and Paula Di Domenico. Copyright © 2016 The Guilford Press. Permission to photocopy this form is granted to purchasers of this book for personal use only (see copyright page for details). Purchasers can download additional copies of this form (see the box at the end of the table of contents).

PART V

Small-Group Coaching Strategies to Support Disciplinary Literacy Instruction

Working with small groups of teachers is an important layer of an effective disciplinary literacy coaching program. When working with small groups such as teams, departments, PLCs, or teachers who all teach the same course, you can tailor your coaching to meet the specific goals and challenges of the teachers and their students. For example, you can meet with eighth-grade ELA teachers to develop lessons to support students' reading of complex texts or high school biology teachers to identify specific disciplinary literacy outcomes they want to address with their students.

Small-group coaching allows you to shift your focus from building knowledge (in large-group coaching) to supporting implementation of disciplinary literacy strategies into teachers' lessons and classrooms. Because you'll only be working with a limited number of teachers at any one time, you will be able to provide more in-depth and intensive support. For example, you'll be able to answer any questions they have, share specific examples that apply to their classes, and discuss the needs of their students. In addition, small-group coaching creates a context in which participating teachers can work collaboratively and support each other as they strive to update their instruction to address the new, more rigorous learning standards.

In Part V, you will learn about six small-group coaching strategies that you can use to support the ELA, science, and social studies teachers you coach. Strategy 6 addresses how you can help teachers determine relevant disciplinary literacy outcomes and create assessment structures aligned to those outcomes. In Strategy 7, you'll learn how to help teachers select complex texts and develop instruction so their students can access those complex texts. Strategy 8 focuses on helping teachers prioritize vocabulary for instruction. Vocabulary instruction tends to be challenging for many teachers due to the enormous number of words that could be taught, so the approach in this strategy will help teachers choose the most important words to teach, as well as develop a plan for teaching them.

In many middle and high schools, common assessments are used for units of study and for midterm and final exams. To address this context, Strategy 9 provides an approach for helping teachers review common assessments so that they align with important disciplinary literacy outcomes and learning standards. In Strategy 10 you'll learn how to develop and implement discussion protocols to meaningfully engage teachers. Finally, Strategy 11 examines how you can help teachers inquire into their disciplines to further their own professional development.

As you use the strategies in Part V, you will be able to provide tailored coaching to meet the needs of small groups of teachers. Then, by layering on the individual coaching strategies described in Part VI, you will be able to provide the individualized support that some teachers will need to infuse disciplinary literacy instruction into their practice.

Determining Disciplinary Literacy Outcomes and Creating Assessment Structures

What Is It?

Disciplinary literacy instructional outcomes are based on standards that are identified as priorities for instruction in a particular course. By working in small teams to identify the disciplinary literacy instructional outcomes for a course, the teachers and the coach can focus on determining how to measure whether or not students have met the outcomes for learning in the unit. The team can set up an assessment structure that delineates how students are expected to make progress toward mastery of the learning outcomes. Until teachers have a clear sense of their discipline-specific instructional outcomes and an understanding of how they will measure these outcomes, determining discipline-specific strategies to support students is difficult. By helping teachers clarify the discipline-specific goals and how to measure those goals, coaches can then focus on how best to support the teachers as they help their students learn to master the discipline. In addition, a clear understanding of the instructional outcomes can also provide an opportunity for teachers to think beyond the activities in the classroom and toward the discipline-specific habits of thinking they would like to address over time.

In short, disciplinary literacy instructional outcomes, also referred to as instructional outcomes, are the foundation of future coaching collaborations, and assessments are determined from those outcomes. Without disciplinary literacy instructional outcomes and assessments, it is difficult to make instructional decisions (Reeves, 2011) or to organize instruction in a manner that allows teachers to support their students by monitoring their progress in developing skills. These assessment structures thus provide an opportunity for teachers to use assessment information to guide future instructional decisions.

Effective assessment structures are important for teachers, students, and coaches. In addition to serving as an instructional guide for teachers, assessment can also serve as an avenue to establish conversations about performance with students (Frey & Fisher, 2011). Elements of effective assessment structures include ensuring that students understand the purpose of the assignment, task, or objective; providing students with an opportunity to check for their own understanding of a concept or skill; and providing a platform for teachers and students to engage in conversations about progress toward the disciplinary learning outcomes (Frey & Fisher, 2011). Furthermore, results from these assessment structures can guide coaching conversations between teachers and coach.

How Do I Do It?

In order to help small groups of teachers select disciplinary literacy instructional outcomes and then create assessment structures, ensure that the teachers have access to the relevant standards. Then ask them to engage in the following steps.

1. Review the purpose for this meeting. Set the expectations for your work together by identifying the norms for the meeting or using a discussion protocol. (See Strategy 10 for an example of using discussion protocols.)
2. Determine the standard from which to write the instructional outcomes. This may come from a curriculum map, a department website, the standards themselves, or a final exam.
3. Review the standard and the teachers' curriculum and ask the teachers to write a narrative regarding what they would like students to be able to understand as a result of their work toward the particular standard. This quick brainstorm writing can help the teachers clarify the goals for the unit.
4. Ask teachers to create a list to identify what success on this objective might look like. Help them identify the criteria for successful mastery or progress toward this standard.
5. Next, ask teachers to consider the students' conditions for learning. That is, help them determine how students will engage in the behavior identified in the discipline-specific instructional outcomes. Help them identify the materials (e.g., texts, videos, graphic organizers) the students will need to engage in the lesson.
6. Then consider and apply the ABCD's of writing instructional outcomes (audience, behavior, condition, and degree) to write summative and formative instructional outcomes.
7. Once the instructional outcomes are set, identify assessment structures for the summative and formative instructional outcomes.
8. Set the stage for the next coaching session by offering to support individual teachers as they adapt, adopt, or create disciplinary literacy strategies for their work with students. (See Strategy 16 for more information about adapting, adopting, and creating disciplinary literacy strategies.)

The Strategy in Action

Linda Shinn, a full-time disciplinary literacy coach, has been working with the teachers on the curricular team for Western Civilization, which is a course offered to high school juniors and seniors. A former English teacher, Linda is a certified reading specialist and supports teachers of all disciplines.

Linda works with each teacher on the Western Civilization team (i.e., Jackie Smith, Renee Klopsmite, Adam Rivers, and Cristian Carrera) in one-on-one coaching sessions, as well as in the small-team structure. During a one-on-one coaching session, Renee expressed some confusion over how best to support students as they engage in writing arguments in history. Renee explained that the team had been teaching content and then teaching students how to write at the end of the unit, and she felt it was taking too much time, as the students did not have enough time to practice their writing. Renee wondered if they could combine the content students needed to learn about Western civilizations while they learned to reason and argue in writing. Linda suggested that they could collaborate at the next team meeting to consider how best to support students' writing by creating disciplinary literacy instructional outcomes.

During the team meeting, Linda began by explaining that they were there to review the upcoming unit to clarify disciplinary literacy instructional outcomes that married both the content of the unit and the skills, particularly writing arguments. Linda explained that Renee wanted to incorporate more writing practice for students and that Linda had offered to support their work if the other teachers were in agreement. Jackie, Cristian, and Adam agreed with Renee's and Linda's suggestions, and the group decided that the goal of their time together would be to brainstorm and generate ideas about what the teachers want students to gain from the unit of instruction and then create disciplinary literacy instructional outcomes to guide their instruction. Once the goals for their work were set, the team began collaborating.

To get the process started, Linda began, "Renee mentioned that her primary concern was to infuse more argumentative thinking and writing as students were learning the content. Which standard do you hope to address through this work?"

Cristian explained that the group was working toward WHST.11-12.1b, which involved developing claims and counterclaims and supplying the most relevant data and evidence for each in a manner that is appropriate to the discipline and anticipates the audience's knowledge level. Cristian added, "We're about to start a new unit on the Crusades. Do you think that they can write an argument on that?"

Linda suggested, "Why don't we begin by defining what the narrative for our unit is? What is it that you want the students to be able to walk away with? Let's each take five minutes to brainstorm a draft of what we expect from students." After 5 minutes of engaging in the quick-write brainstorming activity, Jackie volunteered to share her narrative with the group:

"It's not just that we want the students to understand the Crusades and what the impact of the Crusades were. It's more than that. We also want them to know that there are many factors that influenced the development of European nations. It's not like it was just one thing or one event, though some have more influence than others. They should be able to read texts and then consider the causes of these conflicts and how those were influential."

Renee added, "If we can create opportunities for students to write about their thinking, maybe they would not struggle so much."

"It just takes so much time," Adam said.

Linda moved the conversation forward by saying, "Let's take a look at that narrative. When you say that you want students to understand the Crusades, what does that mean? What would that understanding look like?"

"In my narrative, I added that I want them to review events and sift through evidence to determine the cause-and-effect relationship of the events leading to the development of European nations. We always go back to that. It's the purpose of our course," Renee explained. "I just don't know how to weave it in."

Linda summarized, "So what I hear you saying is that you want the students to consider causal relationships between certain events, including the Crusades. Then you want them to consider how this influenced development of European nations. I also heard that you want students to write arguments to work toward mastery of the standard while considering the impact of certain events on the development of nations. Am I on target?"

"Yes, that's right." Cristian said.

"Okay. And what does success look like?" Linda asked.

"Students need to be able to construct a clear argument based on sound evidence. It can't just be any evidence. Their reasoning must be supported by sound thinking," Jackie added.

After hearing Jackie's response, Linda stated, "Our work may be helped by applying the ABCD's of instructional outcomes. This framework can guide our thinking about the instructional outcomes. In this framework, the 'A' stands for audience, in this case your Western Civilization students. The 'B' is for behavior, or what it is your students should be able to do. The 'C' is for conditions of learning. How will students learn? What will they be doing? And the 'D' is for degree of completion. Here's where you can identify what success on this really looks like. And for this case, let's write this as a summative instructional outcome. This will focus on what the students will be able to do by the end of the unit." After engaging in discussion, the teachers created the summative instructional outcome shown in Figure 6.1.

"Now that we have an idea of what the summative instructional outcome is, we can build formative instructional outcomes that will guide the learning in the classroom," Linda stated. "What will the students need to be able to do in order to meet this summative instructional outcome? Remember, the action verbs will help you determine how to write these instructional outcomes. If you focus on the discipline-specific verbs, you can ensure that you are marrying the content and the skills of the discipline."

Together, the team brainstormed a list of what the students would need to be able to do using discipline-specific verbs whenever possible. Their list is shown in Figure 6.2.

A	Audience	The Western Civilization students
B	Behavior	Compare factors that influenced the development of European nations and argue which was most influential
C	Condition	Given a text set on the Crusades and direct instruction in argument writing
D	Degree	with strong, logical evidence

Summative instructional outcome: Given a text set on the Crusades and direct instruction in argument writing, the Western Civilization students will be able to use strong, logical evidence to compare factors that influenced the development of European nations and argue which was most influential.

FIGURE 6.1. Applying the ABCD's to create a summative instructional outcome.

- Corroborate information across multiple sources.
- Review conflicts and determine their causal relationships.
- Reason and select the best evidence to support claims.
- Recognize causal relationships.
- Write and develop claims and counterclaims.
- Synthesize information across multiple sources.

FIGURE 6.2. Behaviors students will engage in to meet a summative instructional outcome.

From that list, the team then wrote formative instructional outcomes that would support their students' ability to show progress toward meeting the final summative instructional outcome, using the ABCD format. These are provided in Figure 6.3.

Once the team identified the instructional outcomes, Linda suggested that they consider the tasks in which the students would engage that would show the teachers whether or not the students have met the outcomes. The tasks created to support the instructional outcomes are detailed in Figure 6.4. After finalizing the tasks used to measure the instructional outcomes, Linda suggested that they continue their collaboration in individual and small-group coaching meetings to determine how best to instruct students.

They planned to meet as a team in a few weeks to determine whether or not the students were making progress toward meeting the objectives by analyzing the first formative task. Before leaving the meeting, Linda also set up the next individual

- Given a text set on the topic, the Western Civilization students will be able to use sound evidence to explain the conflict during the Crusades and the impact on the development of European nations.
- Given a text set on the topic, the students will be able to use sound evidence and develop a counterclaim when arguing whether or not alliances are necessary for survival of a nation.
- Given a prompt, students will be able to use sound evidence to write an argument as to whether or not defensive alliances and wars lead to the formation of nations.

FIGURE 6.3. Formative instructional outcomes.

Summative instructional outcome: Given a text set on the Crusades and direct instruction in argument writing, the Western Civilization students will be able to use strong, logical evidence to compare factors that influenced the development of European nations and argue which was most influential.

Summative task: Write an essay in which you compare two factors that influenced the development of European nations (conflict over religion and defensive alliances and wars) and argue which was the most influential in the development of European nations. Support your position with evidence from class discussions, texts read in class, and class activities.

Formative instructional outcome	Formative task
Given a text set on the topic, the Western Civilization students will be able to use sound evidence to explain the conflict during the Crusades and the impact on the development of European nations.	Write an essay in which you explain the impact of the Crusades on the development of Western Europe. Support your discussion with evidence from the text(s).
Given a text set on the topic, the students will be able to use sound evidence and develop a counterclaim when arguing whether or not alliances are necessary for survival of a nation.	Revise your alliance essay to elaborate upon your argument of whether or not alliances are necessary for survival of a nation. Be sure to present and develop a counterclaim in your revision.
Given a prompt, students will be able to use sound evidence to write an argument as to whether or not defensive alliances and wars lead to the formation of nations.	Write an essay in which you explain the impact of alliances and conflicts on the development of Western Europe. Support your discussion with evidence from the text(s).

FIGURE 6.4. Tasks aligned to formative and summative instructional outcomes.

meeting with Renee to talk about how best to instruct students and apply strategies related to these disciplinary literacy instructional outcomes.

Tips for Working within Other Disciplines

Several resources that provide general academic terms are available online at websites such as that of the Center for Teaching and Learning (*http://teaching.uncc.edu/learning-resources/articles-books/best-practice/goals-objectives/writing-objectives*). These will help teachers write instructional outcomes. To ensure a disciplinary literacy approach, coaches can also rely on more specific verbs and phrases that reflect each discipline's values. A list of these verbs and verb phrases can be found in Figure 6.5.

Social studies	ELA	Science
corroborate	critique	record observations
source	evaluate	hypothesize
contextualize	argue	predict
synthesize	determine author's purpose	synthesize
consensus	evaluate author's effectiveness	generalize
determine causal relationships	compare the approach	model
examine multiple sources	research	argue
compare the point of view		critique

FIGURE 6.5. Disciplinary literacy action verbs.

Selecting, Assessing, and Scaffolding Complex Texts

What Is It?

The CCSS make clear that students need to read increasingly complex texts (NGA & CCSSO, 2010). Appendix A of the CCSS (*www.corestandards.org/assets/ Appendix_A.pdf*) outlines what constitutes text complexity and provides guidelines for assessing text complexity. As a literacy coach, you may be asked to ascertain the complexity of a variety of disciplinary texts. In the past, reading specialists often used readability formulas such as Fry or Flesch–Kincaid to match readers to a reading level. The CCSS shift away from solely aligning texts to specific reading levels to ensure that students read within a grade-level band of text complexity. For example, Standard 10 for Reading Literature in the 9th- to 10th-grade band states that students should "By the end of grade 9, read and comprehend literature, including stories, dramas, and poems, in the grades 9–10 text complexity band proficiently, with scaffolding as needed at the high end of the range" (NGA & CCSSO, 2010). Increasing the level of text complexity, especially in grades 6–12, is a key instructional shift, especially for teachers who have students who may read one or more grade levels below their peers. Teachers need to become proficient in selecting complex texts for instruction. They must move from leveling texts to match the reader through the use of a readability formula to analyzing texts to ensure that students are reading texts within a defined grade band of complexity. They must also realize that text complexity is more than a quantitative measure. Text complexity, according to the CCSS, comprises quantitative measures, qualitative measures, and reader and task factors (Figure 7.1).

In the CCSS, quantitative measures are reported in Lexile levels. Lexiles can be computed using the website *https://lexile.com*. According to the developers, "the

FIGURE 7.1. CCSS text complexity factors.

Lexile Analyzer® measures the complexity of the text by breaking down the entire piece and studying its characteristics, such as sentence length and word frequency, which represent the syntactic and semantic challenges that the text presents to a reader" (*www.lexile.com/analyzer*). The CCSS has outlined a range of text complexity by Lexile levels (see Figure 7.2). Qualitative factors for text complexity include levels of meaning, structure, language conventionality and clarity, and knowledge demands (see Figure 7.3). Reader and task considerations include cognitive capabilities, motivation, topic knowledge, and strategy knowledge (RAND Reading Study Group, 2002). Appendix A from CCSS is a good resource for coaches to see examples of texts that are analyzed for complexity based on these three dimensions.

Your role as a literacy coach is not to assess every text for teachers but rather to provide tools so that teachers can assess the complexity of the texts that they want to use and suggest potential strategies for helping students learn with challenging texts.

How Do I Do It?

The coach can meet with small groups of teachers from the same discipline to show them the process of assessing texts for complexity and walk them through that process with a text in their discipline. The goal is to build teacher capacity for the

Text complexity grade band in the Standards	Old Lexile ranges	Lexile ranges aligned to the CCR expectations
K–1	N/A	N/A
2–3	450–725	450–790
4–5	645–845	770–980
6–8	860–1010	955–1155
9–10	960–1115	1080–1305
11–CCR	1070–1220	1215–1355

FIGURE 7.2. Text complexity bands.

Dimension	Indicators of complexity	ELA	History	Science
Levels of meaning	Multiple levels of meaning or purpose rather than single meanings	Use of an unreliable narrator Use of literary elements such as allegory or satire	Presence of subtext (i.e., written from a particular perspective)	Multilayered or multistep processes
Structure	Unclear structure that juxtaposes events temporally, uses complex graphics, and/or unconventional text structures	Multiple flashbacks or flash forwards Presence of additional sidebar information about author or context often found in anthologies Gutters and panel nuances in graphic novels	Breaks in chronological narrative (e.g., Watergate) Argument disguised as a narrative in a secondary text Presence of political cartoons, maps, and charts that are integral to narrative in the text	Presence of graphics that are essential to understanding the written text
Language conventionality/ clarity	Use of figurative language, dense or misleading language, archaic terms, and/or technical/ domain-specific vocabulary.	Archaic or contextual language Presence of literary devices such as simile, metaphor, alliteration	Archaic language (e.g., gilded age) Metaphorical descriptions (e.g., lamp of liberty)	Highly technical terminology (e.g., deoxyribonucleic acid) Use of nominalizations to describe processes (e.g., oxidize to oxidation)
Knowledge demands	Presence of multiple perspectives, unknown genres, references to multiple texts, and high disciplinary background knowledge	Allusions to other works of literature Knowledge of genre Knowledge of context of the story	Ability to infer when author information is obscured Knowledge of preceding events	Knowledge of requisite formulas Knowledge of underpinning theories

FIGURE 7.3. Qualitative indicators of text complexity in the disciplines.

assessment of text complexity through the small-group coaching process. We propose a three-step framework for supporting teachers' use of complex disciplinary texts (see Figure 7.4).

Helping Teachers Select Texts

1. Ask teachers to select texts that will support disciplinary literacy instructional outcomes. It is important to approach text selection based on disciplinary literacy instructional outcomes rather than simply trying to select random texts that are complex. For example, an English teacher may want her students to identify how metaphor and simile can convey the theme of a novel. She has decided to focus on this disciplinary literacy instructional outcome during the upcoming unit on courage.

2. Probe teachers to determine the disciplinary skills needed to comprehend the selected text(s). In the above example, once the teacher has selected a text on courage, he or she should review it to be sure the text contains opportunities for students to identify simile and metaphor in relation to the theme of courage.

Assessing for Text Complexity

1. Encourage teachers to reread the entire text before they begin instruction so that they can anticipate potential areas where the text may present challenges for students.

2. Show the teachers how they can calculate quantitative measures using Lexiles (*https://lexile.com/analyzer/*) or how they can enter three 100-word passages into Microsoft Word and run a Flesch–Kincaid readability measure. Remind them

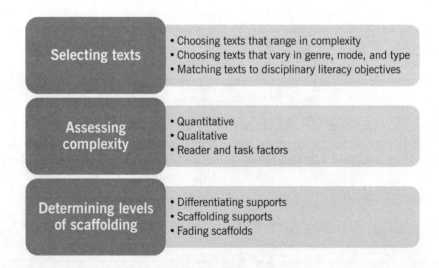

FIGURE 7.4. Three-step process for helping teachers teach with complex disciplinary texts.

to be very cautious. If they enter fewer than three 100-word passages, the readability level will be less reliable. Determine whether the text fits within the grade bands identified in Figure 7.2.

3. Show the teachers how to conduct a qualitative analysis of the text, using the following dimensions: levels of meaning, structure, language conventionality/clarity, and knowledge demands. See Figure 7.3 for indicators of complexity along each dimension for ELA, history, and science.

4. Identify the task that the teachers will have the students do that makes use of the text. The following questions may guide the teachers' thinking:
   - How will the text help students complete the assigned task?
   - What experiences do students have doing this type of task?
   - What will be evidence that students have met the objectives for this task?

5. Help teachers identify reader factors that will affect complexity. Questions that can guide this process include: What experiences have students had with this type of text? What challenges do students have with reading this type/genre of text?

6. Initially, you might want to use Form 7.1 to help teachers document each level of complexity and then ascertain the overall complexity.

Selecting Scaffolds to Support Reading of the Text

1. Once complexity has been determined, teachers should use all three aspects of complexity (i.e., quantitative, qualitative, task and reader factors) to decide whether the text is appropriate to use with students. If they decide to use the text with their students, teachers may need support in how to use the text in relation to other texts. Will other texts be used to frontload information? Will comprehending the selected text be imperative to comprehension of subsequent texts? How will the teacher differentiate for students?

2. Help the teachers determine what strategies might best support learning from text. Make sure the focus remains on student learning from text rather than having the teachers tell students what the text is about. You may need to remind teachers that they should differentiate supports for students, scaffold their use, and eventually fade the support over time.

   A powerful scaffolded approach to reading complex texts that fosters deep understanding, not simply literal comprehension, is close reading. To support students as they learn to closely read the text, the teacher initially provides students with a focus and a strategy as they interact with sections of the text. For example, teachers may instruct students to read the text first for general understanding. Then they may ask students to read a section of text again to notice how the author structured it. A third and fourth close read might help students focus on the author's use of metaphor and simile to help them consider the impact of these devices on the theme. Practices that can support close reading are annotation, asking questions of the text, noting confusions encountered in the text, and having students discuss what they have read (Fisher & Frey, 2012). Close reading should be purposeful and match the teachers' disciplinary literacy instructional outcomes. Close reading is not an isolated exercise to meet the CCSS but rather an approach to reading a text when deep comprehension is needed to build disciplinary knowledge. It is also important for teachers to model close reading for their students and ask text-dependent questions that require a synthesis of ideas within the text.

3. Based on the students' previous experience with the genre of text, the complexity of the text, and strategy use related to the task, remind teachers to use the gradual release of responsibility model (i.e., explicit instruction, modeling, guided practice, group practice, independent practice, and reflection; Pearson & Gallagher, 1983) to keep students moving toward independently constructing meaning with complex texts in the discipline.

The Strategy in Action

Rosa Morales is a literacy coach at Martin Luther King Middle School. She has been a literacy coach for 4 years and was a reading specialist for 4 years prior to that. As a reading specialist, Rosa often worked with teachers to match texts to the reading level of their struggling students. Now teachers often approach her to check the complexity of their texts. Rosa was concerned that she was spending too much time assessing text complexity for teachers and not enough time coaching toward disciplinary literacy instruction. She realized that she should be helping teachers learn to analyze the complexity of texts themselves and that this would give her more time to focus her coaching on disciplinary literacy instruction.

Rosa started to build that teacher independence with members of the seventh-grade language arts team who approached her about Sandra Cisneros's *The House on Mango Street* (1991), a text they wanted to use in an upcoming unit. They were concerned that the text was not complex enough because it had registered at the fifth-grade level according to the Flesch–Kincaid and had a Lexile of 870 in terms of text complexity, which was below the expected Lexile level range for sixth to eighth graders (see Figure 7.2). Yet they knew the text had some complex themes, such as interpersonal and familial relationships and the struggle for self, for their seventh graders to explore.

At their Thursday team meeting, Rosa shared the Text Complexity Evaluation Form (Form 7.1) and explained how it could be used to evaluate the text qualitatively. They agreed to complete the form individually and set a meeting for the following Monday to continue their discussion. The team members came to the meeting with their Text Complexity Evaluation forms completed. As they shared their notes, they realized that the novel was more complex than the quantitative measures indicated because students might need some prior knowledge about Latino Chicago in the 1960s and because the novel contained language that might be unfamiliar to their seventh graders. Rosa then asked, "What is your instructional goal?" Kim, a second-year teacher, struggled a bit because she was so focused on using a complex text. Initially, she said she wanted the students to understand the context of Chicago in the 1960s. Rosa then asked, "How will reading *The House on Mango Street* help the students gain that understanding?" Kim wasn't sure. Rosa used this as an opportunity to discuss the role of reader and task.

By reading parts of *The House on Mango Street* (1991) together as a team, they realized that characterization and setting were important elements of the novel. They all agreed that early in the novel, they wanted students to examine how the author used characterization to address the characters' interpersonal and familial relationships. As the meeting continued, the team decided that focusing more on literary elements, such as development of character and use of setting, would make the reading of the novel more discipline-based. Rosa helped them create a disciplinary literacy instructional outcome that focused on character development and setting. Tom, who had been a member of the language arts team for 6 years, also remarked that they could bring in other complex texts to help develop students' understanding of the setting.

Hearing that the team wanted to have students read a text that would provide context about Latino/a neighborhoods in Chicago, Rosa found a resource from the Illinois History Society titled "The Mexicans in Chicago" by Louise A. N. Kerr (1999). At their next team meeting, they analyzed this informational text and realized that it would provide a good opportunity for students to grapple with a historical source and integrate the information with the novel they were reading. They recognized, however, that students would need supports for reading this complex text. Rosa worked with the team to develop a summarization strategy and a paired discussion protocol that would support students' comprehension of the text. Other possible supports the group discussed are provided in Figure 7.5.

Rosa and the team agreed to meet three more times, once at the beginning of the novel unit to discuss where students were struggling and succeeding with the text and to determine what additional instructional supports were needed; once in the middle of the unit to make any instructional adjustments, such as adding or removing texts or checking on the efficacy of the instructional supports; and once at the conclusion of the unit to reflect on the process and plan for upcoming instructional units.

As a result of her work with the seventh-grade team, Rosa decided to make some resources available to teachers so they could start the text evaluation process on their own. She held workshops and made tutorial videos about calculating quantitative measures of text complexity using Lexile levels or the Flesch–Kincaid readability formula through Microsoft Word. She also created a tutorial related to the qualitative dimensions of text complexity to help teachers begin to consider those dimensions. Rosa now asks teachers, prior to a coaching meeting that involves text

Complexity factor	Possible supports
Unfamiliar vocabulary	See Strategy 8: Prioritizing Vocabulary for Instruction to review the procedures for creating appropriate vocabulary strategies. Provide a glossary of terms. Use a word knowledge strategy such as a Knowledge Rating Guide (Blachowicz, 1986).
Multiple meanings	Incorporate a summarization strategy such as GIST (Cunningham, 2013). Engage in close reading of selected passages in which multiple meanings are present. Use scaffolds such as annotation, modeling through think-alouds, text-based discussions, and asking text-dependent questions. Use a Plot/Concept Relationship Chart (Schmidt & Buckley, 1991).
Unfamiliar text structure	Use text structure graphic organizers such as Herringbone for plot, cause–effect or problem solution charts, or compare-and-contrast charts. Use an Observation/Inference Chart (Nokes, 2008) for visual texts such as photographs, diagrams, or political cartoons. Have students create a timeline of events. Conduct a think-aloud with a parallel text to demonstrate thinking about how you figure out text structure.
High knowledge demands	Use video or photo resources to build a quick base of background knowledge. Begin by having students read a less complex text that provides background knowledge. Use a closed word sort (Templeton, Johnston, Bear, & Invernizzi, 2010) or concept circles (Vacca, Vacca, & Mraz, 2005) to have students create conceptual connections among key ideas prior to reading the text.

FIGURE 7.5. Possible instructional supports for scaffolding the reading of complex texts. Explanations of the strategies in the above chart and their connection to the CCSS can be found in Manderino, Berglund, and Johns (2014).

selection, to prepare for that meeting by completing the Text Complexity Evaluation Form (Form 7.1).

During coaching meetings that focus on text selection, Rosa asks specific questions about the disciplinary literacy instructional outcomes related to the texts the teachers have selected for their students to read. Rosa often asks questions about the specific disciplinary demands that might make a text complex. She has reported that she is able to focus more on reader and task demands as a result of teachers coming to meetings having done some preliminary evaluation of their texts.

Text Complexity Evaluation

Text:	Lexile or Grade-Level Equivalent:

Qualitative Factors	Evidence of Complexity
Levels of Meaning 1 2 3 4 5 Less complex More complex	
Structure 1 2 3 4 5 Less complex More complex	
Language Conventionality/Clarity 1 2 3 4 5 Less complex More complex	

(continued)

From *Collaborative Coaching for Disciplinary Literacy: Strategies to Support Teachers in Grades 6–12* by Laurie Elish-Piper, Susan K. L'Allier, Michael Manderino, and Paula Di Domenico. Copyright © 2016 The Guilford Press. Permission to photocopy this form is granted to purchasers of this book for personal use only (see copyright page for details). Purchasers can download additional copies of this form (see the box at the end of the table of contents).

Qualitative Factors	Evidence of Complexity
Knowledge Demands 1 2 3 4 5 Less complex More complex	
Task Factors 1 2 3 4 5 Less complex More complex	
Reader Factors (experience, motivation, knowledge of the topic, knowledge of strategies)	

Overall Evaluation of Complexity:	1	2	3	4	5
	Less complex				More complex

Prioritizing Vocabulary for Instruction

What Is It?

Secondary disciplinary literacy coaches will answer many questions from teachers regarding how they can best help students learn vocabulary terms. Teachers often report feeling overwhelmed when teaching vocabulary because they have so much content to address and because there are many terms that are requisite to understanding the concepts or engaging in academic thinking in the discipline. Further, there are many discipline-specific language challenges that can make teaching vocabulary terms at the secondary level daunting (Fang, 2012), as each discipline values and uses language differently.

Additionally, the CCSS (NGA & CCSSO, 2010) require more attention to engage with and understand complex texts. So that students can access these complex texts, teachers must provide them with the resources they need to be able to comprehend and produce texts in the discipline, using the language of the discipline (Townsend, 2015). The problem is that many teachers feel that there are just too many words to teach. To support students, teachers often end up creating long lists of vocabulary terms and then attempting to teach all of the terms because they do not know what else to do (Townsend, 2015). Instead of creating a list based on what students might not know, teachers can provide opportunities for students to learn the vocabulary that is essential for understanding in the discipline (Gillis, 2014) by carefully selecting the vocabulary terms to teach. Understanding these challenges with vocabulary selection can help coaches support teachers in the decision-making process. Disciplinary literacy coaches can rely on a decision-making framework to support teachers as they determine which vocabulary terms to select for instruction.

Flanigan and Greenwood (2007) outline a framework that coaches can adapt to help teachers make decisions about how to select the vocabulary terms to use in instruction. Coaches can then help teachers link their vocabulary instruction to specific curricular goals (Townsend, 2015). An adaptation of Flanigan and Greenwood's framework is presented in Form 8.1 and can be used to support teams of teachers as they work to identify which terms to teach and how to teach these terms. After collaborating to select the most appropriate terms to teach, the coach and teachers can work together to determine which strategies will foster students' discipline-specific and academic vocabularies.

How Do I Do It?

1. Use the team's disciplinary literacy instructional outcomes for the lesson or unit as a guide. If the teacher or team does not have a disciplinary literacy instructional outcome, see Strategy 6 to consider how to help teachers create one. Coaches and teachers can work at the lesson or unit level.

2. Consider the terms that students need to know by reviewing the instructional outcomes and objectives, as well as the texts and assessments involved in supporting students as they work toward mastering the instructional outcomes.

3. Complete the vocabulary selection framework.

    a. Ask teachers to consult texts and curricular materials to generate a list of terms students may need to know to meet the instructional outcomes.

    b. Support teachers as they sort the vocabulary words into three categories: critical terms students need to know, words not to teach, and terms which students may need some information about but that do not require deep instruction.

    c. Ask teachers to review the critical terms that require deep instruction and determine when to teach these terms.

    d. Help teachers consider what they want students to know about the term, and then identify strategies that will help students develop that knowledge.

    e. Brainstorm and help the teacher determine how to assess the students' word knowledge.

The Strategy in Action

Carla Pfeiffer is a part-time coach and a part-time reading teacher at Watertown Community High School. She has three release periods each day to work with teachers, and she also teaches two developmental reading courses. Carla has been coaching for the past 5 years and holds a degree in English; she is also a certified reading specialist. Carla is working with a group of English teachers who are planning for their first unit of the ninth-grade curriculum, the short story. The focus of the unit is to teach the students the structure and the genre of short stories. During the unit, the students will analyze short stories and will also write narratives and critiques. There are several vocabulary terms that the students will need to know in order to be successful in this unit, and the teachers were feeling overwhelmed. Tim Anderson, one of the teachers on the team, asked Carla if she would meet with them during their common planning time to consider how best to teach the vocabulary of this unit to the students.

The team consisted of Tim Anderson, who has been teaching for 11 years, Aysha Korian, who has been teaching for 9 years, Anton Brown, who has been teaching for 4 years, and Elias Hidreth, who has been teaching for 20 years.

To begin, Carla asked the team to identify the discipline-specific instructional outcomes of the unit. The teachers explained that during the course of the unit on short stories, students should meet the CCSS standard 9-10.RL.5: "Analyze how an author's choices concerning how to structure a text, order events within it (e.g., parallel plots), and manipulate time (e.g., pacing, flashbacks) create such effects as mystery, tension, or surprise." From that standard, the team had created two disciplinary literacy instructional outcomes, which can be found in Figure 8.1.

The first instructional outcome involved providing students with the opportunity to choose a short story and then examine the author's choices of either text structure, order of events, or manipulation of time. Once the students complete that analysis, they will then write an original passage that would change the impact of the story. The team of teachers explained that students will also reflect on their work and explain how their original passage affects the message and serves to answer the essential question. That is, they will be able to answer, "What does this addition to the story do for the readers?" In addition to the students' choice texts, the teachers would provide students with six short stories and some literary nonfiction to support their understanding of the unit's instructional outcomes.

Having clarified their disciplinary literacy instructional outcomes, the teachers reviewed the standards and the stories and brainstormed terms that the students

---

Disciplinary literacy instructional outcomes
- Given the opportunity to choose a story from a variety of short stories, students will be able to analyze the author's choices concerning how to [student selects one: structure a text, order events, or manipulate time] to create such effects as mystery, tension, or surprise and explain how that works to convey the author's message.
- Given the short story of their choice, students will be able to write an original passage that would change the overall effect/impact of the story if it were added to or substituted into the work, using dialogue, pacing, or description.

brainstorm: word list
genre, narrative, short stories, text structure, mystery, tension, surprise, author's message, effect, dialogue, character dimensions, absurdly, instinctively, efficiently, sedative, bemused, council, circumstances, gesture, hearth, sixpence, proceeding

FIGURE 8.1. Instructional outcome identification for vocabulary framework.

Terms that are critical	Terms that are not critical
author's message, effect, dialogue, character, text structure, mystery, tension, surprise	*genre, narrative, short stories, absurdly, instinctively, efficiently, sedative, bemused, council, circumstances, gesture, hearth, sixpence, proceeding*

FIGURE 8.2. Critical and noncritical terms.

would need to learn throughout the course of the 4-week unit. The team identified 22 terms, as shown in Figure 8.1.

Carla asked the group to sift through the list and determine which terms are so important to the unit that they would spend 15 minutes teaching each of those terms. She explained that these were critical terms that would require deep teaching. Carla pressed the team to identify which terms were important enough to the objective that they were worth that amount of instructional time. She asked the team members to use a chart like the one shown in Figure 8.2 to help guide their thinking. The teachers included the "15 minute" words in the critical term column.

As the teachers were sifting through the words, they determined whether or not students needed to know these terms before or after they started reading the short stories of the unit, and they sorted the words accordingly. Next, Carla helped the team identify what it was they wanted students to know about the terms. Finally, she helped the teachers determine strategies they would use to support the students' learning and how they planned to assess their students' understanding of the terms. The decisions the team made are recorded in Figure 8.3. Form 8.1 is a blank form that coaches can use in their work with teachers.

As a result of applying the vocabulary selection framework with Carla, Tim and the rest of the teachers no longer felt overwhelmed by the vocabulary demands. Tim said, "Now I feel like I can focus on teaching the students to think and write like an author would instead of memorizing a bunch of terms."

"Yeah," Anton added, "I have to say I'm looking forward to teaching this short story unit now."

Disciplinary Literacy Instructional Outcome/Objective

- Given the opportunity to choose a story from a variety of short stories, students will be able to analyze the author's choices concerning how to [student selects one: structure a text, order events, or manipulate time] to create such effects as mystery, tension, or surprise and explain how that works to convey the author's message.
- Given a short story of their choice, students will be able to write an original passage that would change the overall effect/impact of the story if it were added to or substituted into the work, using dialogue, pacing, or description.

Critical before			Critical after		
Term	Behavior	Strategy	Term	Behavior	Strategy
author's message	Explain that an author makes decisions to deliver a message to an audience.	Provide examples and nonexamples and scenarios.	*effect*	Identify and explain the effect a device has on a reader.	Use a graphic organizer to guide thinking about specific devices and their effectiveness.
text structure	Explain narrative structure and how that structure or altering that structure can affect the message of a story.	Provide examples and nonexamples and scenarios.	*dialogue*	Explain how the use of dialogue affects the author's message.	Use a graphic organizer created by the coach and teacher.
tension, mystery, surprise	Draw a connection to how structure affects tension, mystery, and surprise.	Provide examples and nonexamples and scenarios.	*character*	Identify how authors use character as a way to deliver a message.	Use a graphic organizer created by the coach and teacher.

Foot-in-the-Door Terms: *genre, narrative*

Terms not to teach but that students may need exposure to: *short stories, dimensions, absurdly, instinctively, efficiently, sedative, bemused, council, circumstances, gesture, hearth, sixpence, proceeding*

Assessment of Vocabulary Terms: Assess students' scenarios and examples and nonexamples from their vocabulary strategy exercises.

FIGURE 8.3. Vocabulary decision-making framework for the short story unit.

Vocabulary Decision-Making Framework

Disciplinary Literacy Instructional Outcome/Objective

	Critical before			Critical after	
Term	Behavior	Strategy	Term	Behavior	Strategy

Foot-in-the-Door Terms

Terms I don't need to teach but that students may need exposure to

Assessment of Vocabulary Terms:

From *Collaborative Coaching for Disciplinary Literacy: Strategies to Support Teachers in Grades 6–12* by Laurie Elish-Piper, Susan K. L'Allier, Michael Manderino, and Paula Di Domenico. Copyright © 2016 The Guilford Press. Permission to photocopy this form is granted to purchasers of this book for personal use only (see copyright page for details). Purchasers can download additional copies of this form (see the box at the end of the table of contents).

Reviewing Common Assessments

What Is It?

In many middle and high schools, the use of common assessments has become an important aspect of the curricular process. A common assessment is generally developed by teachers who teach the same course so that "student learning will be assessed using the same instrument or process and according to the same criteria" (DuFour, DuFour, Eaker, & Many, 2010, p. 63). When teachers develop a common assessment for a unit of study, they are coming to a shared understanding of what the students will be responsible for learning, and a natural outgrowth of this shared understanding is the use of common instructional strategies to help all students who take the course achieve the specified outcomes.

Coaches often support these teams of teachers in developing common assessments, helping them use the standards, curriculum guides, and disciplinary literacy instructional outcomes to determine what content knowledge, reasoning, and skills should be assessed (Reeves, 2007). After determining what should be assessed, the coach and teachers then work together to decide what type(s) of assessment (e.g., selected response, extended written response, performance) would be most appropriate (Stiggins, Arter, Chappuis, & Chappuis, 2011). Finally, the coach facilitates the process of creating the assessment items and, in the case of extended responses or performance, the scoring rubrics.

However, creating a common assessment is only the beginning of the assessment cycle. After students have taken a common assessment, it is important that teachers meet together to review the results. Once again, the coach can guide the team of teachers as they analyze the results; pinpoint difficulties in terms of student knowledge, reasoning, and skills; and determine what factors might be contributing to those difficulties. Together, the coach and teachers can decide what revisions might be beneficial before the unit is taught again and how disciplinary thinking processes and/or skills might be retaught in an upcoming unit.

How Do I Do It?

When you work with a team of teachers to review a common assessment, you are striving to build capacity. After you facilitate the process with the team once or twice, they should then be able to use that process and the tools you share to review other common assessments without your support. Regardless of the type of assessment data you are reviewing, there are three essential components to the review process: compiling the data, analyzing the data, and determining appropriate revisions.

Compiling the Results

1. Collect the assessment data from the teachers or from the school's assessment management system, if your school uses such a system.

2. Compile the results. Determine how you will share the results. If you use the graphic feature in Excel, you can determine which of several display options will most clearly convey the data. You may want to develop several different displays. For example, assume the teachers have administered an extended-response common assessment and scored it using a rubric. You could display the results in terms of the total score, the scores for each cell of the rubric, or the scores broken down by demographics (e.g., gender, English learner/non-English learner, socioeconomic status). You could also present the results separated by teacher.

3. You may want to work with a teacher from the team on this part of the process so that the teacher can take the lead in compiling the results for a future common assessment.

Analyzing the Results

1. If the team meets on a regular basis, you can use one of those meeting times to analyze the results. If it doesn't meet on a regular basis, you will need to schedule a meeting date and time that works for everyone. Many common assessments include both a selected-response component and an extended-response or performance component. When this is the case, you may need to schedule a separate meeting to review each component.

2. Share the overall results with the teachers and ask them to draw some general

conclusions as to whether the students, on the whole, met the targeted instructional outcome(s). Use the top section of Form 9.1 to record their conclusions.

3. Share the data broken down by rubric cell or group. Ask the teachers to note areas of strength and areas that seemed difficult for the students. Their ideas can be recorded in the middle portion of Form 9.1.

4. Then ask the teachers to brainstorm factors that could have contributed to students' strengths and difficulties. Record their thoughts in the middle portion of Form 9.1. Some possible factors are:

   a. The texts that the students read were not aligned with the content they were expected to learn.

   b. The instruction related to disciplinary thinking and writing was not sufficient for the students to meet the expectations of the extended response or performance assessment.

   c. For selected-response assessments, some items included poor distractors.

   d. For extended-response and performance assessments:
      • Directions for the task were not clear to the students.
      • The category descriptions on the rubric were not clear, leading to inconsistency of scoring across teachers.
      • The students were asked to do a task about which they had received little to no instruction.

Determining Appropriate Revisions

1. A close examination of the factors contributing to student performance strengths and difficulties will help the teachers determine appropriate revisions. Revisions can be recorded in the final section of Form 9.1.

2. Sometimes, revisions to the common assessment may be warranted. For example, items in a selected-response assessment might be deleted or distractors changed. Perhaps the directions for the extended-response or performance assessment need to be clarified and/or expanded. Teachers might also suggest revisions to the scoring rubric language or the scoring process, believing that consistency would be improved if they engaged in some group scoring of a small set of assessments before scoring the rest on an individual basis.

3. Teachers may also decide that revisions are needed in regard to one or more of the following: the instructional outcomes, clarifying instructional outcomes for students, assigned texts, instructional strategies, and methods of teaching those strategies.

4. If revisions are needed in terms of the unit plan, the instructional outcomes, or the common assessment, determine which member of the team will make the revisions and the date by which those revisions should be completed. Add that information to the final section of Form 9.1.

The Strategy in Action

Allen Weinberger is a half-time disciplinary literacy coach at Newton Township High School. Allen taught English for 6 years prior to becoming a coach and continues to teach three periods of English I. He minored in history and thus is pleased that his coaching responsibilities include working with colleagues from both the English and social studies departments.

Last year, Allen and the four ninth-grade global studies teachers worked together to develop disciplinary literacy instructional outcomes and common assessments for all six units of study. They gave the common assessments last year but did not have the time to closely examine the results. This year, the teachers decided that they should focus more on what those common assessments were telling them about their students' ability to meet the disciplinary literacy instructional outcomes for the units. They decided to ask Allen if he could help them analyze the results of the upcoming extended-response common assessment for the comparative government unit.

The common assessment focused on the following CCSS standard: WHST.9-10.1, "Write arguments focused on discipline-specific content." At the end of the unit that focused on five purposes of a legitimate government, students were to read a series of articles about a government and then write an argument citing evidence to support the claim that the government was not a legitimate government. Each teacher scored his or her students' assessments according to the rubric developed by the team. The teachers told Allen that, in addition to the overall scores, they were interested in seeing the breakdown of scores by rubric cell. That would help them determine what aspects, if any, of the common assessment were problematic for the students.

As Allen compiled the data, he noticed that for two of the rubric cells, selecting appropriate purposes of government to discuss and providing evidence, students' scores differed by class. Students in Andrea Titus's class scored higher than the other classes in selecting appropriate purposes of government, whereas students in Winston Mason's class scored higher than the other classes in providing evidence. So Allen expanded the table to include how each class had performed on each rubric cell (see Figure 9.1). From his previous work with this team, Allen knew that the teachers often shared their teaching practices to determine which practices appeared to be most effective in helping their students meet the rigorous standards. Therefore, he knew they would be comfortable seeing the scores broken down by teacher.

Allen began the team meeting by projecting a copy of Form 9.1 on the screen and then distributing copies of the overall scores to each member of the team. Taking a facilitating coaching stance, he asked, "What do you notice about these scores?" The teachers commented that their goal was that at least 80% of the students would score a 75% or higher on this assessment. The results indicated that 82% of the students had scored at or above 75%, so their goal had been met. However, they were concerned that about 8% of the students had scored right around the 50% level and thought that an examination of the results by rubric cell would help them pinpoint

Rubric cells	#1. Topic sentence: Demonstrates understanding of the question.	#2: Applies knowledge of the five purposes of government by appropriately stating why the government was not legitimate.	#3: Provides appropriate evidence (i.e., examples) for each purpose cited.
Scoring	Complete understanding: 2 points General understanding: 1 point Little understanding: 0 points	Includes all four purposes: 4 points Includes three purposes: 3 points Includes two purposes: 2 points Includes one purpose: 1 point Does not include any of the appropriate purposes: 0 points	1 point for each appropriate piece of evidence
All ninth graders	1.75	3.1	3.9
Keiko Hamada's class	1.68	2.6	3.0
Winston Mason's class	1.75	3.0	5.6
Trenton O'Connor's class	1.83	2.7	2.9
Andrea Titus's class	1.73	3.6	3.9

FIGURE 9.1. Assessments results displayed by rubric cell and teacher.

the problem areas. Allen noted their conclusions on the top part of Form 9.1 as they talked.

Allen then carefully explained how he had developed the second data display (i.e., the display of rubric scores broken down by teacher, as shown in Figure 9.1), and the group discussed factors that might have contributed to students' strengths and difficulties. Allen typed these factors onto Form 9.1 and then presented the idea that the results provided an opportunity for members of the team to share their instructional practices with each other. Keiko Hamada said, "Oh, I see exactly what Allen is saying. Look at the student scores from Andrea's class for citing appropriate purposes of government. Almost all of her students earned the total points for this, scoring much higher than the students in the other three classes. Andrea, what did you do to help the students understand all five purposes?" Andrea explained how she had used a series of video clips to show examples and nonexamples of each purpose and guided the students to develop a whole-class example–nonexample chart of the five purposes. She said she would be happy to share the video clips and chart template with the rest of the team.

Trenton O'Connor mentioned that his students seemed to have the most difficulty with citing appropriate evidence and, noting that—on average—Winston's students had provided almost two examples for each purpose, asked Winston what he had done to help his students be successful in this area. Winston described how he had carefully explained and modeled the process before asking the students to find evidence with a partner. The other three teachers noted that they had described the process and shown the students a model of how to write about the evidence, but that they had not actually modeled the thinking–writing process in front of the students. Allen recorded both of these ideas in the revisions section of Form 9.1 and suggested that the group might like to have Winston walk them through his modeling process at a future team meeting.

At the end of the team meeting, Allen asked the teachers to reflect on the review process. The teachers noted that they mainly discussed how instructional practices may be contributing to student success and difficulties. Keiko said that she thought this was very helpful, as they would be continuing to have students make claims and support those claims with evidence throughout the remainder of the year. Trenton said that, in the future, they might want to look more closely at the common assessment task itself to see whether the directions or the texts needed to be changed. Winston added that he would like to examine the scores of those students who did not meet the minimum passing criteria when they reviewed future common assessments. He even offered to compile the data for the next common assessment.

As Allen wrote up the meeting notes, he thought, "This team is well on its way to being able to review common assessment data without my guidance. It sounds like Winston would be willing to facilitate the next review, and I can be more of a listener/participant. And I think the Common Assessment Review Form [Form 9.1] was an effective protocol for the discussion; I will use it again next week when I meet with the English II teachers."

Common Assessment Review Form

Common Assessment Description	
Course:	Unit:
Type (circle one of the following—selected response, extended response, performance [e.g., model, project]—or describe here):	
Teachers participating in the review process:	
Date of review:	
Conclusions about results for all students:	

In-depth analysis: Cells of a rubric Specific group(s):	
Areas of strength	Factors contributing to strengths
Areas of difficulty	Factors contributing to difficulties
Revisions needed	Person in charge of revisions/expected completion date

From *Collaborative Coaching for Disciplinary Literacy: Strategies to Support Teachers in Grades 6–12* by Laurie Elish-Piper, Susan K. L'Allier, Michael Manderino, and Paula Di Domenico. Copyright © 2016 The Guilford Press. Permission to photocopy this form is granted to purchasers of this book for personal use only (see copyright page for details). Purchasers can download additional copies of this form (see the box at the end of the table of contents).

Developing Discussion Protocols

What Is It?

Discussion protocols provide opportunities to structure professional conversations in ways that give each participant a voice. They provide that structure through the types of questions asked, as well as by the use of time parameters. They can be used to brainstorm ideas, develop solutions to identified problems, consider multiple perspectives on a topic, examine student data, or converse about a shared text. Discussion protocols have been used widely as facilitators for classroom talk. Examples include Save the Last Word for Me (Short, Harste, & Burke, 1996), Intra-Act (Hoffman, 1979), or discussion webs (Alvermann, 1991). Discussion protocols for small-group coaching are a way to democratize conversations, keep discussions flowing, and provide a common set of criteria for evaluating the topic, dataset, or text. They are flexible, can be created easily, and efficiently use the time allocated to small-group coaching contexts. The coach selects discussion protocols based on the purpose for the small-group coaching session. A number of free discussion protocols for professional learning can be found at *www.nsrfharmony.org/free-resources/protocols/a-z*.

How Do I Do It?

To implement discussion protocols, there are three steps you need to complete. The first is to prepare for the small-group discussion. Second, you need to facilitate the discussion. Finally, you need to provide time to have group members debrief the discussion. Following are the basic steps for preparing, facilitating, and debriefing professional conversations using discussion protocols.

Preparing to Conduct a Small-Group Discussion

1. Determine who will participate in the discussion. Ideal discussion group sizes range from four to six teachers. Depending on the size of the group and your purpose, you may create subgroups or facilitate a larger group discussion. If you need to create subgroups, consider how you may want to group teachers (e.g., by discipline, with representatives from a range of disciplines, by experience).

2. Identify the purpose for the discussion. A list of broad topics and possible protocols are provided in Figure 10.1. If time permits and you have multiple goals for the session, you might conduct more than one discussion. For example, you might use a discussion protocol to analyze a policy or text and then use a different protocol to analyze student work in light of the text or policy discussed in the first part of the session.

3. Determine the ground rules for the discussion. Ground rules should be simple and concise. The purpose is to encourage discussion, not stifle it. Sample rules can be found in Figure 10.2. It is ideal to provide opportunities for the participants to be involved in the setting of ground rules to ensure greater buy-in to the process. Once ground rules are established, they should be used consistently.

4. Communicate the purpose of the discussion and provide group members with any necessary materials in advance of the discussion.

5. Prepare for the discussion by reading up on the topics to be discussed or analyzing any datasets to be examined.

Facilitating a Discussion

1. Organize the room in a manner that is conducive to small-group discussion. Sample configurations may include having discussion tables if there will be multiple groups, a horseshoe arrangement so all participants can see each other, or seats arranged in a circle.

2. Begin by establishing the purpose for the discussion.

Purpose of discussion	Sample protocol(s)
Analysis of student work	Consultancy: Examining Student Work *www.nsrfharmony.org/system/files/protocols/consult_stud_work_0.pdf*
Analysis of student data	ATLAS: Looking at Data Protocol *www.nsrfharmony.org/system/files/protocols/atlas_looking_data_0.pdf*
Analysis of text or policy documents	Three Levels of Text Protocol *www.nsrfharmony.org/system/files/protocols/3_levels_text_0.pdf*
Inquiry of professional practice	A Change in Practice *www.nsrfharmony.org/system/files/protocols/change_practice_0.pdf*

FIGURE 10.1. Sample discussion protocols.

1. Listen actively.
2. Address discussion members by name.
3. Unless someone is recording notes, please close laptops and silence phones.
4. One person has the floor to talk.
5. Use evidence to support opinions.
6. Maintain confidentiality of what is said in the discussion.
7. Remember we are interrogating ideas, not criticizing individuals.

FIGURE 10.2. Sample ground rules for discussion.

3. Explain the discussion protocol and establish the ground rules for discussion with input from participants. Revisit the ground rules in subsequent discussions.

4. Model each component of the protocol.

5. Keep time for the group.

6. Decide whether you will participate in or observe the discussion.

7. Take notes on the discussion to share during the debriefing process.

Debriefing the Process

1. Plan for 5–10 minutes to summarize the discussion. Highlight the major sources of agreement and/or disagreement. The literacy coach should summarize the main points raised by participants or invite someone else to do so.

2. Debrief the process of using the protocol. Ascertain what elements facilitated discussion and what elements may have shut down parts of the discussion.

3. Plan for any additional follow-up discussion that is needed on the topic.

4. Send a follow-up email that summarizes the key points of the discussion.

The Strategy in Action

Marla Daniels is a new literacy coach at Hillman Middle School. She was a former ELA teacher and seventh-grade team leader. She also has a middle-school endorsement in science. Now she is working with the seventh-grade interdisciplinary team as they strive to address the CCSS. Specifically, the team has been focusing on identification of claims and evidence in informational texts. After observing some team meetings, she noticed that certain voices continually dominated the discussion. These same voices often discussed student work in terms of deficits of the students rather than opportunities to improve curriculum and teaching practices. She sensed that teachers were leaving these meetings frustrated and with few ideas or support for changing practice.

Marla decided to investigate a few protocols to help change the tenor of these meetings. She decided to adapt a protocol called Consultancy to examine student work (see Figure 10.3). By using the protocol, she reframed the purpose for discussing student work from focusing on the perceived deficits in students' reading ability to focusing on students' assets and creating teaching solutions. She modeled the protocol with the team and then took copious notes during the discussion.

Time

Approximately 1 hour

Roles

- Presenter (whose student work is being discussed by the group)
- Consultants (the group)
- Coach (who also participates)

Steps

1. The presenter (teacher) gives a quick overview of the students' work. She or he describes the task, highlights the major issues or concerns, and frames a question for the consultancy group to consider. The framing of this question, as well as the quality of the presenter's reflection on the student work and related issues, are key features of this protocol. An example question might be, "How well does this work represent mastery of identifying a claim and evidence [e.g. CCSS.ELA-LITERACY.RI.9–10.1: Cite strong and thorough textual evidence to support analysis of what the text says explicitly as well as inferences drawn from the text.]?" (5 minutes)

2. The group members individually examine the student work with the question in mind. (5 minutes)

3. The consultancy group asks clarifying questions of the presenter—that is, questions that have brief, factual answers (e.g., "Was this homework or was it completed in class?"). (5 minutes)

4. The group asks probing questions of the presenter. These questions should be worded so that they help the presenter clarify and expand his or her thinking about the issue or question raised about the student work being examined. The goal here is for the presenter to do some deeper analysis of the student work. The presenter responds to the group's questions, but there is no discussion by the larger group of the presenter's responses. (10 minutes)

5. The group members talk with each other about the student work and related issues in light of the questions framed for the group by the presenter. "What did we hear?" "What didn't we hear that we needed to know more about?" "What do we think about the question and issue(s) presented?" Some groups like to begin the conversation with "warm" feedback—answering questions such as "What are the strengths in this student's work?" or "What's the good news here?" The group then moves on to cooler feedback—answering such questions as "Where are the gaps?" "What isn't the presenter considering?" "What do areas for further improvement or investigation seem to be?" Sometimes the group will raise questions for the presenter to consider ("I wonder what would happen if . . . ?" or "I wonder why . . . ?"). The presenter is not allowed to speak during this discussion but instead listens and takes notes. (15 minutes)

6. The presenter responds to what she or he heard (first in a fishbowl format if there are several presenters). A whole-group discussion might then take place, depending on the time allotted. (10 minutes)

FIGURE 10.3. Consultancy Protocol Adapted for Examining Student Work. Adapted from *www.nsrfharmony.org/system/files/protocols/consult_stud_work_0.pdf.* Copyright 2014 by the National School Reform Faculty® (NSRF). Reprinted by permission. NSRF® emphasizes that the protocols are most powerful and effective when facilitated by a trained coach.

Dear 7th-Grade Blue Team,

Thank you so much for a rich discussion about student work last week! I wanted to share the highlights of the discussion with you all so we can move forward in our planning around identification of claims and evidence.

1. The sample provided was meant to be representative of most of Mr. Bryce's students' work on identification of claims and evidence in his Earth Science class.
2. The students did identify claims consistently but appeared to select the supporting evidence more haphazardly.
3. Others confirmed that their students also identify claims well but struggle with finding the best evidence to support a claim when they read informational texts in their classes.
4. The group members agreed that we all need to be more explicit about modeling and asking for the best evidence so that students do not treat all evidence as equal.

If you have questions or have more points to add to this summary, please add and reply to all on this email. I look forward to our meeting next Tuesday at 3:00 p.m. in the media center.

Marla

FIGURE 10.4. Sample follow-up email.

After the group discussed the protocol, Marla allowed 5–10 minutes for the group to debrief the process and suggest improvements for the next meeting. Marla informed the group that she would email a synopsis of the main points of the discussion (see Figure 10.4).

Over the next month, Marla and the seventh-grade team continued to use a version of the Consultancy protocol to structure their conversations. After using the modified Consultancy protocols, team members have reported feeling that they have a much greater voice in the process. Cedric Larson, the seventh-grade social studies teacher, reported that, "As a new teacher, I feel like my voice is heard, and I am not afraid that I might be speaking too much or too little."

Facilitating Teacher Inquiry into the Disciplines

What Is It?

Middle and high school teachers typically experience two types of professional development. The first revolves around general teaching strategies. Examples might include writing across the curriculum, cooperative learning, or teaching with technology tools. A second, more rare form of professional development includes opportunities to learn about content in their discipline. Examples include experts from disciplines (scientists, writers, historians) providing lectures about individual topics in their field of study or conferences focused on disciplinary content. In the first type of professional development, teachers are expected to apply their own content to the teaching strategies being presented. In the second type of professional development, teachers are expected to have knowledge of the teaching strategies to render the content accessible to their middle or high school students.

Shulman (1986) explained the knowledge bases of content and teaching as pedagogical content knowledge (PCK). PCK refers to combining a teacher's content knowledge (history, science, literature) and his or her knowledge of pedagogy to be able to effectively make disciplinary content accessible to middle and high school students. Additionally, a disciplinary literacy approach to instruction means creating developmentally appropriate opportunities for disciplinary learning for middle and high school students. Examples might include working with primary sources in history, conducting a lab in science, or engaging in critical analysis of literature in English. Teachers need opportunities to develop their PCK and create meaningful disciplinary literacy lessons and units of study. As a disciplinary literacy coach, you can serve an important role in developing teachers' ability to take their content knowledge and use it to teach for disciplinary literacy.

Middle and high school teachers do not regularly engage in expert practices the way historians, literary critics, or scientists do, and although they may have experienced those practices in their teacher preparation programs, most of their coursework focused on teaching the subject, not producing knowledge in the discipline (Moje, 2008). Teachers often plan and use texts for learning based on limited conceptions of expert practice as well as on their own experiences (Di Domenico, 2014). One way to provide opportunities to examine disciplinary knowledge for teachers is to engage them in the types of disciplinary inquiry in which they want their students to participate. The quest to investigate gaps in information and to seek answers to problems drives the knowledge that is produced, communicated, and critiqued in the disciplines. It is important for teachers to read and write as disciplinary insiders (Buehl, 2011) if they are to expect the same from their students.

In small-group settings and especially in content-area teams, you can facilitate opportunities to build teachers' PCK by encouraging teacher inquiry activities. Teacher inquiry in their disciplines can serve multiple purposes. First, it can help break down an artificial distinction that you as a coach are supporting only general teaching practices because you do not possess background in all of the disciplines. Your role, however, is to support teacher's development of PCK, which includes their own content knowledge in relation to how they will teach that content. Second, inquiry allows you as the coach a window into the discipline and can build your knowledge for subsequent disciplinary literacy coaching. For teachers, inquiry allows opportunities to make their tacit thinking and reading explicit, which will help them to identify the disciplinary reading and writing in which they want their students to engage.

How Do I Do It?

As a disciplinary literacy coach, you will have opportunities to provide small-group coaching to content-area teams or departments. You can suggest that in order for you to effectively support their team or department, you would like to better understand what reading, writing, and thinking look like in their discipline. It is also important for the coach to communicate to the teachers that they will benefit from their own inquiry in their discipline by uncovering potential roadblocks for student learning and identifying the skills needed for students to deeply learn the subject matter. Facilitating teacher inquiry is a great opportunity to give teachers a strong voice in their own professional development. Following are some guidelines to facilitate the process.

1. Have teachers select a focus of inquiry. Encourage teachers to decide on the topic and skills on which they want to focus. Examples of topics are the industrial revolution, states of matter, or epic poetry, and examples of skills are argumentation, synthesis of multiple sources, or supporting text-based discussion. Figure 11.1 provides some specific disciplinary examples.

Discipline	Inquiry questions	Disciplinary practices
English	What literary devices does Steinbeck use in *The Grapes of Wrath?*	Reading for literary devices
	How is Nick Carraway an unreliable narrator in *The Great Gatsby?*	Use of an unreliable narrator
	What elements of symbolism are used in the film *The Graduate?*	Examining symbolism in literature
Science	What causes erosion?	Constructing models of scientific processes
	How are flowers pollinated?	Writing scientific explanations
	What are the steps in the water cycle?	Reading nonlinguistic scientific representations
Social studies	What sources best explain the rise of industrialization?	Evaluating primary and secondary sources
	Was George Pullman an idealist or an opportunist?	Constructing historical arguments
	What caused the French Revolution?	Representing causal relations between events

FIGURE 11.1. Possible inquiry questions and skills in the disciplines.

2. Probe the group regarding their beliefs about the importance of the topic; the nature of the inquiry practices they plan to use, such as investigating scientific processes, using primary sources to create a historical argument, or uncovering themes in literature; and their reasons for conducting such inquiry. It is important to uncover teachers' beliefs about learning in the discipline because their beliefs may differ from each other's. Those differences provide grist for discussion about the nature of learning in the discipline. Then ask the teachers to identify texts that are related to the topic. Have the teachers share why they would need to read those texts to learn the content. This uncovers their beliefs about the role of text in learning in the discipline.

3. Next, have the teachers collaboratively read the texts and produce some outcome of the inquiry, such as a written response, a representational model of a process, or a structured debate or discussion. For example, if a group of chemistry teachers decides that the topic they want to investigate is the role of ionic and covalent bonds in binding molecules together, then follow up by asking how they would represent their learning. Options might include creating a written explanation, constructing three-dimensional models, or discussing the role of bonds in chemical processes. Once a decision is made, be sure to have teachers follow through and construct their representations.

4. After the inquiry, have teachers reflect on their own processes. You may want to ask them to identify obstacles that made learning challenging, what strategies they used, and what made representing their knowledge easy or challenging.

5. Next, shift the discussion to why they would want to have students engage in this type of learning. What might make this type of learning challenging for students? What supports might be necessary?
6. Begin to plan for instruction by using the teachers' own inquiry as a guide for the types of disciplinary literacy supports that will be needed during instruction.

The Strategy in Action

The U.S. history team at Addams High School has been working to shift instruction toward the type of inquiry that is emphasized in the C3 Framework from the NCSS (2013). Dimension 3 is focused on evaluating sources and using evidence. The U.S. history team decided they wanted to start with the beginning of this dimension and, in particular, Standard D3.2.9–12: "Evaluate the credibility of a source by examining how experts value the source." The team was struggling to envision how they would teach the ways experts might value sources. Jen Carcetti, a 17-year veteran teacher and the lead U.S. history teacher, decided to approach the school's literacy coach, Russell Bell, because Russell had worked successfully with the world history team in the past on using strategies to help read primary sources. Some members of the world history team were also members of the U.S. history team and agreed that Russell might be able to help this team as well. Russell Bell is a third- year literacy coach and former ELA teacher.

Jen explained to Russell that the C3 was a shift in thinking for the team and that they needed help to shift their practice. Russell suggested that they use the next four PLC meetings to provide ample time to work on evaluation of the credibility of sources. He asked Jen to go back to the U.S. history team to select a topic for exploration and to bring some sources to evaluate. They then set the next four meetings on Wednesday mornings for 45 minutes during PLC time for teachers. On the first Wednesday the team met, and the five teachers, including Jen, had all decided they wanted to investigate the Vietnam War. The teachers brought in a number of sources, including video clips, political cartoons, newspaper articles, and an excerpt from a historians' account of the war. Russell began by asking why they thought the topic of Vietnam was important to study. Elena McNulty remarked, "We never get to focus in depth on this topic!" Nerese Campbell, a teacher with 10 years of experience, stated, "The outcome of this war set the tone for the next 30 years of American life." Jen added, "I don't know that any of us have really studied the war since college, as we rarely have a chance to teach this topic with any depth."

Russell wrote the reasons on the board and asked if everyone agreed with Nerese's conclusion about the impact of the Vietnam War. A lively conversation followed in which many of the teachers expressed disagreement about the impact. Russell knew his role was to facilitate the group, so instead of providing his opinion, he restated the key ideas presented by the group and asked whether historians agree on the impact of the Vietnam War. The team agreed that the study of history was not about memorization of facts but about studying different perspectives and interpretations of historical events. With the remaining few minutes, Russell asked the group to decide on four sources that would be challenging to read and evaluate in order to determine the causes for American intervention in the Vietnam War. The group decided on a primary source from Ho Chi Minh, a recorded phone call between President Lyndon B. Johnson and Secretary of Defense Robert McNamara, a video clip from the documentary *The Fog of War* (Morris, 2003), and an excerpt from a historian's account of the war. Russell then studied those four texts the next week to familiarize himself with the content.

The following Wednesday the team met again. Russell thought the historian's account might be a good place to start because the source contained a number of references to primary documents and gave an overall account of the impact of the war. The team took 5 minutes to reread the text. Russell then asked two teachers to read a part of the text aloud and share their thinking as they read. Jen volunteered, along with Elena McNulty, a teacher with 8 years of experience. Jen began reading the introduction aloud and stopped and said, "I don't know who this historian is, so I'm not sure if I trust this source." Jen resumed reading and came to a statistic about the number of Vietnamese killed in the war. She said, "I never knew that number was so high! I always read about the number of Americans killed in our textbook." Elena then began to read and came to a passage in which the author stated that Vietnam has not recovered from the war. Elena asked, "When was this written? Because I thought I read that tourism was on the rise in Vietnam." Nerese Campbell exclaimed, "Now I want to read those other sources to see if they add new information!" Russell had been taking notes and shared what had been stated. "It seemed to me that as you are reading this source, you asked a number of questions. You asked if the source is to be trusted, when it was written, and why other texts might say different things about the event." Russell also had done some research prior to the meeting and explained that in his research he learned that historians always ask questions about the source, what others have said about the topic, and when the source was written (Wineburg, 1991). "That seems really consistent with what you all have done here today. Next week we will dig further into these sources."

The third Wednesday, the team met again, and they were buzzing to discuss the sources more. Jen said, "I think I speak for the group when I say that all week we had conversations in the hallway about how we were reading these sources, and that is how we want our students to read." Russell then stated, "Before we get to your students, how would you represent your learning about Vietnam from these sources?" The group agreed that first they should construct a timeline of key events that explains why the United States intervened in the Vietnam War based on the information provided in the four sources. Russell recorded their work as a team and created a timeline based on the sources that they had read. After the timeline was constructed, Russell asked, "How did you decide on these events?" The group explained that based on their readings, they chose events that were backed up in multiple sources. Russell then added, "It seems to me that based on last week and this week, you have identified some ways that you evaluate the credibility of a source. Now we can focus on how students can construct a timeline about why the United States intervened in the Vietnam War by evaluating sources like historians. We can also discuss how you can support their learning."

The final Wednesday meeting was dedicated to designing instruction that taught students how to evaluate the credibility of a source. Russell asked, "What made the reading challenging for you and what would make it challenging for your students?" Nerese responded that before this inquiry experience she wasn't really aware of how she was reading and that students might need a guide for evaluating sources. Russell had done some further research on evaluating sources and shared a strategy called SOAPStone (Figure 11.2). The strategy explicitly asks students to evaluate the source based on the speaker, the occasion, the intended audience, the purpose, and the significance of the event. Finally, students also read the text for clues about the tone of the source and what might be inferred from the author's tone. Thus the SOAPStone strategy covered the categories that the teachers had discovered during their own inquiry, as well as a couple of additional categories. The group agreed that this would be a great way to introduce this C3 standard to students. They also discussed how they would explain and model the SOAPStone strategy before having the students apply it, first in pairs and then independently.

The group decided that this was a great way to use their PLC time. Thomas Bailey, a second-year teacher on the team, remarked that it was refreshing to do some inquiry on their own and then think about what challenges students might also have. Elena said "Russell never acted like an expert but only offered suggestions and did ancillary research for the group. He really respected our expertise." Russell also reflected that he learned so much about how history teachers approach their discipline that he now feels more prepared to coach other teams in the history department.

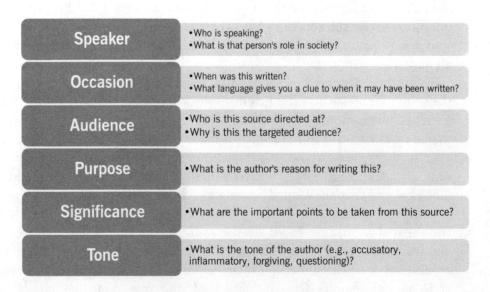

Speaker	•Who is speaking? •What is that person's role in society?
Occasion	•When was this written? •What language gives you a clue to when it may have been written?
Audience	•Who is this source directed at? •Why is this the targeted audience?
Purpose	•What is the author's reason for writing this?
Significance	•What are the important points to be taken from this source?
Tone	•What is the tone of the author (e.g., accusatory, inflammatory, forgiving, questioning)?

FIGURE 11.2. The SOAPStone strategy.

PART VI

Individual Coaching Strategies to Support Teachers with Disciplinary Literacy Instruction

Individual coaching is often considered the "gold standard" of coaching because you are able to provide exactly what a teacher needs at a particular point in time. By taking an individualized approach to coaching, you can help teachers actually implement disciplinary literacy instruction in their own classrooms with their own students. Some teachers may be eager to try new instructional strategies they learn about in large-group and small-group coaching experiences, but they may struggle with exactly how to put those ideas into action. That's precisely when you will want to use individual coaching strategies.

Individual coaching works best when it flows directly from small-group coaching activities so that teachers can layer and deepen their understanding and application of disciplinary literacy instruction. The individual coaching layer allows the coach to adjust and provide the "just right" support and encouragement to help teachers update their daily instructional practice to address disciplinary literacy in meaningful ways. Although individual coaching can be quite time-consuming, it can lead to powerful outcomes for both teacher practice and student learning.

In Part VI you will learn about six coaching strategies you can use to support individual teachers. In Strategy 12, you'll learn about helping teachers create essential questions to guide their teaching and their students' learning. Strategy 13 focuses on how you can develop questions with objectives to guide your coaching conversations with individual teachers. Strategy 14 presents an approach for extending the gradual release of responsibility model (Pearson & Gallagher, 1983) so teachers can organize their instruction of complex strategies, skills, or tasks. Strategy 15 discusses how coaches can use three levels of think-aloud to help teachers uncover and understand their thinking processes when completing disciplinary literacy tasks. The teachers can then use those understandings to make that thinking transparent for their students. In Strategy 16, you'll learn how to help teachers adopt, adapt, and create effective strategies for disciplinary literacy instruction. Finally, Strategy 17 provides guidance on how to use the coaching cycle to engage teachers in intensive coaching.

Part VI provides you with a core set of strategies to support individual teachers. By layering these strategies on top of the large-group and small-group coaching activities you implement with teachers in your school, you can provide the targeted support teachers need to update and align their instruction with the disciplinary literacy demands of the new learning standards.

Creating Essential Questions

What Is It?

Essential questions are a way to frame instructional units that support student inquiry (McTighe & Wiggins, 2013). They are questions framed by teachers that encourage deep conceptual thinking about the subject matter being studied. Literacy coaches can use teachers' essential questions to gain a broader perspective of their unit design or to help teachers create a unifying theme for their instruction.

Essential questions can guide student inquiry and frame the types of disciplinary thinking needed to answer the questions. Student inquiry is an essential part of disciplinary practice. For example, inquiry in ELA may focus on broad themes and be framed by essential questions such as "What does it mean to have courage?" or "How is love a universal language?" whereas in science it may be an inquiry into natural phenomena framed by essential questions such as "What are the consequences of erosion?" or "How are cells the building blocks of life?" Essential questions serve to frame the types of inquiry that are common in the disciplines, thus functioning as an avenue for disciplinary thinking and practice (Bain, 2008; Buehl, 2011). Regardless of the discipline, the CCSS, the C3 Framework, and the NGSS make it clear that inquiry is critical in the disciplines and should be based on reading, writing, and discussing disciplinary texts. The type of inquiry that teachers create for their students will influence the essential questions teachers use as a part of their instructional design.

Types of Inquiry

According to Martin-Hansen (2002), there are four major types of inquiry. Teachers may choose to use any combination of these types of inquiry for disciplinary literacy instruction. The type of inquiry that teachers seek to have students engage in can be greatly supported by well-matched essential questions.

1. *Open inquiry.* This is student-centered inquiry that is based on student-generated questions. Essential questions are important to frame the unit of study and are the impetus for the questions generated by individuals or small groups.
2. *Guided inquiry.* This is inquiry in which the teacher poses the questions that students investigate. Essential questions are critical for framing an inquiry that does not lead to single answers.
3. *Coupled inquiry.* The inquiry starts off as guided but moves to open inquiry. Essential questions are critical to supporting students as they move toward the open inquiry portion in which they generate their own questions.
4. *Structured inquiry.* This is very prescriptive inquiry that leads students to similar findings. Essential questions are critical to make the overall inquiry meaningful and not simply a collection of more discrete questions.

An understanding of the general approaches to inquiry described above is critical for disciplinary literacy coaches when helping teachers determine the type of inquiry they want to use. More important, you will use this knowledge to help teachers understand how the use of essential questions will undergird the inquiry process. Essential questions are an important bridge from content-only instruction to disciplinary literacy instruction because they provide pathways for student use of disciplinary habits of thinking and practice. Questions that pose intellectual problems in the disciplines can be framed in three ways (Figure 12.1). As a disciplinary literacy coach, you can use these ways of framing to help teachers develop their essential questions.

How Do I Do It?

Generating essential questions that move beyond content acquisition and include critical disciplinary literacy skills can be challenging for teachers. For you as a disciplinary literacy coach, helping teachers create strong questions that build disciplinary literacy skills is important. You can do this by encouraging teachers to focus on questions that require displays of disciplinary thinking and practice to construct content knowledge (see Figure 12.1 for examples in each discipline). You can also use teachers' existing essential questions as a starting point and work to match them to their disciplinary literacy instructional outcomes.

	Definition	ELA	Science	Social studies
Binary essential questions	Questions that ask someone to choose a side or take a position and evaluate the person, policy, or event using that position.	"Was Holden Caulfield, in *The Catcher in the Rye,* an unreliable narrator?"	"Is erosion preventable?"	"Was the Montgomery bus boycott successful?"
Causal essential questions	Questions that ask *why* or *how,* to show causal reasoning or describe a chain of events.	"How was Holden Caulfield, in *The Catcher in the Rye,* an unreliable narrator?"	"Why is erosion an issue?"	"Why was the Montgomery bus boycott successful?"
"To what extent" essential questions	Questions that ask students to acknowledge all sides of an issue and use evidence to explain the degree of their response.	"To what extent was Holden Caulfield, in *The Catcher in the Rye,* an unreliable narrator?"	"To what extent is erosion an issue on the coasts?"	"To what extent was the Montgomery bus boycott a critical event in the civil rights movement?"

FIGURE 12.1. Types of disciplinary inquiry essential questions.

Supporting Disciplinary Inquiry through Essential Questions

1. Help the teacher determine disciplinary instructional outcomes. The development of essential questions can help refine disciplinary instructional outcomes because they require consideration of both content and process. If questions focus heavily on knowledge recall, you can ask the teacher to explain what disciplinary habits of mind or skills students would need to answer the essential question.

2. Ask the teacher to decide what types of assessments will provide evidence that students met the disciplinary literacy instructional outcomes (see Strategy 6). It is important that assessments measure the content and processes identified in the disciplinary instructional outcome. Throughout the unit, it should be evident to students that their inquiry will lead them to a better understanding of the essential questions and ensure that they have the skills, strategies, and thinking needed to demonstrate their understandings on the summative assessment. Essential questions that are too abstract will be disconnected from daily learning activities and the summative assessment.

3. Probe the teacher to determine the type of inquiry in which he or she wants students to engage. Essential questions are an excellent way to encourage a disciplinary inquiry approach rather than teaching for content memorization (Buehl, 2011). If a teacher wants students to engage in open inquiry, ask how the essential questions will help students generate their own questions. An example of an essential question that supports more open inquiry in history when the focus is on civil rights might be, "How are our inalienable rights protected?" Students could then choose any number of rights to investigate. If the teacher wants more guided or structured inquiry for his or her students, ask how the questions used during

the inquiry help students answer the overarching essential questions. Examples might be, "How does the Constitution define our rights?" and "What is the difference between people's rights and people's responsibilities?" These types of questions could be applied to any number of civil rights topics.

4. Use Form 12.1 with the teacher to help determine possibilities for essential questions. It is helpful to brainstorm a number of questions and then discuss how the questions require disciplinary literacy and how they support inquiry in disciplinary concepts. You can also ask probing questions, such as, "How long would it take students to answer this question?" or "Will students ever be able to reach a tentative answer to the question?" You play an important role in helping the teacher determine the scope of his or her essential questions.

5. Encourage the teacher to answer the question him- or herself. You might also ask, "In what areas will students struggle?" or "What scaffolds can you provide students when they struggle?" Throughout the unit you can follow up with the teacher to see whether the essential questions are working, whether they need to be refined, or whether they need to be altered. It is important that teachers realize that essential questions are not set in stone but rather can be continually refined to better address the disciplinary literacy instructional outcomes.

6. Once you and the teacher have selected the essential question(s), your coaching focus will shift to how the teacher will use the essential question(s) to plan for instruction. It is important that the essential question(s) be connected to disciplinary literacy instructional outcomes, disciplinary literacy instruction, and assessment. Using backward design planning (Wiggins & McTighe, 2005), begin by deciding how students will be assessed and what role the essential question(s) will play in both formative and summative assessments. Then you can move on to planning the instruction, referring back to the teacher's essential question(s) to be sure that instruction is supporting the disciplinary literacy practices needed to answer the questions. If the teacher struggles to explain this, you may use this as an opportunity to engage in more coaching about disciplinary literacy instruction.

The Strategy in Action

Tina Kim has been a high school literacy coach for 2 years and was a reading specialist for 3 years prior to full-time coaching. During individual coaching sessions, she has found that many teachers are focused on topics rather than inquiry. She has discovered, however, that asking teachers about their essential questions is a good starting point to help teachers plan for disciplinary inquiry. Recently, Seth Dixson, a 4th-year science teacher, approached Tina about working together on his science curriculum. Seth was struggling to make sense of the NGSS that his department has been working on incorporating into all science courses. Seth admitted that he has been very focused on content-based instruction. He typically frames lessons and units to correlate with the textbook chapters, such as states of matter, motion, and acids and bases. When Tina asked Seth what his essential questions were, he responded that he typically asked questions that would lead to direct answers, such as "What is the atomic weight of carbon?" His response indicated to Tina that Seth did not have a clear understanding of the characteristics of an essential question that leads to deeper thinking about the topic. Given the focus on inquiry in the NGSS, Tina redirected her question and asked how Seth might engage his students in inquiry. She explained the four different types of inquiry. Together they examined the standards, and Seth remarked that he had often prescribed inquiry in a really small way by asking series of discrete questions. He said he wanted to be sure that all of his students reached the same conclusions.

Tina thought that Seth might be ready to move toward more guided inquiry to begin meeting the NGSS. She began by asking Seth to select a unit of study and describe what his disciplinary literacy instructional outcomes were. Seth chose to focus on his physical science class and a unit on simple machines. Seth indicated he was most comfortable beginning with structured inquiry. Tina wanted to meet Seth where he was in terms of comfort and felt that designing good essential questions would be a way to support Seth's structured inquiry approach to simple machines. Together they filled out Figure 12.2 as they worked. Seth indicated that he wanted students to understand the advantages of using inclined planes, levers, and pulleys.

Type of Question	Binary ☐		Causal ☑		To What Extent ☐
Type of Inquiry	Open ☐	Guided ☐	Coupled ☐	Structured ☑	
Content Needed to Investigate the Question	*Pulleys, levers, inclined planes, point-slope formula, measurement*				
Disciplinary Habits of Thinking Needed to Investigate the Question	*Hypothesis testing, model building, calculation*				
Possible Essential Questions	*Seth's Essential Questions* *What makes an inclined plane efficient?* *How is a pulley a simple machine?* *Is a lever better than an inclined plane?* *Tina's Essential Questions* *Why do people use simple machines?* *When are simple machines most effective?* *To what extent is a simple machine most efficient in a given situation?*				

FIGURE 12.2. Tina's and Seth's essential questions.

He was very clear about the content, so Tina shifted focus to what disciplinary habits of mind students would need to learn about simple machines. Seth focused most on the fact that students would have to model, test, and retest their machines. There would also be a fair amount of calculations of efficiency needed to evaluate the effectiveness of the simple machines they investigated.

Seth suggested some typical questions he might ask, including "What makes an inclined plane efficient?", "How is a pulley a simple machine?", and "Is a lever better than an inclined plane?" Tina also began to compile a list of possible essential questions. Some included "Why do people use simple machines?", "When are simple machines most effective?", and "To what extent is a simple machine most efficient in a given situation?" They realized that Seth had good structured questions to guide inquiry at the lesson level but that perhaps the types of questions Tina generated were more appropriate at the unit level. They decided that a good essential question for the unit would be, "Why do people use simple machines?" They noted that, regardless of the inquiry question for a specific lesson, the students could link it back to this overarching question.

Next, Tina asked Seth to determine his assessments and connect those back to his essential question. Seth decided that on his formative assessments for each simple machine, he would ask students to explain why people would use that particular machine. Now that Seth had determined the habits of thinking that would be focused on during the unit and had created an essential question, as well as the formative assessments, he felt ready to teach the unit.

At the conclusion of the unit on simple machines, Tina asked Seth to reflect on his essential question based on student responses on their formative assessments. She asked, "Did student responses demonstrate that students met your disciplinary literacy instructional outcomes?" Seth stated that, although students could explain why people might use a pulley, he really wanted the students to explain how a pulley would increase efficiency. He decided that the essential question that he and Tina initially created about why people used simple machines was better suited to hook students into the inquiry. However, upon reflection, Seth realized that changing his essential question from "Why do people use simple machines?" to "How do simple machines increase efficiency?" would better support his students' use of inquiry. He made a note on his science curriculum to use this new essential question when he taught the unit the following year.

For his upcoming unit on wave energy, Seth offered several possibilities, as he and Tina brainstormed essential questions that would encourage scientific thinking and real-world connections. As the year progressed, Tina continued to help Seth create essential questions that encouraged scientific thinking, moving toward a more facilitative coaching stance by the end of the year. Seth was clearly on his way to independently creating essential questions to meet the inquiry demands of science and the NGSS.

Developing Essential Questions Template

Type of Question	Binary ☐	Causal ☐		To What Extent ☐
Type of Inquiry	Open ☐	Guided ☐	Coupled ☐	Structured ☐
Content Needed to Investigate the Question				
Disciplinary Habits of Thinking Needed to Investigate the Question				
Possible Essential Questions				

From *Collaborative Coaching for Disciplinary Literacy: Strategies to Support Teachers in Grades 6–12* by Laurie Elish-Piper, Susan K. L'Allier, Michael Manderino, and Paula Di Domenico. Copyright © 2016 The Guilford Press. Permission to photocopy this form is granted to purchasers of this book for personal use only (see copyright page for details). Purchasers can download additional copies of this form (see the box at the end of the table of contents).

Developing Questions with Objectives

What Is It?

Questions with objectives is a coaching strategy designed to empower coaches to engage in focused and productive conversations with teachers. When implementing this strategy, coaches brainstorm, draft, and organize questions that will promote constructive coaching conversations. Well-crafted questions can lead to new insights (Tofade, Elsner, & Haines, 2013) and focus thinking (Christenbury & Kelly, 1983). These questions can provide an opportunity for the coach to respectfully participate in collaborations with teachers while ensuring that the focus remains on improving instructional opportunities for students. Questions with objectives may also foster teacher reflection on their current practice, which can help coaches determine how best to support teachers.

Coaches can use questioning to enter conversations with teachers, clarify their own understanding about a teacher's practice, and deepen the teachers' understanding and thinking about their discipline, their students, and their instruction. Thus, in this strategy, the questions coaches ask are aligned with specific objectives such as "to gain an understanding of the teacher's view of students" or "to determine teacher's use of text." Questions with objectives can be general in nature, or they can be more discipline-specific, depending on the teacher's needs and the coach's collaboration with that teacher.

By preparing a written list of questions to facilitate coaching conversations, coaches can ensure that the limited time they have with teachers is spent productively. As coaches gain experience, they may internalize the questions, but the practice of brainstorming questions and using those questions to guide coaching conversations is one that will benefit coaches who have varied levels of experience.

How Do I Do It?

Coaches who are using questions with objectives need to brainstorm and plan prior to coaching conversations, apply these questions in conversation with a teacher, and reflect on the effectiveness of questions after the coaching conversation.

Brainstorming and Writing Questions with Objectives

1. Reflect on the teacher's stated goal. Consider general topics that may create the opportunity for coaching conversations related to that goal. Once you brainstorm the topics, you can create questions to foster conversations about these general teaching topics for use with any teacher. Some examples of general topics might include:

   a. Using formative assessment
   b. Modeling
   c. Using and removing scaffolds
   d. Differentiating instruction

2. Additionally, coaches can choose to brainstorm discipline-specific topics and questions. For example, a coach working with an English teacher might brainstorm questions regarding writer's workshop, author's purpose and choice, or identification and evaluation of rhetorical strategies. On the other hand, a coach working with a social studies teacher might ask questions about corroboration, sourcing, or contextualizing sources.

3. Other topics that coaches might brainstorm and prepare questions for include district initiatives, topics related to student performance, or text selection.

4. Coaches are encouraged to avoid writing questions to which they already know the answers. These can be off-putting and position the coach in the role of expert and the teacher in the role of student. Instead, coaches will want to create questions that are open-ended and that will build dialogue in an attempt to engage the teacher in reflective thinking in order to improve educational opportunities for students. Examples of questions with objectives are listed in Figure 13.1.

Applying the Questions in Conversations with Teachers

1. Once you brainstorm a list of questions related to specific objectives, keep adding to that list so that you have a comprehensive resource when you are meeting

Objective	Questions
Gain an understanding of the teacher's perspective of the lesson.	"What went well today? What do you wish had gone differently?" "How did your students respond to . . . ?"
Gain an understanding of the teacher's plan and the context surrounding this plan.	"Walk me through this plan." "Where is this plan in the context of your curriculum?"
Gain an understanding of the teacher's view of his or her students.	"What will your students need to be successful on this?" "Which students may need scaffolds? What scaffolds are you planning to use? When will you remove these scaffolds?"
Determine the teacher's plan for the formative use of assessment.	"How will you know if students understand the information?" "Will students have a second chance to demonstrate their learning if they don't get it the first time?"
Identify the teacher's feedback loop.	"Will you assess students or provide feedback? When and how?" "How will the students be expected to respond to your feedback?"
Discern students' independence in learning.	"What are the students responsible for during the lesson? What are you responsible for?"
Identify teacher's use of modeling in the classroom.	"Will you provide a model for students? What will it look like?" "Will you be modeling for students? What will the students be doing while you are modeling?"

FIGURE 13.1. Examples of general questions with objectives.

with teachers. While you do not need to have the list of questions displayed, it is helpful to tuck a small list into your notebook or save it to your desktop on your computer so that you can easily access the questions when working with teachers. Over time, you will become less reliant on the questions written on paper to engage in effective communication with the teachers you coach.

2. Once you have brainstormed a general list of questions, you can tailor the list for your work with a specific teacher. By having specific questions with objectives for each teacher, you can ensure that the teachers will feel valued and that their time was well spent. For instance, if you know that a teacher is going to work on student assessment, prepare questions that will help the teacher deepen his or her thinking about assessment. If you are working with a science teacher who has been modeling how to write a lab report, create questions that will help the teacher unpack this practice and reflect upon his or her modeling.

3. As you engage in a conversation with a teacher, ask questions that will best support that teacher's work toward his or her goals and the goals he or she has set for

the students. By keeping the questions centered on student needs and the teacher's goals, you can ensure a productive conversation.

Reflecting on the Effectiveness of the Questions

After the coaching session, reflect on the effectiveness of the questions. Consider which questions helped you gather information that you could use to support the teacher in the decision-making process and which questions helped the teacher reflect and feel supported with the changes she or he was making. By reflecting on your coaching practice, you can revise your list of questions related to specific objectives—keeping those that are effective and eliminating those that are not.

The Strategy in Action

Luis Contreras, a former English teacher, was entering his second year of instructional coaching at Portmont Middle School. When reflecting on his first year of coaching, he was happy with his work for the most part. Nevertheless, he felt like he was leading teachers with his ideas and acting more as a consulting coach (Lipton & Wellman, 2007) than a collaborator. In an attempt to move toward more of a collaborative stance, Luis thought he would try writing some general questions with objectives and then think specifically about the science team he would be working with each week, writing some more specific questions for them as well. This way, he could foster conversations with individual teachers, as well as with the teams of teachers he would be collaborating with in the near future.

Because the district was focusing on using formative assessment structures as a school improvement goal, Luis knew he would want to engage teachers in conversation about formative assessment. He also thought he wanted to ask about student independence in learning and teachers' use of modeling in the classroom. In addition, he reflected on the fact that he was not always sure about a teacher's perspective on the lesson. He wanted to create questions that would help his understanding of this. With these four objectives as a starting point, Luis created a two-column chart to help organize his thinking. His final list of questions aligned to specific objectives can be found in Figure 13.1. Luis knew that he could rely on these questions when meeting with teachers of any discipline.

Confident that this list of questions about general topics would help him begin his work with individual teachers, Luis moved on to think about the science team he would be working with this semester. He knew that the team's stated goals were to have students engage in scientific inquiry, to build models to explain scientific phenomena, and also to write explanations using evidence. Luis developed objectives based on these goals and then brainstormed a list of questions aligned to those objectives (see Figure 13.2). He planned to use these questions to start conversations with the science teachers at the next team meeting or with other teachers from the science department.

During his first meeting with Sally Winskinski, a biology teacher, Luis was able to begin the coaching conversation by including some of the questions from the list in Figure 13.2. When Sally set the meeting with Luis, she explained that she would like to review her plan to ask students to engage in creating a model of photosynthesis. To begin, he asked her to describe her instruction about photosynthesis to this point. He then asked:

Luis: How much practice have the students had constructing models?

Sally: This is their first attempt.

Luis: What do you wish they knew about creating models?

By using this question, Luis was able to help Sally clarify her expectations and outcomes for students' work with modeling. After understanding Sally's expectations, Luis was able to go on and ask questions about the tools students would be able to use and whether or not the students had choice in how they represented the model. This helped Sally think through how she planned to support students as they built their photosynthesis models.

As Luis headed back to his office after their conversation, he reflected that the three big questions he had asked resulted in Sally's being able to create a clear plan for how she would introduce models and support the students as they created their models.

Objective	Questions
Determine how teachers are preparing students to create models.	"What do the students currently know about creating models? What do you wish they knew?" "Will the students work independently or in teams? How will you share your expectations with your students?"
Help teachers reflect on their practice.	"Which aspect of student learning does this focus on?" "How will you push students' thinking?"
Consider how teachers will support students as they build models to explain a phenomenon.	"When will students receive feedback on the process?" "Will students have choice in the representation of this model?" "What tools will the students use?"
Write with evidence to support a position.	"What is a well-supported statement?" "What counts as evidence in science?" "Is all scientific evidence equal?"

FIGURE 13.2. Discipline-specific questions with objectives in science.

Tips for Working within Other Disciplines

In the previous section, you saw how Luis developed both general and science-specific questions with objectives. You may also find it helpful to prepare a list of discipline-specific questions with objectives for other disciplines that are the focus of your coaching. Examples of discipline-specific questions with objectives in social studies and ELA can be found in Figure 13.3

Social Studies	
Objective	**Question**
Determine teacher's use of text.	"What are your criteria for text selection?" "How many texts will students read on a topic?"
Determine teacher's view of text.	"Will the students critique the argument of the text?" "Will students analyze the historical context of primary source documents?"
Determine use of models/modeling of norms and conventions.	"How will students know what evidence is sound?" "Will you present historians' models of reasoning, or write to show how you reason in front of students?"
Consider multiple points of view.	"Whose view are the texts told from?" "Is there a balance? If not, does that matter?"
ELA	
Objective	**Question**
Determine teacher's approach to feedback.	"At what point (or points) in the writing process do students receive feedback?" "How do you explain to students how they should use the feedback they receive?"
Consider students' role in the writing process.	"Will students confer with you? With others? Walk me through what this would look like."
Determine use of models/modeling of norms and conventions.	"Will students use mentor texts? If so, what mentor texts do you plan to use?" "Will there be modeling?"
Consider multiple approaches.	"Will students see more than one example of an author's ability to manipulate structure (flashback, multiple views)?" "Will students be expected to use multiple structural approaches in their own writing?"

FIGURE 13.3. Discipline-specific questions with objectives in social studies and ELA.

Applying the Extended Gradual Release of Responsibility Model

What Is It?

The extended gradual release of responsibility model is a coaching strategy that provides the teacher with a template for organizing instruction of complex strategies, skills, or tasks. It is a template based on the gradual release of responsibility (GRR) model (Pearson & Gallagher, 1983) and includes all elements of that instructional strategy. By extending the traditional GRR model, coaches and teachers can collaborate to provide students with incremental instruction designed to help students master more complex skills or tasks.

The steps in the GRR model are designed to support students as they develop ownership of literacy strategies. The GRR model has also been used to guide students toward the development of skills required by the standards. For example, the CCSS, NGSS, and C3 Framework call for students to demonstrate proficiency of complex skills such as writing and defending arguments, critiquing the reasoning of others, and building models to illustrate scientific phenomena. By using explicit instruction, modeling, guided practice, individual performance, and reflection, teachers can support students as they work to master these complex skills. Nevertheless, some of these skills are too complex to complete in one cycle of the GRR model. By collaborating with a coach, teachers can apply the elements of the model to more complex tasks through using the extended scaffold described in this strategy.

Stage in the GRR model	Recommended number of minutes
Explicit instruction	5 minutes
Modeling	5–10 minutes
Guided practice	5–10 minutes
Collaborative work	10 minutes
Independent work	15 minutes
Reflection	5 minutes

FIGURE 14.1. Timeframe for the GRR model for a 50-minute class.

The GRR model can take place during one class period or over several days. Kirmes (2009) suggests that if the process is going to be used during one class period, a teacher might consider the time frames presented in Figure 14.1.

Some skills and strategies would fit well within the time frames identified in Figure 14.1, whereas others might require more recursive instruction. For example, a teacher might provide explicit instruction and modeling for 5 and 10 minutes, respectively, but provide students with two class periods or more to work on this skill in a collaborative group or with a partner. Further, some teachers may choose to purposefully reorder the steps in the model to allow students to engage in collaborative inquiry before they receive direct instruction (Grant, Lapp, Fisher, Johnson, & Frey, 2012).

Often, when secondary coaches collaborate with teachers, they realize that many of the discipline-specific skills are complex and thus require teachers to expand their thinking regarding how to use the GRR model. The extended GRR model is a scaffold coaches and teachers can use in their collaborations to ensure that students can learn complex skills. In this strategy, coaches first consider the teacher's knowledge of the GRR model, as well as the teacher's instructional goals. Next, the coach and teacher review the standards and the skills required to meet those standards. The coach and the teacher then create an instructional plan that will foster student mastery of those skills. Finally, the teacher and coach implement the plan and reflect on its effectiveness.

How Do I Do It?

When collaborating with a teacher who wants to teach a complex skill, secondary disciplinary literacy coaches can use the extended GRR model to help the teachers organize a plan for instruction. The following five steps can guide you through this collaborative process.

1. Consider the teacher's current context.

   a. Before meeting with a teacher, it is important to consider the teacher's familiarity with the GRR model (Pearson & Gallagher, 1983). If the teacher has not used this model in the past, you will want to start by reviewing the model with the teacher and explaining each step in the process, using concrete examples from the teacher's discipline to ensure that the teacher understands how the model works.

   b. Next, you'll want to consider the teacher's goal. What is it that the teacher is trying to accomplish? You will also want to determine what instruction the teacher has already provided and how much practice the students have already had with this skill or task. This will help you and the teacher determine a starting point. For instance, if the teacher is just introducing the skill, she may want to begin with explicit instruction and modeling. If she has already provided some explicit instruction and modeling, she may want to focus on ways to provide guided and collaborative practice.

   c. After listening to the teacher, review the standard or goal to create a disciplinary literacy instructional outcome with the teacher. Write that instructional outcome at the top of the Extended GRR Model Form (see Form 14.1).

2. Consider the skills students need to master the instructional outcome.

   a. Once you have an understanding of the teacher's disciplinary literacy instructional outcome, you will want to identify the skills that students would need to master that goal and the tasks that would help the students develop those skills. Write the tasks in the row labeled "Steps in the GRR Model" on Form 14.1.

   b. Next, brainstorm a possible sequence of instruction that would lead students toward proficiency on this standard or disciplinary literacy instructional outcome. Use the identified skills to determine how many cycles of the GRR model you will need to organize into the extended GRR model. Because a complex task is often composed of several skills, these skills may need to be taught and practiced separately using the GRR model so that the students can meet the final goal. The extended GRR model can help the coach and teacher organize multiple uses of the GRR model into a coherent plan for instruction.

3. Consider the instructional plan. Once you've identified the elements for which the students will need direct instruction, collaborate with the teacher to complete the rest of the extended GRR model (see Form 14.1). That is, consider how the teacher will do the following:

   a. Explicitly instruct the skill or task

   b. Model, including selecting which materials/instructions teachers will use to share the model with the class

   c. Have the class help the teacher

   d. Have students engage in collaborative work, with a partner or in small groups

    e. Ask students to work independently

    f. Guide the students toward reflection

4. Implement the plan by supporting the teacher through each step of the extended GRR model, based on the teacher's knowledge.

      Once you and the teacher have identified the plan, work with the teacher to implement the plan by supporting the teacher as she or he moves through the extended GRR model. Some teachers may need support with each step. Other teachers may only need support modeling, while still others may just need support providing feedback to students as they engage in collaborative work. Many teachers will readily tell you with what steps they would like help. In other cases, careful observation and reflection will help you determine how best to support the teacher with whom you are collaborating.

5. Reflect on the process. You and the teacher will need to reflect on the process regularly by reviewing student work completed during each phase and adapting instruction as necessary.

The Strategy in Action

Angela Mondato is a full-time secondary disciplinary literacy coach who was a former English teacher and has been coaching for 8 years. She is collaborating with Christina Jones, a veteran social studies teacher who has 20 years of experience. These colleagues from West Charleston High School are collaborating around a discipline-specific literacy skill. In a meeting earlier during the week, Christina explained that she wanted her ninth-grade social studies students to consider how religion can influence conflict by studying the Israeli–Palestinian conflict. She explained that her students had been studying religion, and she wanted them to be able to independently answer this overarching question by studying multiple texts from diverse perspectives on this topic. She wanted the students to be able to explain how various authors, based on their points of view, address this conflict. Prior to writing an essay that explains how religion might affect conflict, she wanted the students to demonstrate that they understood how an author's point of view might influence the information he or she decides to include in the text. Angela and Christina engaged in the following steps to apply the extended GRR model.

    1. *Consider the teacher's current context.* First, Angela asked Christina to identify what she wanted her students to get out of the lesson. To begin this discussion, Angela stated, "I'd like to clarify what I heard you say at our meeting earlier this week. You'd like your students to study the approaches of more than one author, and these authors have more than one point of view about the Israeli–Palestinian conflict." Christina answered that she would like them to do this and also collect information about the conflict as they are engaging with the texts. She wanted them to address this information in an essay later, when they would explain how

religion influences conflict, using this conflict as an example. Christina explained that she wanted her students to work toward mastering the CCSS.ELA-Literacy. RH 9-10.6 standard that reads, "Compare the point of view of two or more authors for how they treat the same or similar topics, including which details they include and emphasize in their respective accounts" (NGA & CCSSO, 2010). Christina explained that she felt that this was incredibly complex thinking for her students, many of whom many of whom struggle with reading and writing. While her students have summarized an author's message after reading a text, they were not yet critical of the author's message and did not recognize how an author's perspective might affect his or her message. Together, Angela and Christina brainstormed a list of possible instructional outcomes that would allow students to demonstrate progress on Christina's stated goal. They clarified that their disciplinary literacy instructional outcome would read, "Given several texts written from various points of view on the Israeli–Palestinian conflict, ninth-grade social studies students will be able to compare and contrast each author's point of view and determine how that perspective influences the information that was presented in the text."

2. *Consider the skills students need to master the goal.* Angela and Christina realized that there were many skills embedded in this instructional outcome. Angela asked Christina to reflect on her knowledge of her students. What would the students need to know to accomplish this goal? Christina and Angela brainstormed the following list:

- Recognize that authors have specific points of view based on who they are and when they are writing.
- Recognize that an author's perspective influences his or her selection and presentation of information.
- Demonstrate understanding of the author's message and recognize his or her point of view.
- Compare and contrast each author's point of view and presentation of information.

Once students were able to do this, they could use what they learned from text and previous lessons on religion to write an explanatory essay regarding how religion influences conflict.

Christina explained that she worried about how best to organize and deliver this instruction to her students. Angela suggested using the extended GRR model template to organize her goals and her sequence of instruction. They began by entering the instructional outcome and the four tasks that the students would be expected to accomplish (see Figure 14.2).

3. *Consider the instructional plan.* After reviewing the complex goal and the skills required to meet that goal, Angela and Christina realized that the students needed to engage in multiple steps to reach the instructional outcome. Angela modeled how to complete the first column of this framework (see Figure 14.2). Next, she and Christina worked together to determine how to organize instruction for the rest

of the unit. After Christina and Angela reflected on the instructional sequence and steps in the framework, they predicted how many 50-minute class periods students would need to complete each task. Their final decisions can be found in Figure 14.2. Because the texts they would be reading contained the important content of the course, Christina felt confident that she was utilizing sound disciplinary literacy instruction and teaching students the skills of the discipline to master the content of the course.

4. *Implement the plan by supporting the teacher through each step of the GRR model.* After completing the chart, Angela asked Christina to walk her through how she planned to deliver the direct instruction and modeling phase of the process. During a previous collaboration, Angela had helped Christina talk through a think-aloud, so Angela asked Christina to walk her through one of the think-alouds one more time. After completing this process, Christina explained that she felt prepared to implement the direct instruction and modeling steps of the lesson but wanted to talk through how to give feedback to students as they worked collaboratively and independently. Angela shared some approaches that she had seen work for other teachers in the building, and Christina noted that several of those approaches seemed to fit in with her teaching style. She said that she now felt prepared to teach the series of lessons, and they ended their planning session by scheduling a meeting midway through the implementation to discuss how the plan was working.

5. *Reflect on the process regularly by reviewing student work during each phase and adapting instruction as necessary.* After collecting the students' first formative task, Christina and Angela met to discuss the students' progress and adapt instruction as necessary. In this case, the students were able to identify the source but struggled to consider how this influenced the author's message. Angela and Christina collaborated to determine how Christina could reinforce this understanding before the next lesson. Angela and Christina continued to collaborate throughout the remainder of the unit. At a coaching meeting near the end of the unit, Christina reflected, "You know, I really felt overwhelmed by the task. I wasn't sure I was going to be able to help my students accomplish the instructional outcome. Using this framework guided my instruction and helped me feel confident that I could take this on. I was always skipping steps before, and I think that by breaking students' learning opportunities down into smaller steps, we all benefited."

Tips for Working within Other Disciplines

English

English teachers might use the extended GRR model to help students analyze rhetoric an author uses and how that use of rhetoric crafts the author's message. English teachers might also use this process to help students master the following standard (or work toward mastery of the standard): RL.9-10.5, "Analyze how an author's choices concerning how to structure a text, order events within it (e.g., parallel

Instructional Outcome: Given several texts written from various points of view on the Israeli–Palestinian conflict, ninth-grade social studies students will be able to compare and contrast authors' points of view and determine how that perspective influences the information that was presented in the text.

Steps in the GRR Model	Explicit instruction	Teacher does alone
Task: Given texts from a variety of viewpoints on the Israeli–Palestinian conflict, explain the author's position and explain what information you applied to reach this decision. **Time:** One lesson, two class periods	Define point of view. Articulate objectives for the unit and explain why it is important that students recognize the point of view an author holds. Explain when and why students would want to pay particular attention to point of view.	Using a text on the Israeli–Palestinian conflict, teacher models how to source the document and how he or she identifies the author's point of view. She or he considers knowledge of author, title, and word choice and shows students how to engage in this thinking.
Task: Given texts from a variety of viewpoints, explain how the author uses information to support his or her point of view. Consider whether or not a source can be neutral. **Time:** One lesson, two class periods	Connect to the previous lesson's reflection. Explain that an author includes and/or excludes information that would help his or her argument and his or her view of a situation and that it is important to consider this when using text to build an understanding of the topic.	Using a text on the Israeli–Palestinian conflict, the teacher will model how to determine the evidence the author uses and explain how this use of evidence supports the author's message.
Task: Write an objective summary of the text; include a clear description of the author's point of view. **Time:** One lesson, one class period	(Students have written summaries earlier in the course.) Teacher explains how to craft a summary that includes a description of the author's point of view. Also, teacher explains why this is an important consideration for this instructional outcome.	Teacher models how to include information about the author and point of view in the summary of the text students had previously written.
Task: Compare and contrast each author's viewpoint. Determine how the point of view influences the information that was presented in the text. **Time:** One lesson, one class period	Teacher explains that one compares and contrasts two or more things to come to a greater understanding. Teacher explains that when comparing and contrasting, one should have units for comparison. In this case, students could compare author's point of view, presentation of evidence, use of language to describe each side of the conflict, where the author places emphasis, and how the author constructs the argument.	Using a compare-and-contrast graphic organizer, the teacher models how to identify units for analysis, in this case author's point of view, presentation of evidence, use of language to describe each side of the conflict, where the author places emphasis, and how the author constructs the argument. Teacher models just one of these, using multiple texts for comparison.

Teacher models with input from the class	Using a text on the Israeli–Palestinian conflict, students in the class help the teacher source the document and identify the author's point of view. Together, they consider knowledge of author, title, and word choice and how to engage in this type of thinking.	Using a text on the Israeli–Palestinian conflict, the class helps the teacher determine the evidence the author uses and explains how this use of evidence supports the author's message.	The class helps the teacher include information about the author and point of view in the summary of the text.	Class helps the teacher with a second unit of analysis.
Students work on task in groups	Using a text on the Israeli–Palestinian conflict, students working in pairs source the document and identify the author's point of view. Together, they consider knowledge of author, title, and word choice.	Using a text on the Israeli–Palestinian conflict, students working in pairs determine the evidence the author uses and explain how this use of evidence supports the author's message.	Students working in pairs include information about the author and point of view in the summary of the text.	Students working in pairs complete a third unit of analysis.
Students work independently	Using a text on the Israeli–Palestinian conflict, each student sources the document and identifies the author's point of view while considering knowledge of author, title, and word choice. Each student is provided with feedback.	Using a text on the Israeli–Palestinian conflict, each student determines the evidence the author uses and explains how this use of evidence supports the author's message. Each student is provided with feedback.	Each student includes information about the author and point of view in the summary of the text. Each student is provided with feedback.	Each student completes the graphic organizer for a fourth unit of analysis. Each student is provided with feedback.
Reflection	Students reflect on how understanding the author's point of view affected their understanding of the construct.	Students reflect on whether or not they believe a source can ever be neutral. They also explain how the position an author takes affects his or her argument.	Students reflect on the importance of sourcing and acknowledging this information.	Students synthesize their comparison and explain how this understanding builds their conceptual knowledge.

FIGURE 14.2. Example of the extended GRR model.

plots), and manipulate time (e.g., pacing, flashbacks) create such effects as mystery, tension, or surprise." Disciplinary literacy instructional outcomes for this standard may include:

- Given a selection of short stories, students will select a short story and explain one of the following: author's choice of structure, order of events, or use of time to create mystery, tension, or surprise.
  - Discrete skills or cycles of extended gradual release might include:
    - Identifying author's choice of structure for the text,
    - Explaining how author's choice to manipulate time affects the audience,
    - Explaining how author's choice of flashback can create mystery.

Science

Science teachers may use this process to help students master the following NGSS standard: HS ESS3.1, "Construct an explanation based on evidence for how the availability of natural resources, occurrence of natural hazards, and changes in climate have influenced human activity." Disciplinary literacy instructional outcomes might include:

- Given instruction on the occurrence of natural hazards (such as tsunamis, flooding, and forest fires) and access to resources to guide investigations, students will conduct research to determine and then explain, using evidence from this research, how these natural disasters have influenced human activity.
  - Discrete skills or cycles of extended gradual release might include:
    - Explain the characteristics of natural hazards,
    - Identify various types of natural hazards,
    - Engage in research using online resources,
    - Use evidence to support an explanation in writing,
    - Write an explanation of how natural disasters have influenced human activity.
- Given time to conduct research and access to resources to guide investigations, students will conduct research to determine how availability of resources and changes in climate have influenced human activity.
  - Discrete skills or cycles of extended gradual release might include:
    - Explain the role of climate and natural resources in human activity,
    - Engage in research using online resources,
    - Use evidence to support an explanation in writing,
    - Write an explanation, using evidence that explains the role of climate change in influencing human activity.

Extended GRR Model Template

Instructional Outcome:

Steps in the GRR Model	Task: Time:	Task: Time:	Task: Time:
Explicit instruction			
Teacher does alone			

(continued)

From *Collaborative Coaching for Disciplinary Literacy: Strategies to Support Teachers in Grades 6–12* by Laurie Elish-Piper, Susan K. L'Allier, Michael Manderino, and Paula Di Domenico. Copyright © 2016 The Guilford Press. Permission to photocopy this form is granted to purchasers of this book for personal use only (see copyright page for details). Purchasers can download additional copies of this form (see the box at the end of the table of contents).

Extended GRR Model Template *(page 2 of 2)*

Teacher models with input from the class	Students work on task in groups	Students work independently	Reflection

Implementing Three Levels of Think-Aloud

What Is It?

Three levels of think-aloud is a coaching strategy that will help teachers unlock their habits of thinking in order to make it transparent for students. Teachers possess tacit knowledge of the processes in which they engage to make sense of content in the disciplines, but they often don't explicitly share this knowledge with their students. While think-alouds can facilitate transfer of this knowledge for students, it is sometimes difficult for teachers to provide the narrative, or the *why* and the *when* of the processes, along with an explanation of *how* they are thinking during the think-aloud. Additionally, think-alouds are sometimes beyond the students' ability. That is, the teacher models the process as an expert would take on the task—not as a novice who is learning the process would. The model of the process needs to match the audience and be delivered in a way that makes it possible for the students to understand and complete the task.

Think-alouds are used to model processes for students (Davey, 1983) and offer insights on not only *how* to do something, but *why* and *when* to complete certain tasks or cognitive processes. In think-alouds, it is the process that becomes the focus instead of the product. By sharing the thought process with students, they can learn how to transfer the skill to new contexts.

How Do I Do It?

When teachers are struggling to help students transfer their knowledge to new situations, a coach can employ the three levels of think-aloud strategy to help determine information that would help with that transfer process. This knowledge would include not only how to engage in the process but also when and why the student would engage in the process. The steps involved in the three levels of think-aloud strategy follow and are summarized in Figure 15.1.

1. The teacher identifies a process that needs to be modeled for students.
2. The teacher performs a think-aloud of the process for the coach. The coach records this think-aloud verbatim.
3. The coach and teacher review the think-aloud, note areas that are lacking narrative (i.e., the *how*, *why*, and *when*), and revise to include any missing elements in the think-aloud text.
4. Prior to using this think-aloud, the teacher asks an average-performing student in the class to engage in a think-aloud of the task for the teacher. The teacher might approach a student and ask, "Would you be willing to walk me through how you approach this process? I'd like to take notes so that I can see how students approach this type of problem." Then the teacher can take notes as the student shares his or her thinking with the teacher.
5. The teacher and coach discuss the differences between the teacher's process and the student's process. These differences are recorded, and the teacher's think-aloud is revised to clarify steps of process that were problematic for the student and/or to incorporate language from the student's think-aloud that might make the process clearer for other students.
6. The teacher models the process using the revised think-aloud for the whole class.
7. The teacher guides a student through the process for the whole class to observe so that the class can learn from the student's think-aloud as well.

	Level 1	Level 2	Level 3
Action	• The teacher engages in a think-aloud with the coach. • The coach records the think-aloud verbatim. • The teacher and coach review and revise the think-aloud to include information on *what*, *how*, and *why* to engage in the process identified in the think-aloud.	• The teacher asks a student to engage in a think-aloud. • The teacher records the student's think-aloud. • The teacher and the coach review the student's think-aloud to identify requisite knowledge for students.	• The teacher engages the whole class in the revised think-aloud. • The teacher may also decide to coach a student through the process in front of the class.
Purpose	• Unlock teachers' tacit knowledge.	• Identify student's knowledge. • Highlight teacher's tacit knowledge.	• Provide think-aloud for students.

FIGURE 15.1. Three levels of think-aloud.

The Strategy in Action

Jesse Kantopoli is a former social studies teacher who is in his 2nd year as a full-time disciplinary literacy coach. Sienna Bergman is a science teacher with 11 years of experience. She has been teaching chemistry to students at Horace Mann Senior High for 7 of those years. Lately, she had been frustrated by her students' inability to transfer knowledge from one situation to the next. She had been using the GRR model (Pearson & Gallagher, 1983) for the entire academic year, but she felt that her students were not making progress on their goals. She would go through the cycle and students would perform well, but when asked to transfer the same thinking to a new context, students struggled to engage in the same type of thinking in that new context. One of the most challenging concepts was teaching students how to analyze and interpret data, which is Practice 4 of the NGSS. Sienna wanted her students to be able to both interpret and create visual representations of data. Even though she used the GRR model to teach these skills in October and reviewed the process in November, it is now January, and her students continue to struggle to analyze and interpret each new table or graph they encounter.

After listening to Sienna, Jesse wondered how she was engaging in the think-aloud component of the GRR model (Pearson & Gallagher, 1983). He wondered whether or not Sienna was providing students with enough narrative to allow them to transfer their thinking to a new context. Jesse suggested that they engage in three levels of think-aloud to support students' ability to transfer their knowledge.

Level 1: Teacher Think-Aloud

Sienna explained that her objective was to provide a think-aloud for students that would help them read and interpret a table and graph. She then began to model her think-aloud, describing how she would interpret a table and graph. As Sienna talked, Jesse wrote her think-aloud:

> "Starting off, looking at the graph, there is a title. It says 'Showing the effusion rate versus the molecular mass of the gases.' I look over to the side to see what gas effusion is. It explains that it is when the gas moves to an area of lower pressure through a small hole.
>
> "Looking at the table, it lists the gases, the effusion time, the molecular mass, and the density, and the molecular speed. So you can see that as the mass goes up, the effusion time goes up. The more mass it has, the longer it takes to effuse. And then the density is also going up. And then the average molecular speed goes down. So basically, what we're looking at is the smaller the mass, the faster the speed. And so the faster the speed, the less time it takes for the effusion to occur.
>
> "Looking at the graph, the x-axis is the molecular mass, the y-axis is the rate of effusion. Just looking at the first coordinate that the highest rate of effusion is at the smallest molecular mass. And then as you move across, the

molecular mass gets higher, the rate of the speed or effusion decreases. So basically, the smaller the mass, the greater the rate of effusion."

After reviewing the think-aloud, Jesse realized that Sienna's think-aloud would help students interpret this graph but that students were likely unaware of how to apply this type of thinking to new situations. Jesse used questions with objectives (see Strategy 13) to help Sienna identify areas in which she was not explaining the *how* and *why* in addition to the *what* in her think-aloud narrative. Together, Jesse and Sienna reviewed her think-aloud and added details to ensure that she included information in the narrative that would allow students to transfer their thinking to a new situation. The **bold text** indicates additions they made to the think-aloud:

"Starting off, looking at the graph there is a title. It says, 'Showing the effusion rate versus the molecular mass of the gases.' **I look at the title to see what the graph is going to tell me. I look to make sure I understand what it is going to be about—and I look at the title to see if it is going to fit my purposes. Will it tell me what I need to know?** I look over to the side to see what gas effusion is. It explains that it is when the gas moves to an area of lower pressure through a small hole. **If you don't know what a word in the title means, you want to make sure you know it before you move on. Check the page to see if the word is shown in bold print with a definition or if it is defined along the side of the page in a sidebar. Check a glossary, the Internet, and so on. You have to know what all the words mean to understand the graph.**

"**After I read the title, my next step is to check the table that is located right next to the graph for any patterns because any extra information provided by the author is going to help me understand the graph. In this case, I'm checking the table for patterns.** Looking at the table, it lists the gases, the effusion time, the molecular mass, and the density and the molecular speed. **These are the titles of the columns. They are going to play a big role in the chart.** So you can see that as the mass goes up, the effusion time goes up. The more mass it has, the longer it takes to effuse. And then the density is also going up. And then the average molecular speed goes down. So basically, what we're looking at is the smaller the mass, the faster the speed. And so the faster the speed, the less time it takes for the effusion to occur. **Getting this information from the table helps me preview the information I'll get in the graph.**

"**After reading the table, I'm ready to read the graph. The first thing I do is see how the axes are labeled.** Looking at the graph, the *x*-axis is the molecular mass, the *y*-axis is the rate of effusion. **Then we check to see what the points [or bar graphs, or whatever is used to represent values] are. I notice by** just looking at the first coordinate that the highest rate of effusion is at the smallest molecular mass. And then as you move across, the molecular mass gets higher, and the rate of the speed or effusion decreases. So basically, the smaller the mass, the greater the rate of effusion. **I come to this understanding before I even try to** solve a problem or answer any questions. I want to make sure I know what the graph says before I try and do anything with that information."

After Sienna and Jesse reviewed the new think-aloud, Jesse wondered if this think-aloud was covering all the thinking students did not know how to do. He suggested that Sienna also engage in the second level of think-aloud to provide her with insight into her students' abilities.

Level 2: Teacher Analyzes Student Think-Aloud

The next day, Sienna asked one of her students to explain how he reads and interprets a table and graph. She noticed that the student:

- Did not note the title.
- Did not check to see what the axes were labeled.
- Began to answer questions prior to reading the graph/table.
- Did not try to interpret the "main idea" of the graph/table.

Sienna brought this information back to a meeting with Jesse, and, together, they revised her think-aloud to ensure that all of those components were included and would be shared at a level that is appropriate to her students' abilities.

Level 3: Teacher Delivers Think-Aloud to the Whole Class

Finally, Sienna delivers her new think-aloud to the class. To ensure that she is modeling appropriately for her audience, she also shares a second table and graph and coaches a student through a think-aloud of the process. Sienna then completes the GRR model related to the reading of tables and graphs.

- Students work in groups with a third table and graph.
- Students work independently with a fourth table and graph.
- Students reflect on their ability to interpret tables and graphs.

During one of their coaching sessions later that month, Jesse asked Sienna to describe how her students were doing regarding their graph interpretation skills. Sienna explained, "I'm so glad that we went through the three levels of think-aloud process. My students know where to start now. While a few students need a quick reminder, most of them are able to at least start their interpretation without any help from me. They are well on their way to mastering the process."

Adopting, Adapting, and Creating Strategies

What Is It?

Disciplinary literacy coaches support teachers in determining what types of strategies students need to be successful in meeting the course instructional outcomes, and then they adopt, adapt, or create a strategy appropriate to the context (Gillis, 2014a). It is important to remember that some students need to be instructed in general literacy strategies. These students need support to comprehend the text used during instruction. For example, a struggling reader may need more support with a text that is on grade level but is above her reading ability. Also, an advanced reader might need to rely on a general literacy strategy when he is challenging himself with more complex text. On the other hand, all readers will likely require discipline-specific strategies to support their engagement with the texts in their courses.

As a disciplinary literacy coach, you will frequently be asked to support teachers who work with both types of students: those who need help in comprehending the text and those who are engaging in discipline-specific reading, writing, and thinking. These needs should be the basis of strategy selection and implementation (Faggella-Luby, Graner, Deshler, & Drew, 2012).

All students are entitled to learning strategies that will support them as they navigate the specific complexities of consuming and then producing texts in the disciplines (Shanahan, 2015). Although there are many resources regarding general literacy strategies (e.g., Fisher, Brozo, Frey, & Ivey, 2014; Keene & Zimmermann, 2007) and some resources available for disciplinary literacy–specific strategies (e.g. Manderino, Johns, & Berglund, 2014; Shanahan, 2015), disciplinary literacy coaches will likely collaborate with teachers to adopt, adapt, or create strategies appropriate for their curriculum, goals, and students.

To begin to understand how to engage in this work, it is important to determine the definition of the term "strategy." Tierney and Readence (2005) explain that a strategy is an instructional approach meant to guide students through learning. These instructional strategies are connected to specific behaviors the instruction is intended to target. A coach can help a teacher consider which specific structured activity will help the students engage in the behavior embedded in the disciplinary literacy instructional outcome.

How Do I Do It?

1. When working with the teacher, determine what the teacher's disciplinary literacy instructional outcome is (see Strategy 6).

2. Explain to the teacher that strategies involve a strategic behavior and a structured activity. You can explain that when teachers ask students to engage with a vocabulary strategy, they are focusing on a strategic behavior (e.g., making connections, recognizing relationships, visualizing) and employing a structured activity (e.g., four-square chart, concept circles, drawing pictures) that helps students to engage in that strategic behavior.

3. Collaborate with teachers to identify the strategic behavior that is embedded in the disciplinary literacy instructional outcome.

4. Adapt, adopt, or create a structured activity that will support the teachers' instruction of this behavior.

The Strategy in Action

In each of the following examples, we focus on a coaching strategy shared in this book to illustrate how to engage in strategy adoption, adaptation, or creation. Though slightly different approaches, each involves the coach collaborating with the teacher to identify the strategic behavior necessary to be successful and then to connect that behavior to a specific structured activity that will foster students' success in engaging in that behavior.

Adopt

In Strategy 14, Angela Mondato and Christina Jones collaborated to apply the extended GRR model to guide Christina's students' work. Once the instructional sequence was established, Angela and Christina continued the coaching conversation to consider which strategies might support Christina's students as they engaged in each step of the extended GRR model. To begin, Angela asked Christina to clarify the behaviors in which students needed to engage to be successful. She asked Christina to focus on the behaviors that challenged the students.

Christina said that her students often struggle to organize their thinking when reading multiple texts. One of the goals included in the extended GRR model involved asking students to do the following: "Given texts from a variety of viewpoints, explain how the author uses information to support his or her point of view. Consider whether or not a source can be neutral."

Christina explained, "My students struggle to see how the texts can provide information through the synthesis and comparison of multiple points of view. They tend to read the texts as discrete units and struggle to see how ideas can be developed by reading multiple texts and that thinking can be refined by viewing texts from multiple points of view. Is there anything that can help with that?"

"What I hear you saying is that students need a way to organize information so that they can consider multiple texts to answer questions about the topic. Is that right? Is that the behavior that you'd like to target?" Angela asked.

Christina agreed that focusing on that behavior would allow students to successfully engage in the task. Angela then suggested that they show students how to use an inquiry chart (Hoffman, 1992). This chart helps students consider a topic or question from multiple texts and multiple points of view. An example of an inquiry chart can be found in Form 16.1.

Angela and Christina decided to adopt the inquiry chart to support her students since the behavior targeted in the chart matched the strategic behavior in which she wanted her students to engage. This chart will enable Christina to support her students as they work toward a larger, more complex disciplinary literacy instructional outcome. Angela explained that Christina's students would likely benefit from instruction in how to create the questions used to guide information gathering while reading and recording that information in the inquiry chart. As she reviewed the chart and the instructional outcome, Angela asked, "Once your students have completed the information-gathering task, will they know how to summarize across multiple texts?" "Not really," Christina replied. "Should I model how to do that?" Christina's question moved the discussion from determining which tool to use to determining an effective mood to create successful experiences for students.

Adapt

In Strategy 15, Jesse Kantopoli, a disciplinary literacy coach, and Sienna Bergman, a high school science teacher, worked to implement three levels of think-aloud to support students as they honed the skills of analyzing and interpreting data. After sharing the think-aloud with students, Sienna reported that students were better able to transfer their thinking to new graphs and tables but that they struggled to make hypotheses about what they were seeing. Sienna explained that she wanted students to make observations about what was presented in charts, graphs, or tables. She then wanted students to think about what those observations meant and make an inference about their observations. Finally, she wanted her students to predict how that information would influence the phenomenon under study.

Jesse considered structured activities that he knew that might target the behaviors Sienna identified. Jesse knew that an observation, question, and inference (OQI) chart is a three-column chart to help organize students' thinking, and he had recommended that teachers use this chart in the past. Nevertheless, he knew that Sienna wanted the students to observe, infer, and then predict how that information would take on new meaning in a new context. Because the OQI chart did not exactly match the behaviors Sienna identified, Jesse and Sienna collaborated to adapt the chart into one that would match the targeted behavior embedded in the disciplinary literacy instructional outcome. They called this adaptation the observation, inference, and prediction (OIP) chart, and it would be used to support students' interactions with graphs, tables, and charts. The OIP chart can be found in Form 16.2. By focusing on the discipline-specific behaviors in which Sienna wanted her students to engage, Jesse and Sienna were able to adapt an existing chart to ensure that it would support students' discipline-specific thinking.

Create

In Strategy 8, Carla Pfeiffer, an experienced disciplinary literacy coach, worked with the ninth-grade English team to apply the vocabulary decision-making framework to select vocabulary terms to teach during a unit on short stories. After the team meeting, Carla collaborated with Aysha Korian to determine how best to support students in reaching the goal she set for students.

Aysha and her team wanted their students to be able to understand the term "dialogue." To this end, they wanted to provide several chances for students to identify and analyze an author's use of dialogue and how its use influenced the author's message. Aysha explained that the behavior she wanted students to target was to "think deeply about how the author uses dialogue. I mean, they know what dialogue is. It would take two seconds for them to understand that. They need to learn how to recognize dialogue as a tool that authors use to produce an intended effect. That's the true disciplinary view of that term."

Since neither Aysha nor Carla knew of a structured activity that focused on that specific behavior, they decided to create a graphic organizer that would guide students' thinking regarding the use of dialogue in the text. This graphic organizer can be found in Form 16.3. After they brainstormed how to create the graphic organizer, Aysha and Carla decided to try using the graphic organizer to ensure that it would work to help them meet their disciplinary literacy instructional outcome. They selected Section 3 of John Steinbeck's *Of Mice and Men* to determine how Steinbeck's use of dialogue conveyed his overall message. Since the students had read this novel earlier in the semester, Aysha thought that she could use this example as a model for her students to refer to when they are examining how authors use dialogue during the short story unit. After reviewing the completed organizer, Aysha felt confident that it would provide her students with the support they needed to be successful.

Inquiry Chart

Topic:	Question 1:	Question 2:	Question 3:	Comments:
What I already know:				
Text 1:				
Text 2:				
Text 3:				
Text 4:				
Text 5:				
Summary:				

From *Collaborative Coaching for Disciplinary Literacy: Strategies to Support Teachers in Grades 6–12* by Laurie Elish-Piper, Susan K. L'Allier, Michael Manderino, and Paula Di Domenico. Copyright © 2016 The Guilford Press. Permission to photocopy this form is granted to purchasers of this book for personal use only (see copyright page for details). Purchasers can download additional copies of this form (see the box at the end of the table of contents).

Observation, Inference, and Prediction Chart

Observation	Inference	Prediction

From *Collaborative Coaching for Disciplinary Literacy: Strategies to Support Teachers in Grades 6–12* by Laurie Elish-Piper, Susan K. L'Allier, Michael Manderino, and Paula Di Domenico. Copyright © 2016 The Guilford Press. Permission to photocopy this form is granted to purchasers of this book for personal use only (see copyright page for details). Purchasers can download additional copies of this form (see the box at the end of the table of contents).

Impact of Dialogue Graphic Organizer

Author's Message/Theme:

Example of Dialogue Used	Effect of That Dialogue	Connection to the Author's Message

How would this message have been different if the author had not used dialogue?

From *Collaborative Coaching for Disciplinary Literacy: Strategies to Support Teachers in Grades 6–12* by Laurie Elish-Piper, Susan K. L'Allier, Michael Manderino, and Paula Di Domenico. Copyright © 2016 The Guilford Press. Permission to photocopy this form is granted to purchasers of this book for personal use only (see copyright page for details). Purchasers can download additional copies of this form (see the box at the end of the table of contents).

Using the Coaching Cycle

What Is It?

The traditional coaching cycle, which grew out of the work of elementary coaches, is composed of a progression of activities that includes goal setting, modeling, co-planning, co-teaching, observation of the teacher by the coach, and a follow-up conference to debrief and determine next steps (Casey, 2006; Elish-Piper & L'Allier, 2014; Toll, 2004). Working together on a targeted goal over a period of time enhances teacher practice and increases student learning (Bean, 2009; Biancarosa, Bryk, & Dexter, 2010). In our work, we have seen many elementary coaches implement the cycle as outlined above, and we have seen them modify this model to fit the needs and preferences of the teachers with whom they are working. The coaching cycle at the secondary level (see Figure 17.1), based on the teacher-initiated model described in Part III, includes all of the activities common to the elementary model but is purposely designed to be flexible to work within the schedules of the participants, as well as to accommodate teacher needs and preferences. Notice that, in the secondary coaching cycle, co-planning is included under collaboration, whereas modeling, co-teaching, and observation may be activities within the implementation stage.

Although secondary literacy coaches sometimes are able to move through the entire coaching cycle, they often focus on just one, two, or three components of the cycle. For example, a teacher may be hesitant to have her coach observe her teach but is very willing to work with the coach to co-plan a series of lessons and to have a conference with the coach about how those co-planned lessons helped her students achieve the instructional outcome. In this case, the coach and teacher would be engaging in the collaboration and follow-up components of the cycle. In another

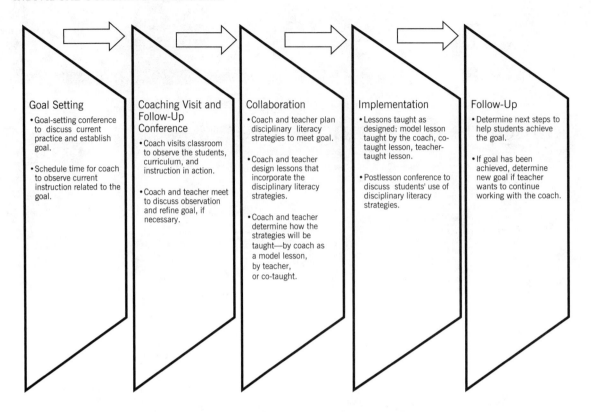

FIGURE 17.1. Coaching cycle at the secondary level.

scenario, a teacher might be very willing to have the coach model, co-teach, or observe. However, his coach only spends two periods a day coaching, and neither of those periods coincides with his teaching schedule. Therefore, unless the coach could arrange for a substitute to cover her own class, it would be difficult for the coach to model, co-teach, or observe in this teacher's classroom. In this case, it is likely that the coach and the teacher would engage in a goal-setting conference, collaborate to co-plan, and hold a follow-up conference to discuss the lesson implemented by the teacher.

How Do I Do It?

You may be able to follow the full coaching cycle, or you may decide to adapt the cycle. We offer the following guidelines to help you differentiate your coaching to fit the needs of the teachers with whom you work.

1. Always begin with goal setting. When you develop the goal together, you and the teacher gain a shared understanding about the purpose of your future work. This shared understanding provides direction for the work and increases the likelihood that the teacher's goal will be achieved.

2. Use teacher input to determine what aspects of the coaching cycle would be most beneficial. Asking the following questions can help establish your coaching plan.

    a. "What can I do to support you as you work toward this goal?"

    b. "Would it be helpful for me to see your students in action before we move forward with our work?"

    c. "What do you think might be the most difficult part(s) of your work related to this goal: the planning of instruction, the delivery of the instruction, your ability to make observations as you teach, reflecting on your instruction?"

3. Use the teacher's responses to the questions listed above to help determine whether you should make a coaching visit, what type of collaborations would be most helpful, and whether—as well as how—you might be involved in the implementation of instruction. Teacher and coach schedules will also need to be considered, as modeling, co-teaching, and observation require that the coach be available when the teacher is working with the students specified in the goal.

4. Carry out the coaching cycle that you and the teacher developed. The teacher is counting on you to participate as planned, so it is important that you be on time for all co-planning meetings, that you model or co-teach or observe on the days when these activities have been scheduled, and that you follow up any in-class coaching activity with a conference or conversation with the teacher. You may need to tell your principal or district curriculum coordinator that you cannot attend some meetings because you are committed to being in a teacher's classroom at that time. Following through with your coaching commitments builds trusting relationships with teachers—and we have seen how the word about coaches who respect their commitments spreads throughout a building, encouraging other teachers to approach their coach for support.

5. Regardless of the steps of the coaching cycle you use with a particular teacher, always end the cycle with a follow-up conversation, summarizing progress toward the teacher's goal, what his or her next steps will be in terms of that goal or related to a new goal, and whether you will continue to be involved in those next steps.

The Strategy in Action

Because it is highly likely that the coaching cycle will need to be modified to fit teacher and coach schedules and teacher preferences, we present three different scenarios in which specific steps of the coaching cycles are highlighted. We hope these scenarios will enable you to see how you can most effectively use some or all parts of the coaching cycle.

Focus on Goal Setting

Whenever a coach begins to work with a teacher, it is important for them both to have a clear understanding of the purpose or goal of their work. This goal establishes the parameters for their collaborations and can clarify which steps of the coaching cycle are essential for accomplishing that goal. Developing a SMART goal (DuFour et al., 2010) is a good approach to goal setting, as it requires the teacher to be Specific about the goal, to ensure that the goal is Measurable, Attainable, and Relevant, and that it can be accomplished in a Timely fashion. Discussing these elements ensures that the coach and the teacher have a shared understanding of the goal and often delineates areas in which the coach can provide support to the teacher.

Let's see how Angela Mondato, the literacy coach from West Charleston High School, and Christina Jones, a social studies teacher, developed a SMART goal before they began the work described in Strategy 14. Christina approached Angela for assistance, saying that she felt somewhat overwhelmed with planning instruction related to a new instructional outcome from the ninth-grade social studies curriculum. Angela suggested that they meet to discuss Christina's concerns and began their discussion by helping Christina determine the specific goal and her needs in relation to that goal. Angela showed Christina the SMART Goal-Setting Template (see Form 17.1) and explained how completing the form together would enable Angela to learn more about the instructional outcome and to think about ways she could help Christina develop instruction related to that outcome.

Christina quickly explained the instructional outcome and how that outcome was directly related to a CCSS (see Figure 17.2). Their discussion of the measurable and attainable aspects highlighted areas in which Angela could be of assistance. Christina said, "I would love to have all of my students earn a 3 or a 4 on the rubric of the summative assessment, but I know that is not realistic. However, I am concerned that the task is so difficult that not even 80% will receive an acceptable score." Angela responded, "You're right, reading multiple texts and then comparing and contrasting the multiple perspectives presented in those texts is a complex task, but I think if we break it down into smaller tasks that lead to the final task, the students can be successful. Perhaps determining those smaller tasks is something we can do together." Christina agreed that this would be very helpful and also asked whether they could discuss appropriate instructional methods to address and assess each of the tasks. These additional coaching activities were added to the SMART Goal-Setting Form (see Figure 17.2). Christina synthesized all of the information from the form to write her SMART goal at the bottom of the form. She said, "I think everything is clear now" and immediately began to examine her schedule to find a time when she and Angela could start to unpack the individual tasks embedded within the instructional outcome.

In terms of the coaching cycle, Christina and Angela began their cycle with goal setting. To accomplish that goal, there was no need for Angela to visit the classroom, so the coaching visit and follow-up conference step was omitted from their cycle. The collaboration step was essential to their work as they determined the key tasks and how to assess them. In terms of implementation, Christina did all of the teaching. Angela offered to observe some of the teaching, but Christina said she did not

SMART Goal Considerations	My Plans
SPECIFIC	Instructional outcome: *Given several texts written from various points of view on the Israeli–Palestinian conflict, ninth-grade social studies students will be able to compare and contrast authors' points of view and determine how those perspectives influence the information that was presented in the texts.* Specific standard(s) to be addressed: *CCSS.ELA-RH 9-10.6*
MEASURABLE	How will students demonstrate progress toward this goal? *At least eighty percent (80%) of the students will score a 3 or 4 on the 4-point scale rubric for the final essay.*
ATTAINABLE	Is this goal challenging and meaningful, yet "do-able"? *Because there are many steps involved to achieve the standard, it will be challenging for me to teach and for the students to accomplish. Outlining a clear instructional path will ensure that students will achieve the instructional outcome.*
RELEVANT	This goal aligns with district and/or school priorities because *it focuses on a Common Core State Standard and on our goal to have students consider sourcing and contextualizing, two habits of thinking used by historians.*
TIMELY	Timeline for meeting this goal: *I have two weeks to plan before beginning instruction. I expect it will take 7 to 10 days to address this instructional outcome.*
Strategies to Work toward the Goal	My action plan to work toward this goal: • *Gather the texts that students will read.* • *Plan instructional tasks.* • *Develop formative and summative assessments.*
Coaching Support Needed to Work toward Goal	The literacy coach will do these things to support my work toward this goal: • *Angela and I will determine a progression of tasks that will lead to the instructional outcome.* • *Angela and I will determine how to guide the students through each task and design the formative assessments.* • *Angela and I will meet to discuss the results of each formative assessment and make adjustments to the instructional plan as needed.*

Summary of My SMART Goal: *In order for at least 80% of my students to be able to read multiple texts and successfully compare and contrast authors' points of view and determine how those perspectives influence the information that was presented in the texts, I will work with Angela to break down the task into reasonable steps and to determine appropriate instruction and assessment for each step. I will also discuss the formative assessment results with Angela to determine what changes would improve future instruction.*

FIGURE 17.2. SMART Goal-Setting Template completed with Christina Jones.

think that was necessary. However, Christina did find the follow-up step, in which she and Angela reviewed the formative assessments, to be extremely helpful. After their discussion about the second formative assessment, Christina told Angela, "Our joint examination of the results revealed patterns I had not seen on my own, and I now know what things to review as I move on." Results of the summative assessment indicated that 84% of Christina's students earned scores of 3 or 4, a higher percentage than the goal set by the ninth-grade team. Thus, based on the targeted goal and Christina's preferences, the combination of goal setting, collaboration, and follow-up was an effective coaching cycle.

Focus on Coaching Visit and Follow-Up Conference

Although Angela, the coach in the previous scenario, did not make an initial coaching visit to Christina's classroom, such a visit often can be a critical part of the coaching cycle. This was the case for Sean Chapman, a 4th-year coach from Wadsworth High School, while working with a team of 10th-grade science teachers. With a background in English and an endorsement in ESL, Sean's coaching was often at the small-group level, helping the team think through ways to incorporate disciplinary literacy strategies into their instruction. This semester, the team was focusing on life science, and their instructional outcome was for students to build a model that shows the stages of mitosis (NGSS.LS1.B) and to be able to explain their model to an external audience (CCSS.SL.9-10.4). In conjunction with the reading of their laboratory notebook and an article about mitosis, teacher Gabriel LeMont built and explained a model of the interphase stage of mitosis. His students were now ready to begin their own model building of the final four stages of mitosis, but Gabriel was unsure of the type and amount of support he should give them. He asked Sean if they could meet to discuss this issue. When they met, Sean and Gabriel spent just a few minutes developing the following SMART goal: *In order for all of my students to be able to successfully build the five-part model of mitosis and explain it to an external audience, I will work with Sean to determine the amount and type of support that would facilitate their work.* In line with the next step of the coaching cycle, they agreed that Sean should visit Gabriel's classroom on the following day to see how Gabriel provided feedback on the building of the model for the prophase stage. Whenever he went into a classroom to observe, Sean liked to complete a coach's observation form (see Form 17.2). Sean filled in the top of the coach's observation form, noting the purpose for the observation and the names of three students selected by Gabriel for close observation. The first two columns of Figure 17.3 show how Sean completed the form as he observed.

The follow-up conference was held on the day after the observation. Sean's coaching colleague Luis Contreras, whose work is described in Strategy 13, had shared his method of questions with objectives at a district coaching retreat, and

Teacher: *Gabriel LeMont*   **Date:** *October 23, 2014*

Course: *Life Science*   **Period:** *4th*

Purpose of Observation: *To document the type and amount of feedback that Gabriel gives about the students' prophase models, paying special attention to Alicia Hargrove (High Achiever), Martin Sobold (Struggling Student), and Katrina Melinoski (EL).*

Standard(s) Addressed: *New Generation Science Standard LSI.B. 9–10.*

Observations	Comments	Possible Actions (Developed by coach and teacher collaboratively)
Number of students to whom feedback was provided *Comments:* *"You are coming along."* *"That's not quite right."* *"Are you sure about this (pointing to some part of the model)"?* *"How many chromosomes should you have?"* *"What are you missing from your model?"* *"Did you check this with the information in your lab notebook?"* *Told six students to get on task* *Non-feedback activities:* *1. Looked for additional materials needed by students.* *2. Told students what to do with completed models— one at a time.* *3. Told students what to do after completing model— one at a time.*	*✓✓✓✓ ✓✓✓✓ ✓* *11 out of 24* *✓ (Student kept working.)* *✓✓✓ (Martin—He frowned.)* *✓✓✓ (Katrina—She shrugged and kept working.)* *✓ (Student asked a peer.)* *✓✓ (Martin) (Both looked at a peer's model.)* *✓ (Checked and changed model)* *Did not give feedback to Alicia*	1. *Be sure all materials are laid out; that will give me more time to provide feedback.* 2. *Perhaps there was too much time given for the task. Think about setting a time limit.* 3. *Provide more specific feedback. Refer them to the laboratory notebook and the article when they would be helpful.* 4. *Be sure to get to those students who typically struggle with the concepts.* 5. *In 45 minutes, shouldn't I be able to get to all 24 students?*

(continued)

FIGURE 17.3. Observation completed by Sean Chapman in Gabriel LeMont's class.

Next Steps		
Teacher		
• Give a time limit for the model building.		
• Before beginning, tell students what to do with finished model and what to do when finished.		
• Give specific feedback related to		
o Missing component(s)		
o Resources to use (not a peer)		
Coach		
• Do a similar observation when students are working on the anaphase model.		
• Know what the anaphase model should look like before observing.		

FIGURE 17.3. *(continued)*

Sean decided to use that technique with Gabriel. As they reviewed the data, he asked the following questions to help Gabriel define his current feedback practices:

- "You gave feedback to 11 of 24 students in a 45-minute period. How does this number compare to your expectations?"
- "Would you say that the type of feedback you gave was general or specific or did it vary?"
- "Were the students able to revise or move forward with their models on the basis of your feedback?"
- "How do you think your feedback to Alicia, Martin, and Katrina fit their levels of need?"

In responding to the questions, Gabriel made several comments about ways he could improve his feedback, and Sean offered a few ideas as well. Sean wrote notes about these possible actions in the third column of Figure 17.3. Gabriel said that, because it was so helpful to see exactly what he had said and to whom, he wondered if Sean could observe again while the students were working on the third phase of the model. Sean agreed, and they wrote that down under Next Steps at the bottom of the observation sheet. He also wrote down the steps Gabriel planned to take to improve his feedback (see the Next Steps section of Figure 17.3). As Gabriel left the meeting, he told Sean, "I knew my feedback was not as specific as it needed to be if students were to be successful with their model building. I'm excited to try some of the ideas we talked about and see how it impacts their future models."

When you examine this set of activities in terms of the coaching cycle, you see that it basically involved the first two steps: goal setting and coaching visit with follow-up conference. These two steps are often sufficient when the teacher's goal is related to a question he or she has about student response to instruction or feedback. However, these relatively short-term interactions can often lead to additional opportunities for coaching. For example, Gabriel may want to meet with Sean to co-plan and even co-teach the instruction related to the latter part of the instructional outcome: presenting the mitosis models to external audiences.

Focus on Collaboration and Implementation

Many coaches consider the collaboration and implementation steps of the coaching cycles as the "heart of coaching." Let's see how Carla Pfeiffer focused on these two steps in her work with Aysha Korian, a ninth-grade English teacher. Two weeks earlier, Carla had worked to help the ninth-grade ELA team learn the process of selecting essential vocabulary and determining which vocabulary to teach deeply (see Strategy 8). Last week, Carla moved to individual coaching with one member of that team, Aysha Korian, focusing on how to provide deep teaching of some specific words from the upcoming short story unit. The development of a graphic organizer to provide deep instruction about the word "dialogue" (as discussed in Strategy 16) was the beginning of the collaboration step of the coaching cycle. Even though Aysha knew which words she wanted to teach deeply and had an organizer to help her teach one of those words, she was still unsure of how to provide the exact instruction. Because Carla had been a member of the ELA team prior to becoming a coach/reading specialist, she offered to (1) co-plan the lesson with Aysha, (2) model the deep teaching of the word "dialogue" with Aysha's first-period students, (3) confer with Aysha about the modeled lesson during third period, (4) observe Aysha teach the same lesson to the sixth-period students, and (5) talk with Aysha about her lesson at the end of the day. Although these activities would require a relatively large time commitment, Aysha thought that this set of activities was exactly what she needed to move forward with deep teaching of other vocabulary for the short story unit—and for future units as well.

As is true of all good teachers, Carla and Aysha wanted to be sure they were prepared to teach the lesson. As part of the collaboration step of the coaching cycle, they took about 20 minutes to co-plan the lesson using the Co-Planned Lesson Template (see Form 17.3). Their completed co-planned lesson can be seen in Figure 17.4. In this example, Carla planned to model the lesson with one group of students, and Aysha planned to teach the same lesson to another group of students. Note that this same template can be used to co-plan a lesson that the coach and teacher want to co-teach. You merely need to add the name of the person responsible for teaching each part of the lesson. In co-taught lessons, the coach often teaches the more difficult aspects of the lesson so the teacher can observe those instructional practices.

Carla began the implementation step of the cycle by modeling the co-planned lesson. Whenever a teacher observes the coach modeling, the teacher should complete a teacher observation form. Form 17.4 provides a template for a teacher's observation of the coach. Notice that the form asks the teacher to list specific aspects she wants to observe; this ensures that the teacher is looking at aspects she thinks will improve her practice or her students' learning. When Aysha observed Carla, she wanted to focus on the way Carla explained the effect of dialogue, an aspect of the lesson that Aysha was less confident she could explain on her own. She also wanted to see how Carla introduced the collaborative work, as Aysha had not yet asked her students to engage in collaborative activities. Aysha found her completed observation form to be very useful when she and Carla conferred during third period. In just

Teacher: _Aysha Korian_   **Coach:** _Carla Pfeiffer_   **Date:** _November 3_

Course: _English_   **Periods:** _1st (Carla teaches) and 6th (Aysha teaches)_

Purpose or objective of lesson: _To help students gain a deep understanding of the term "dialogue"_
What do you expect the students to be able to do as a result of the lesson? _To identify and analyze an author's use of dialogue and how its use conveys the author's message_
Standard/s to be addressed: _CCSS RL.5.9–10_
What academic vocabulary will be emphasized during the lesson? _dialogue, author's message_

Instructional Steps by Teacher and Students
Label direct instruction (DI), modeling (M), guided practice (GP), collaborative work (CW), independent work (IW), and reflection (R).

Teacher	Students
Note: This is a 15-minute lesson.	
1. _Remind students of the instructional outcomes for the short story unit. Explain how a deep understanding of the term "dialogue" will be needed to accomplish the instructional outcomes. Explain with examples how the use of dialogue conveys the author's message (DI)._	1. _Actively listen and respond to questions._
2. _Introduce the graphic organizer (Form 12.3) that will help students document the effect of dialogue on author's message._	2. _Students find each section on their own organizers as the teacher describes it._
3. _Remind students of "The Man in the Well" by Ira Sher, a short story they have recently read. Tell them the author's message and write it on the graphic organizer._	3. _Actively listen and copy onto their own organizers._
4. _Read three pieces of dialogue, determine the effect of that dialogue, and how it connects to the author's message._ _a. First piece—modeled_ _b. Second piece—guided practice_ _c. Third piece—collaborative work_	4a. _Actively listen and complete their own organizers._ 4b. _Contribute ideas and complete their own organizers._ 4c. _Work with a partner to complete their own organizers._
5. _Guide students in brief discussion of how the message would have been different if the author had not used dialogue._	5. _Contribute ideas and fill in their own organizers._

(continued)

FIGURE 17.4. Lesson co-planned by Carla Pfeiffer and Aysha Korian.

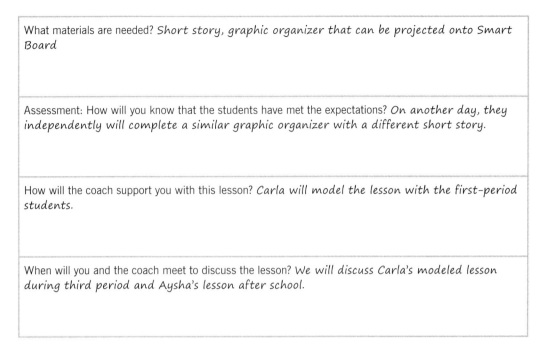

What materials are needed? *Short story, graphic organizer that can be projected onto Smart Board*

Assessment: How will you know that the students have met the expectations? *On another day, they independently will complete a similar graphic organizer with a different short story.*

How will the coach support you with this lesson? *Carla will model the lesson with the first-period students.*

When will you and the coach meet to discuss the lesson? *We will discuss Carla's modeled lesson during third period and Aysha's lesson after school.*

FIGURE 17.4. *(continued)*

20 minutes, Aysha was able to share what she had observed, ask Carla the questions she had written down, and decide how her observation of Carla would affect the way she planned to teach the same lesson later in the day. To maintain a consistent focus, Carla suggested that she use the same observation form when she observed Aysha teach during sixth period. When they met after school, Carla used examples from her completed observation form to confirm Aysha's belief that she had clearly conveyed the importance of dialogue to her students. Carla also asked questions to help Aysha reflect on the day's activities and solidify her next steps related to the instructional outcome. Engaging in both the collaboration and implementation steps of the coaching cycle built Aysha's confidence that she could plan and provide deep instruction of key vocabulary.

Determining the Most Effective Use of the Coaching Cycle

The three scenarios you just read highlight how it is not always necessary to follow the entire coaching cycle to help teachers achieve their goals. As a coach, you can determine how to adjust the coaching cycle by carefully considering the following factors: the teacher's goal, the teacher's preferences, and teacher's and coach's schedules.

SMART Goal-Setting Template

SMART Goal Considerations	My Plans
SPECIFIC	Instructional outcome: Specific standard(s) to be addressed:
MEASURABLE	How will students demonstrate progress toward this goal?
ATTAINABLE	Is this goal challenging and meaningful, yet "do-able"?
RELEVANT	This goal aligns with district and/or school priorities because . . .
TIMELY	Timeline for meeting this goal:
Strategies to Work toward the Goal	My action plan to work toward this goal:
Coaching Support Needed to Work toward Goal	The literacy coach will do these things to support my work toward this goal:
Summary of My SMART Goal:	

From *Collaborative Coaching for Disciplinary Literacy: Strategies to Support Teachers in Grades 6–12* by Laurie Elish-Piper, Susan K. L'Allier, Michael Manderino, and Paula Di Domenico. Copyright © 2016 The Guilford Press. Permission to photocopy this form is granted to purchasers of this book for personal use only (see copyright page for details). Purchasers can download additional copies of this form (see the box at the end of the table of contents).

Coach's Observation Template

Teacher: _____   Date: _____

Course: _____   Period: _____

Purpose of Observation: _____

_____

_____

Standard(s) Addressed: _____

Observations	Comments	Possible Actions (developed by coach and teacher collaboratively)

Next Steps

Teacher

Coach

From *Collaborative Coaching for Disciplinary Literacy: Strategies to Support Teachers in Grades 6–12* by Laurie Elish-Piper, Susan K. L'Allier, Michael Manderino, and Paula Di Domenico. Copyright © 2016 The Guilford Press. Permission to photocopy this form is granted to purchasers of this book for personal use only (see copyright page for details). Purchasers can download additional copies of this form (see the box at the end of the table of contents).

Co-Planned Lesson Template

Teacher: _____ **Coach:** _____ **Date:** _____

Course: _____ **Period:** _____

Purpose or objective of lesson:
What do you expect the students to be able to do as a result of the lesson?
Standard(s) to be addressed:
What academic vocabulary will be emphasized during the lesson?

Instructional Steps by Teacher and Students

Label direct instruction (DI), modeling (M), guided practice (GP), collaborative work (CW), independent work (IW), and reflection (R).

Teacher	Students

(continued)

From *Collaborative Coaching for Disciplinary Literacy: Strategies to Support Teachers in Grades 6–12* by Laurie Elish-Piper, Susan K. L'Allier, Michael Manderino, and Paula Di Domenico. Copyright © 2016 The Guilford Press. Permission to photocopy this form is granted to purchasers of this book for personal use only (see copyright page for details). Purchasers can download additional copies of this form (see the box at the end of the table of contents).

Co-Planned Lesson Template *(page 2 of 2)*

What materials are needed?
Assessment: How will you know that the students have met the expectations?
How will the coach support you with this lesson?
When will you and the coach meet to discuss the lesson?

Teacher's Observation Template

Teacher: _____ Coach: _____ Date: _____

Course: _____ Period: _____

Lesson Description: _____

_____

Standard(s) Addressed: _____

Specific Aspects I Want to Remember to Document (e.g., coach's language, specific students' responses, gradual release of responsibility): _____

_____

Specific Aspects Noted Above and Additional Important Practices	Observations	Questions

How will this observation affect my own practice?

From *Collaborative Coaching for Disciplinary Literacy: Strategies to Support Teachers in Grades 6–12* by Laurie Elish-Piper, Susan K. L'Allier, Michael Manderino, and Paula Di Domenico. Copyright © 2016 The Guilford Press. Permission to photocopy this form is granted to purchasers of this book for personal use only (see copyright page for details). Purchasers can download additional copies of this form (see the box at the end of the table of contents).

PART VII

Profiles of Highly Effective Disciplinary Literacy Coaches

In the first six sections of this book, we presented key ideas and strategies related to disciplinary literacy coaching in middle and high schools. We've discussed important information about adult learning theory, the change process, and layers of coaching (i.e., coaching with large groups, small groups, and individual teachers). We've also shared specific coaching strategies that can be used to support middle and high school teachers in English, science, and social studies. In this final section, we present portraits of seven highly effective disciplinary literacy coaches to illustrate additional key aspects of literacy coaching, such as working with an administrative team, getting into classrooms, and differentiating coaching to meet teacher needs and goals. Each profile highlights a challenge that is commonly experienced by literacy coaches and offers practical tips and tools to help you address and overcome that challenge.

Profile 1 illustrates how a literacy coach can establish and maintain administrator support for literacy coaching at the school level. Profile 2 focuses on how a disciplinary literacy coach can apply the layered approach to coaching to build teacher knowledge and to enhance instructional practice. Profile 3 offers a range of practical ideas for getting into classrooms to work directly with teachers. Profile 4 discusses how a coach can differentiate coaching to meet the needs and goals of different teachers, including new teachers. Profile 5 offers practical suggestions for how the coach can reassure, connect with, and support teachers who may feel nervous about or hesitant to engage with the literacy coach. Profile 6 shares a collection of useful coaching tools to help you stay organized and effective in your work with teachers at your school. Finally, Profile 7 provides ideas for building a professional network to serve as a support system for your work as a disciplinary literacy coach. Collectively, these profiles offer advice and best practices from highly effective literacy coaches. We hope these profiles will encourage and support you as you face challenges and setbacks, as well as successes, in your own coaching.

Establishing and Maintaining Administrator Support

Bahar Humadi is an experienced reading specialist at Hanover Middle School. A year ago, her school district reviewed the roles and responsibilities of the reading specialist and raised the idea of including a focus on literacy coaching. Hanover Middle School was selected to pilot the literacy coaching program. Bahar was excited about her new focus, but she was also nervous about how to announce her new role to the teachers. In addition, she was worried about how to get started with coaching her colleagues, some of whom she had taught with for almost 10 years. They knew her as a reading teacher, and now she would be working with them on disciplinary literacy in English, science, and social studies. She wondered whether they would be open to the coaching program, and she realized that she would need the support of her school's administrative team—Mr. Hernandez, the principal, and Miss Anderson, the assistant principal. Bahar wanted to make sure that all three of them were on the same page about literacy coaching and that, as administrators, they were prepared to support the literacy coaching program at Hanover Middle School. Bahar knew that her school administrators were very busy, so she scheduled a 30-minute meeting and prepared an agenda to help structure their discussions to make sure the meeting would be productive. She carefully selected agenda items to ensure that they would leave the meeting with a shared understanding of the goals and vision for the coaching program. Bahar knew that she was expected to spend three class periods coaching and three periods providing small-group reading intervention for struggling readers. She wanted to discuss which class periods she would be coaching to ensure that her coaching times correlated with the team meeting times for the teachers with whom she would be working. She knew that this might require some tweaking of the original schedule, and she wanted to be sure to discuss it with the administrative team to get their support.

Another topic that Bahar wanted to discuss related to teachers' understanding of her role. Bahar felt that the teachers would wonder what she'd be doing in her new role because she would no longer be teaching six periods like all of the other teachers in the building. She was concerned that they might conclude that she had three "free" periods, and she wanted to make it clear that she would be actively meeting with, working with, and supporting teachers during these times. She also wanted to clarify the types of support she would be able to offer through the coaching program so the teachers knew how she would be available to support them.

Bahar knew that she was expected to support all of the English, science, and social studies teachers in grades 6, 7, and 8, but she realized that she would need to determine a plan to prioritize how to spend her coaching time. She didn't want to scatter her time across all of the teachers doing "random acts of coaching" that would have little to no impact on teacher practice and student learning. She wanted to set specific coaching priorities so her coaching support could contribute to positive outcomes for student learning. Bahar knew that she had to get her administrators' support to enact this model of targeted coaching. Furthermore, she was interested in talking with her administrators about how they could demonstrate that literacy coaching was a high priority in the school so that teachers would participate fully. Because there were so many items to discuss in a 30-minute meeting, Bahar created a meeting template (see Form 1). She then shared her template with the administrative team several days before the meeting so they had a chance to think about the topics she wanted to discuss at the meeting.

Their initial meeting was very productive, and her principal, Mr. Hernandez, suggested that they schedule a short monthly meeting to touch base and make sure that they were on the same page and able to stay out in front of any issues. Bahar was hesitant at first because she did not want to appear that she was always in the principal's office or meeting in private with the administrative team. Miss Anderson, the assistant principal, suggested that they meet in one of the team planning areas, with the door open, to show that they were not discussing personnel matters, observations, or anything confidential. She also suggested that they include team leaders in the meetings depending on the topics to be addressed. Bahar felt this plan made sense, and they agreed to try it and then assess it at the end of the semester.

At one of their early monthly meetings, the conversation quickly led to the topic of how to separate literacy coaching from supervision and evaluation (Toll, 2004). Initially, some teachers hinted to Bahar that they were worried that information from coaching activities would be reported back to the principal or assistant principal to be used in their official evaluations. Although Bahar assured these teachers that she was not an evaluator and did not share specific information with the principal or assistant principal about any teacher's instruction or classroom management, she felt some teachers were still concerned. The administrative team agreed that this concern needed to be addressed directly and quickly so the teachers knew that

FIGURE 1. Administrator–teacher–coach relationship model. Adapted from Elish-Piper, L'Allier, and Zwart (2009). Copyright 2009 by the Illinois Reading Council. Adapted by permission.

Bahar's coaching support was not part of supervision or teacher evaluation. Bahar offered to consult some of her literacy coaching resources, and she found a model that clearly illustrated how the literacy coach is neither a supervisor nor an evaluator (Elish-Piper et al., 2009). In this model (see Figure 1), the administrator doesn't discuss teacher observations with the literacy coach, and the literacy coach doesn't report back to the administrator after observations or conferences with a teacher. In this model, the literacy coach is a supportive colleague for teachers to think and problem solve with—not a supervisor or an evaluator. Mr. Hernandez and Miss Anderson agreed that this model would be appropriate for use at Hanover Middle School, and they discussed plans to share and explain the model at an upcoming all-school faculty meeting.

At the end of Bahar's first year of coaching at Hanover Middle School, the school district announced that literacy coaching would also be implemented at the district's two other middle schools. Bahar contacted the other middle school reading specialists who would be transitioning to literacy coaching responsibilities in the coming year. Knowing how essential the support of her administrative team had been to her early coaching efforts, Bahar made a list of the most important suggestions she could offer these new coaches about how to work with their administrative teams to establish and nurture the literacy coaching program at their schools (see Figure 2).

When she met with the new coaches, one of the first things Bahar shared was the literacy coaching program vision, goals, and approach that she and her school's administrative team worked together to develop (see Figure 3). Mr. Hernandez shared this document at a whole-school faculty meeting, and then he and Miss Anderson followed up with each of the teams to make sure all of the teachers understood the coaching program at Hanover Middle School. Bahar explained to the new coaches in her district, "Having an official coaching program vision, goals, and approach has helped tremendously. It's helped me keep my focus, and it's helped the teachers understand what I'm doing and why I'm doing it. Having an official document like this has clarified that coaching is an important priority at my school." In addition, Bahar asked the new coaches if they would like to meet once a month after school to

1. Meet with your principal and assistant principal as soon as possible to start planning for literacy coaching at your school. Developing a vision, goals, and structure for the coaching program will establish a firm foundation for this new adventure.

2. Meet regularly, but be sure to do it "in public" so it's clear to teachers that you are not talking about them behind closed doors.

3. Discuss how you will separate literacy coaching from evaluation. Develop a plan to share and discuss this with teachers. It is essential that everyone—administrators and teachers—understands and agrees that literacy coaches are not administrators!

4. Develop a strategy to set coaching priorities. Review student assessment data, learning standards, and district and school goals to identify possible priorities. Discuss these priorities to get administrator "buy-in."

5. Ask your principal and assistant principal to publicly support literacy coaching. Some ways they can do this are:
   a. Showing up at professional development sessions the literacy coach facilitates.
   b. Referring to literacy coaching in positive ways at faculty meetings, team meetings, and PLC meetings.
   c. Encouraging teachers to participate in the literacy coaching program.

FIGURE 2. Working with school administrators to promote literacy coaching success.

Hanover Middle School (HMS) Literacy Vision:

To enable all HMS students to develop the literacy skills needed to become independent, self-directed, successful learners in all disciplines.

Goals:
1. To teach students to read actively, strategically, and effectively in each discipline.
2. To increase students' academic and technical vocabularies in each discipline.
3. To develop students' writing skills so they can communicate effectively in each discipline.
4. To help students become metacognitive and strategic about their own learning.

Approach:

The HMS Literacy Coaching Program provides job-embedded, ongoing professional development support for teachers so they can help their students meet the goals listed above. The HMS Literacy Coaching Program is:

• Collaborative,
• Focused on supporting and enhancing teaching and learning, and
• Supportive, not evaluative.

FIGURE 3. Sample literacy coaching program vision, goals, and approach.

share their coaching experiences, challenges, and strategies for working effectively with the administrators. The other coaches agreed, and Bahar was thrilled to realize that next year she would have colleagues and supporters she could talk with who understood the work she was doing as a coach.

As she prepared to start her second year of literacy coaching, Bahar reflected on her accomplishments and challenges. She noted that "without the support of Mr. Hernandez and Miss Anderson, I would have felt like I was on an island. Knowing that they support and believe in the literacy coaching program, and me, helped me feel confident, optimistic, and excited about taking on my new coaching responsibilities. Having their support, understanding, and endorsement made all the difference to getting my coaching off the ground!"

Administrator Meeting Template

Coaching Consideration	Notes
Vision and Goals for Coaching Program	
Time and Schedule for Coaching • When coaching will be scheduled • Adjustments to other aspects of schedule	

Beginning Coaching Priorities
• Consider:
  o Data, including needs assessment
  o District and school goals
  o Standards	

Announcing Coaching Program and Types of Coaching Support to Teachers	When? Who? How?
Other Important Issues to Be Addressed	

From *Collaborative Coaching for Disciplinary Literacy: Strategies to Support Teachers in Grades 6–12* by Laurie Elish-Piper, Susan K. L'Allier, Michael Manderino, and Paula Di Domenico. Copyright © 2016 The Guilford Press. Permission to photocopy this form is granted to purchasers of this book for personal use only (see copyright page for details). Purchasers can download additional copies of this form (see the box at the end of the table of contents).

Applying the Layered Approach to Coaching

After 2 hectic years of literacy coaching, Ebony Wilson came to a realization. She simply could not work with every teacher at Roosevelt High School on every goal or challenge they identified. With an enrollment of slightly more than 2,000 students and almost 40 teachers to coach in the disciplines of English, social studies, and science, Ebony reported feeling "like a chicken with my head cut off—running from one end of the building to the other and not really making a difference." In consultation with her school's administrative team, including the English, social studies, and science department chairs, Ebony discussed the idea of taking a layered approach to coaching (Allen, 2006). She shared two main reasons for her interest in using the layered coaching model. First, she wanted to use her time more efficiently to address important disciplinary literacy goals. Second, she wanted to provide a depth of support to help teachers truly understand, embrace, and use disciplinary literacy instructional practices with their students. The administrative team agreed, and Justin Bolland, the chair of the social studies department, asked Ebony if she'd be willing to start with his department in the area of writing. Ebony agreed and left the meeting excited to put this approach into action.

The following week, Justin invited Ebony to attend a PLC meeting of the social studies department at which the teachers were discussing the expectations of the CCSS for history/social studies as well as the C3 Framework for Social Studies State Standards. The teachers knew that the standards required students to do more writing in social studies, but they were not certain what the actual expectations were or how to provide instruction aimed at those standards. Justin explained, "We need to figure out ways to increase writing instruction for students in our classes. I know this will look different if you are teaching a freshman world history class, a junior

U.S. history class, an advanced placement (AP) U.S. history class, and so on. We need to make sure that writing expectations and instruction become part of what we do in the social studies department here at Roosevelt." Caitlyn Warner-Ross, a teacher in the department, said, "I think I need to step up the research that students do in my world history classes, but I'm not sure where to start." Several other teachers agreed, and Ebony smiled, thinking that this would be an ideal opportunity to implement the layered coaching approach.

Ebony replied, "I'm happy to work with your department on writing expectations and instruction. We can start at a department or PLC meeting as a whole group to look more closely at the writing expectations and to discuss ways to increase writing instruction in your classes. I can then meet with smaller teams to focus on a specific class such as world history, so we can look at setting measurable goals in terms of writing and integrating those goals into an upcoming unit. Finally, I can work with any individual teachers who'd like to co-teach those writing-focused lessons in their classes. Does that sound like a plan?"

Justin replied with an enthusiastic, "Yes!" and most of the teachers nodded in agreement.

Ebony left the meeting feeling encouraged that the layered coaching approach would be a perfect way to address the goals and needs of the social studies department regarding writing instruction. She then went back to her office to sketch out her plans for implementing the layered coaching model. Over the next week, Ebony spoke with Justin several times to get his input, and she also spoke with several of the social studies teachers to make sure that what she was planning would meet their needs.

At the next social studies department meeting, Ebony was given 30 minutes to work with the teachers regarding writing expectations and writing instruction. She began the large-group coaching session by sharing Table 4 from the C3 Framework (National Council for the Social Studies, 2013) that provides "Connections between the C3 Framework and the CCR Anchor Standards in the ELA/Literacy Common Core Standards" (p. 20). Using the C3 dimensions of developing questions and planning inquiries, gathering and evaluating sources, developing claims and using evidence, communicating and critiquing conclusions, and taking action, she facilitated a discussion about what the standards expected of students (and teachers) related to writing.

Ebony then asked the teachers to work in small groups to discuss the types of writing-intensive assignments they give, the types of writing instruction they provide, and the gaps they see for writing in their social studies courses. After the small groups had about 10 minutes to talk, Ebony asked each group to share the most important ideas from their discussion. As the groups shared, Ebony wrote notes on the white board. She then suggested, "This is a really good foundation for what the standards expect students to do with writing in social studies and where you are as a department with writing instruction. I think we're now ready to take it to the individual course level because there is a big difference between your freshman world history and AP U.S. history."

Justin readily agreed, and he suggested, "I think the teachers of two courses should take this to the next level and work with Ebony on developing instructional goals and model lessons. Since we are all concerned about our two required courses, I think we should begin there with world history and U.S. history. We can then add other courses in the near future."

Ebony waited to hear the teachers' responses, and they concurred that focusing on these required courses made the most sense. Ebony then agreed and told the teachers she'd follow up with them to schedule a time to meet with those who taught world history and another time for those who taught U.S. history.

When Ebony met with each of these teams, she worked with them to take the expectations from the writing standards and create measurable writing goals. She continued to use the small-group layer of coaching as she collaborated with the teachers over the next few weeks to address those writing goals within the upcoming unit of instruction. During this process, Ebony took on the role of collaborator, but she did find herself taking the lead in locating resources and typing up the writing portions of the unit plans. Knowing that her schedule was more flexible than the teachers' schedules, she was comfortable with taking on more responsibility for these tasks. In addition, by taking on some of these time-consuming tasks, she thought she could keep the group's momentum moving forward.

Next, Ebony contacted the teachers for each of the courses and offered to co-teach the unit or any of the lessons. In addition, she extended an invitation to meet with any individual teacher who wanted to co-plan and co-teach additional lessons related to writing in their courses. Caitlyn was the first teacher to ask Ebony for individual coaching support. Caitlyn explained, "With the freshmen in my world history class, this is all new to them. I am comfortable with the unit we created together, but I am stumped on how I can plan other lessons or units to address writing in my class." Ebony scheduled a time to meet with Caitlyn during her planning period, and they developed a plan for working together to address Caitlyn's concerns. A few days later, Rayvon Webb, a U.S. history teacher, also contacted Ebony, asking her for more help with planning instruction for writing arguments.

As Ebony reflected back on this process, she was pleased with the layered coaching approach for several reasons. First, because she worked with the whole department, all of the teachers were able to learn about the writing expectations of the new standards. This created a shared understanding and sense of urgency to address writing instruction in their classes. In the small groups, she had been able to guide the teachers to take their knowledge of the standards and apply it to creating measurable goals related to writing and to incorporate those writing goals into an instructional unit. Finally, by working one-on-one with some of the teachers, she had been able to provide the specific support those teachers needed to address writing more fully in their classes. An unexpected but positive outcome for Ebony was that she now understood the social studies curriculum and knew all of the teachers in that department.

One afternoon, Justin stopped Ebony in the hallway. He explained, "I'm seeing more writing instruction in our world history and U.S. history classes, but I'd like

- Keep the focus on meeting the standards and supporting student learning.
- Start with a willing department.
- Ensure you have support from the department chair.
- Make sure at least some of the teachers in the department are on board from the beginning.
- Schedule large-group coaching during already scheduled meetings such as department meetings or PLC meetings so teachers don't feel as though coaching is just one more thing that has to be done.
- Recruit willing teachers to participate in small-group coaching.
- Work with willing teachers for individual coaching.
- Encourage teachers who participate in small-group or individual coaching to share their experiences with their colleagues to help spread coaching across the department.

FIGURE 1. Insights and tips for implementing a layered coaching approach.

that to be true across our whole department. Any chance you'd be willing to work with the teachers of the other social studies classes?" Ebony smiled and responded, "Absolutely. Let's look at schedules and make this happen."

Ebony was so pleased with how the layered coaching approach had worked that she mentioned it to her colleague, Maria Reyes, the literacy coach at the other high school in the district. Maria was intrigued by the idea and asked Ebony to share the most important insights and tips that made her experiences with layered coaching a success (see Figure 1).

Getting into Classrooms

Diana Lopez is a new disciplinary literacy coach at Morgan Community High School (MCHS). She was an English teacher for 9 years before becoming a literacy coach, but this is her first year at this school. Diana is the only literacy coach in her high school, and she is expected to spend 100% of her time engaged in literacy coaching. During her first few weeks at MCHS, Diana spent most of her time trying to meet teachers, learn about the curriculum, and understand how the school operated. She started her coaching with large-group activities such as doing short professional development presentations at department meetings and leading article study groups for the science, social studies, and English departments. The teachers were excited to read and discuss the articles, but when Diana tried to follow up with the teachers to get into their classrooms to help them plan and teach lessons using the new ideas from the articles, they politely but consistently declined. After several months, Diana began to worry that she could not become an effective literacy coach if she could not get into classrooms and do some heavy coaching (Killion, 2009, 2010) that would affect student learning in positive ways.

Diana scheduled a meeting with her principal, Mrs. O'Leary, and her assistant principal, Mr. Walton, to discuss her concerns. They agreed that the large-group coaching Diana was doing seemed to be working well but that she needed to devote her efforts to working with small groups and individual teachers. Diana said she would review articles and books about literacy coaching to see what suggestions she could find for getting into classrooms. She also mentioned that she had a friend who had been a literacy coach for 3 years in a high school in another state. Diana said she would talk to her friend to see if she could offer any practical suggestions of things that had worked for her to gain access to classrooms. Mrs. O'Leary also agreed to "talk up" the disciplinary literacy coaching program so the teachers knew it was an important and valued initiative at MCHS.

While reviewing the coaching resources (e.g., Bean & DeFord, 2012; Elish-Piper et al., 2009; Frost, n.d.), Diana realized that, because she was new to the school, none of the teachers had ever seen her teach. They didn't know whether she was an effective teacher or whether she knew how to work well with their students and in their disciplines. She determined that she needed to establish her credibility as a teacher with her colleagues. At department meetings and in the school's teacher announcements, she volunteered to go to the classroom of every teacher she was supposed to coach to do a short lesson on vocabulary, writing-to-learn strategies, or using technology to build background knowledge. She framed this invitation as a way to get to know the students, and several of the teachers took her up on her offer. As she prepared, she made sure to meet with the teacher, discuss the curriculum, learn about the students in the course, and align the lesson with some aspect of disciplinary literacy. After each lesson, she debriefed with the teacher to see how he or she thought the process went and whether he or she wanted to schedule a follow-up modeled lesson, to co-teach a lesson, or to co-plan a lesson. These short lessons led to a few additional teachers inviting Diana in to model a lesson in their classrooms; however, quite a few teachers still declined to work with Diana beyond the large-group coaching she did with their departments. Throughout her first year at MCHS, Diana tried many approaches to gain access to classrooms, and those that she found most effective are summarized in Figure 1.

Diana also asked teachers to fill out a survey to help her learn what types of coaching support they wanted (see Form 1). The survey served two main purposes. First, it helped Diana identify which teachers were interested in working with her. Second, it clarified the range of coaching support she could provide. Diana now distributes the survey at the beginning of each semester to ensure that she is regularly reaching out to all teachers to offer coaching support.

Strategy	Description and considerations
How Can I Help? survey	Create and distribute a survey to see what types of coaching support teachers are interested in using. The survey can also include topics related to specific disciplinary literacy practices or standards. See Form 1 for a sample survey.
Be visible	Walk the halls. Eat in the teachers' lunch room, at different times, if possible. Visit the library/media center, department offices, and teacher work rooms frequently. By making yourself visible, you can initiate conversations with teachers and start to lay the groundwork for collaborative working relationships that include individual coaching in classrooms.
Share technology resources	Many teachers spend lots of time looking for the "just right" video, website, or technology tool. Make lists of the best technology resources for certain purposes and courses, and share these with teachers. This may then lead to co-planning, co-teaching, or modeling how to use those technology resources.
Focus on a student or a specific class	Offer to assess, observe, or provide instruction to a student or small group of students about whom the teacher has concerns. Meet with the teacher to share your insights and suggestions for supporting the student(s). Offer to model, co-plan, or co-teach a lesson that supports the student(s). If a teacher identifies a specific class that is challenging to teach, offer to visit the class to observe the students and to meet with the teacher to discuss your observations and to collaboratively identify strategies to address those challenges.
Take on the role of learner	Ask teachers if you can visit their classrooms or meet with them to learn about their curriculum and students. Ask questions such as, "What are the bottlenecks in your class where student learning gets stopped?" You can then offer to work with the teacher to investigate how to address these challenges.
Bond over life outside the classroom	Let the teachers get to know you. Have casual conversations about your families, hobbies, travels, or interests. Even talking about a TV show, movie, sports team, favorite restaurant, or current event can begin to lay the groundwork for positive working relationships with teachers.
Provide "crunch time" support	There are predictable crunch times, such as the first day of school, open houses, report cards, final exams, and parent–teacher conferences. Offer to help teachers prepare their classrooms, organize materials, or even grade assignments. Doing so will show that you are willing to "roll up your sleeves" and work. Teachers will appreciate your help and will be likely to invite you back to their classrooms for coaching support.
Establish yourself as a helpful resource by getting creative	You can offer to cover a teacher's classroom so she or he can observe in a colleague's classroom or meet with another teacher to collaborate. Offer to track down texts or instructional resources for classroom activities. If you have chocolate or coffee in your office, invite teachers to stop in any time they need a pick-me-up. These types of helpful activities will lead to conversations, positive relationships, and opportunities to visit classrooms.
Start with willing teachers	If you start with willing teachers and make sure they are pleased with the coaching support you provide, they will share these experiences with their colleagues. Eventually, the word will spread about the value of working with the literacy coach.

FIGURE 1. Useful strategies for getting into classrooms.

How Can I Help? Survey

Dear Teachers:

As the literacy coach at our school, there are lots of things I can do to support your professional development and teaching, especially related to disciplinary literacy practices. Please review this list and identify those coaching activities that you believe will be most helpful to you this year. Please put a check mark (✓) next to any coaching activities that you are definitely interested in and a question mark (?) next to any activities about which you'd like more information.

I would like to collaborate with you about one or more of the following:

_____ Selecting vocabulary   _____ Addressing text complexity

_____ Examining student work   _____ Developing discussion protocols

_____ Creating essential questions   _____ Other (please specify):

I would like you to do one or more of the following:

_____ Model a lesson in my classroom   _____ Co-plan with me

_____ Co-teach with me   _____ Observe specific students in my class

I would like coaching support:

_____ As soon as possible   _____ Within a month   _____ Let's set a meeting to plan a time.

The best time for me to meet with the literacy coach is:

_____ Before school   _____ My plan period   _____ After school   _____ Other (specify)

I am most interested in coaching related to these aspects of disciplinary literacy:

_____ Comprehending discipline-specific texts   _____ Viewing and representing

_____ Conceptual and technical vocabulary   _____ Engaging in disciplinary talk

_____ Habits of thinking in the discipline   _____ Other (please specify)

Please return this survey to my mailbox in the office as soon as you have completed it. Thanks!

From *Collaborative Coaching for Disciplinary Literacy: Strategies to Support Teachers in Grades 6–12* by Laurie Elish-Piper, Susan K. L'Allier, Michael Manderino, and Paula Di Domenico. Copyright © 2016 The Guilford Press. Permission to photocopy this form is granted to purchasers of this book for personal use only (see copyright page for details). Purchasers can download additional copies of this form (see the box at the end of the table of contents).

Differentiating Coaching to Support All Teachers

Dontrell Moore is an experienced disciplinary literacy coach at Walker's Grove Community High School. He is currently in his 4th year of coaching, and, before that, he was an English teacher at a nearby high school for 16 years. Before he started coaching, Dontrell completed a certificate of graduate studies at the local state university in instructional coaching, and he has also taken several courses and workshops specifically about literacy coaching. When we recently saw Dontrell at a meeting, we asked him how his coaching was going. He reported, "I had a breakthrough at the beginning of last year. I realized that just like teaching students where one size doesn't fit all, coaching teachers is the same. I needed to think about the teacher and whether she was new or experienced. I had to think about her challenges and goals. I had to consider her teaching style and discipline, and a bunch of other things. I realized that just like differentiating instruction for students, I could and really should differentiate coaching for the teachers." He went on to explain, "Once I stopped looking for the perfect coaching strategy, I was able to relax and take a more strategic approach to finding the right type and amount of support for a teacher or group of teachers at a specific point in time. I was able to let go of some of my previous frustrations when teachers didn't respond as I thought they would or should. I am now able to approach my coaching more strategically by listening carefully and considering what I know about the teacher and the discipline."

Dontrell shared how, in his 3rd year of coaching, he began using four key considerations to help him differentiate coaching for the teachers with whom he works (Moran, 2007). These four considerations are (1) teacher experience, (2) discipline, (3) goals and challenges, and (4) disposition. Dontrell went on to explain that "there isn't a perfect formula to differentiate how I provide coaching, but I've found some useful practices that have really enhanced my effectiveness with coaching lots of different teachers. For example, in the area of experience, I have learned that when I work with newer teachers, they tend to prefer for me to take more of a consulting stance where I offer specific advice for what has worked for me or other experienced teachers. They tend to want me to guide them through the process of co-planning and then co-teaching lessons. On the other hand, more experienced teachers often like me to take on more of collaborative stance where we work as partners or even a facilitative stance where I'm more of a sounding board for them so they can figure things out almost independently. In terms of the discipline, I make sure that I always remember that the chemistry teacher is most concerned about teaching chemistry content, skills, and strategies. Discipline has to come first in any coaching conversations or it won't lead to anything. Obviously, teachers' goals and challenges need to be front and center in all coaching so it is relevant, meaningful, and productive for teachers. I also consider teachers' dispositions—things like whether the teacher is quiet and prefers to work alone or is outgoing and collaborative." For a summary of Dontrell's insights about differentiating coaching support for teachers, see Figure 1.

Dontrell explained that once he realized that coaching was not a cut-and-dried endeavor, he was able to change his expectations and those of the teachers in his building. At the end of our conversation, he said, "I stopped looking for the perfect coaching strategy or feeling frustrated when teachers didn't want the type of support I was offering. I now think of coaching as a type of matchmaking—finding the right approach or type of support for a teacher at a particular moment in time."

Characteristic	Strategies for coaching
Experience	New teachers • New teachers tend to want to be told what works and how to do it. Taking a consulting stance generally works well with most new teachers. • Check in with new teachers often. They tend to become overwhelmed easily, and they appreciate knowing that the coach cares and is available to support them. Veteran teachers • Experienced teachers tend to want the coach to take a collaborative stance (in which the teacher and coach are partners) or a facilitative stance (in which the teacher leads the process and the coach is a sounding board). • Veteran teachers often decline to work with the coach, but they tend to be most receptive when the coach acknowledges the teachers' expertise and asks to learn from and with the teacher. Experience with a strategy or initiative • When teachers do not have experience with a strategy or new initiative, they tend to need more encouragement and reassurance from the coach. Two useful strategies are sharing concrete examples and connecting these teachers with others who have already implemented the strategy or made strides with the new initiative.
Discipline	Discipline is the first consideration. • Teachers' approaches to instruction, classroom organization and management, and interactions with students are framed around their disciplines. • Always begin coaching conversations with teachers by addressing the disciplinary content, skills, and processes the teacher wants to address in instruction. • Situate the teacher as the expert in the discipline. If your background is in another discipline, don't try to get the teacher to think like you. It won't work! • Avoid saying negative things about other teachers' disciplines. For example, don't say, "I don't understand algebra at all. It's so hard and confusing!"

Goals and challenges	Begin with teacher goals and challenges.
	• Frame all coaching around specific goals and/or challenges that teachers have identified.
	• Even with hesitant teachers, asking questions such as, "What goals are you working toward with your students and how can I help?" and "When you think about the goals you want your students to reach, what challenges do you face?"
	• Two great prompts to use with teachers are:
	  o "What can I do to support you as you work on your goals?"
	  o "How can I help as you work to overcome that challenge?"

Disposition	Dispositions affect everything.
	• Teacher attitudes, state of mind, and natural inclinations are important considerations when working in a coaching relationship.
	• Listen carefully and observe closely to learn more about how teachers think, work, and react in different situations.
	• If you are uncertain about how to work best with a teacher or group of teachers, ASK! Some prompts you can use are:
	  o "What role would you like me to take? Leader, partner, or facilitator?"
	  o "How would you like to structure our collaboration so that it works best for you?"
	  o "What do you want me to know about working effectively with you?"

FIGURE 1. Differentiating disciplinary literacy coaching.

Working with Hesitant Teachers

When we first met Crystal Jones, she was in the middle of her first year as a literacy coach at Morton Hills Middle School. Prior to becoming a literacy coach, she had been a sixth-grade ELA and social studies teacher at the school for 9 years. When the new literacy coaching position was announced the previous spring, she immediately applied. Crystal had recently earned her M.S.Ed. in literacy education, which included several courses focused on literacy coaching, and this coaching position would give her an opportunity to apply her new knowledge and skills. In the fall, Crystal worked closely with her school's administrative team to announce the literacy coaching program and to clarify how she could support teachers. Overall, she told us that she is pleased with how things are going with coaching at her school; however, she is concerned about some teachers who seem hesitant, or even resistant, to work with her. She has tried many of the suggestions that she learned about in her graduate program and in articles and online sources she has read. She's had some success with these approaches, but they have not worked with all of the teachers. She feels that she needs to go beyond just surveying the teachers about how she can help, making herself visible, and volunteering to come into classrooms to model or co-teach. As Crystal recently said to her principal, Mrs. Valerie DeVaney, "I feel like I need to understand why the teachers are hesitant and sometimes even resistant to coaching so I know what to do to reach out to them. They are friendly with me, but they seem to 'run in the other direction' when they hear me talking about coaching!" Mrs. DeVaney agreed and encouraged Crystal to talk to other coaches in the district and to look for articles or books that address this topic. Crystal said she would also contact her professor from the literacy coaching classes she had completed to see if he had ideas about working with hesitant teachers.

After consulting various resources and talking with other coaches and her professor, Crystal realized that there are several common reasons why teachers may be hesitant to engage with literacy coaching in general (Knight, 2009; Toll, 2014). Given that her charge is to work with English, science, and social studies teachers, she realized that disciplinary matters can also contribute to why teachers hesitate to engage in coaching. Crystal listed these reasons on a chart to help her begin thinking about how she could address these issues in her interactions with the hesitant teachers. She then created a list of suggestions to help in addressing each of the reasons so she'd have a starting place to talk to and work with these teachers. As the semester went on and Crystal was able to try the suggestions, she updated her list to show those that were the most effective for building connections with the hesitant teachers in her school (see Figure 1).

Crystal also kept in mind that the change process can be challenging and stressful for teachers (and coaches, too) but that there are fairly predictable stages that teachers progress through as they encounter a new initiative. She realized that she tended to think that a teacher was hesitant or even resistant to change when he or she may have just been trying to figure out what disciplinary literacy coaching is or how to implement it. Crystal realized that if her coaching support was not answering the specific questions that teachers have, they might become "stuck" and unable to move forward, which could look a lot like resistance. By listening carefully to what teachers said and the types of questions they asked, Crystal found that she could identify which stage of the change process the teacher was at so she could adjust her coaching approach and stance accordingly. Figure 2 provides a summary of how Crystal approached hesitant teachers who were at each stage of the change process.

Crystal was also concerned that hesitant teachers would interact with her as a resource for information or materials but would not agree to work with her on the more intense, intentional, and meaningful aspects of coaching—in other words, heavy coaching (Killion, 2009, 2010). She found that by listening carefully to what the teachers said and considering possible reasons for the teachers' comments, she was usually able to develop a response that was directly aligned to the situation. She frequently used Toll's (2014) variation of "the Question" by asking, "When you think about the understanding that you want your students to have when they learn [insert discipline here], what gets in the way?" (p. 68). She often found that this question opened the door to having a meaningful conversation with the teacher that then led to more in-depth coaching opportunities. Several samples of how Crystal used "the Question" effectively with hesitant teachers are presented in Figure 3.

Crystal is now in her 3rd year of coaching at Morton Hills Middle School. When we asked her if she had any new insights about working with hesitant teachers, she responded, "The ideas in this profile still work remarkably well. What I have learned over the past few years is that if a teacher continues to decline to work with me, I can't take it personally. I just need to find the right time and situation

Causes of hesitation or resistance	Suggestions for moving beyond the causes of hesitation or resistance
Teacher questions the value of disciplinary literacy instruction and disciplinary literacy coaching.	• Enlist other teachers who embrace the value of disciplinary literacy instruction and coaching so they can share their perspectives. • Promote proven and powerful teaching strategies that are easy to plan and implement. • Explain the expectations and ramifications of disciplinary literacy instruction on teaching and testing. • Provide or collect outcome data when possible to show the impact of disciplinary literacy instruction. • Talk with the teacher about his or her concerns about disciplinary literacy instruction to get a better sense of the specific things the teacher finds troublesome.
Teacher doesn't have the time or energy to implement disciplinary literacy instruction or to work with the coach.	• Acknowledge that the teacher feels overwhelmed and/or overscheduled. • Be respectful of the teacher's time. • Focus on a small number of effective instructional practices that are easy to plan and implement. • Streamline the work involved with implementing disciplinary literacy instruction. • Promote collaboration so that no teacher feels he or she needs to work alone. • Share resources and offer to complete organizational tasks such as preparing materials to free up the teacher to work on the instructional aspects.
Teacher believes his or her expertise and experience are not valued.	• Invite and value teacher voice and input. • Provide teacher choice related to disciplinary literacy instruction. • Provide meaningful opportunities for teachers to share, network, and engage in professional conversations related to disciplinary literacy instruction.
Teacher is at a different stage of the change process from that at which coaching support is being offered and provided.	• Listen carefully to what the teacher says to determine the stage of the change process at which the teacher is currently operating. • Adjust coaching to address that stage of the change process (see Part II, subsection on "Understanding the Change Process"). • Use the ideas offered in Figure 2.
Teacher is concerned that disciplinary literacy instruction will diminish the emphasis on the discipline.	• Begin by talking about what the teacher wants to accomplish in his or her teaching. • Take the stance that literacy is a tool to help the teacher and students meet disciplinary goals and outcomes. • Acknowledge and embrace the teacher's role as the expert on the discipline. • Don't force a strategy or lesson on a teacher. If he or she doesn't think it is appropriate, honor the teacher's professional judgment.

FIGURE 1. Addressing causes of teacher hesitation or resistance.

to connect with the teacher. Over time, the teachers hear from their colleagues that I helped them with this or that, and they come to me and say, 'Hey, can you help me with that, too?' Probably the best advice I got was from a book that offered the reminder 'Q-TIP: Quit Taking It Personally' [Elish-Piper & L'Allier, 2014, pp. 202–203]. Teachers' hesitancy is about the change, the new approach to disciplinary literacy, and the thousand other demands on their time. It's not all about me, and that helps so my feelings don't get hurt and I can hang in there until it's the right time and situation for each teacher."

CBAM stage	Focus of concern	Question	Sample coaching activities to support teachers
Awareness	Self	What is it?	• Clarify the definition of disciplinary literacy. • Share examples of disciplinary literacy practices in the teacher's content area.
Information	Self	How does it work?	• Share, review, and discuss the relevant learning standards. • Highlight the role that disciplinary literacy plays in the standards. • Share examples of lessons focused on disciplinary literacy practices in the teacher's discipline.
Personal	Self	How does this affect me? What is my plan to do it?	• Confer with the teacher to discuss and help develop specific plans for and assignments related to disciplinary literacy. • Work with the teacher to set realistic goals and provide coaching support to reach those goals.
Management	Implementation	How can I master the skills and fit it all in?	• Connect the teacher with a peer who is already implementing disciplinary literacy instruction. • Model lessons in classrooms. • Co-plan lessons and units of study. • Co-teach lessons and units of study.
Consequence	Results	Is it worth it? Is it working?	• Review assessment data and student work to determine impact. • Provide professional development to address areas in which student performance does not meet standards.
Collaboration	Results	How do others do it?	• Provide time and space for teachers within a discipline to share lessons and resources. • Provide time for the teacher to visit another classroom to observe a peer's practice.
Refocusing	Results	Is there anything else that's better?	• Engage the teacher in self-assessment. • Encourage the teacher to research ways to enhance practice or build on disciplinary literacy instruction.

FIGURE 2. Using the CBAM stages to guide coaching.

Teacher's statement	Possible reasons for the teacher's statement	Coach's response
"I don't have time to teach this reading and writing stuff. Shouldn't that be done in their ELA class?"	The teacher doesn't understand the purpose of disciplinary literacy.	"You're right. They do teach a lot of reading and writing strategies in the ELA classes. But what they teach doesn't specifically address your discipline. *When you think about the understanding you want your students to develop in [insert discipline here], what gets in the way?*"
"There's nothing I need help with."	The teacher does not have any specific goals. The teacher is hesitant to open up his or her practice to others. The teacher does not want to disclose that he or she does not understand or know how to implement a specific disciplinary literacy instructional approach or strategy.	"*When you think about the understanding you want your students to develop in [insert discipline here], the type of teaching you want to do, or the kind of classroom you want to have, what gets in the way?*" "I'd like to learn about your work for my own sake. Because I coach so many teachers in different disciplines, I need to learn what instruction and learning look like across our school. Can we talk about your course and expectations so I can learn more about what you and your students are doing?"
"No offense, but you don't teach in my discipline. I'm not sure that you can teach me anything that applies to my classes."	The teacher doesn't understand the purpose of disciplinary literacy coaching. The teacher is focused on the course content and not the skills, strategies, and habits of thinking used in the discipline.	"No offense taken. I'm here to help, and I've already worked with several of the teachers in your discipline. They have found it helpful when we worked together on . . ." "I have been looking at the curriculum in your discipline and at the common assessment results. I noticed that one area where students seem to struggle is. . . . I'd like for us to talk about *what gets in the way of the students' understanding* in this area so we can work together to figure out some solutions."

FIGURE 3. Using "the Question" to respond to hesitant teachers.

Using Tools and Tips for Productive Coaching

Beth Glawinski is a full-time disciplinary literacy coach at Franklin Middle School. She has been coaching for 4 years and previously worked at Franklin as a reading specialist. Beth is one of three disciplinary literacy coaches in her school district. Each coach is assigned to a different middle school, but they get together monthly to meet with Jacqui Brady, the district's coordinator of professional development. At these monthly meetings, Beth and the other two coaches, Stephen Jordan and Joan Marie Pappas, share their successes and challenges. Last month at their meeting, Beth lamented, "I feel like I'm swimming upstream as fast as I can, but I don't seem to have enough time to do everything on my to-do list." Stephen agreed and added, "I try to spend as much time as I can in classrooms and in conversations with teachers, but that means I never have time to get organized." Joan Marie chimed in, "A lot of the time I feel like I'm reinventing the wheel as I create yet another form, protocol, or resource. There's got to be a better way!"

Upon hearing their concerns, Jacqui suggested that they start each of their monthly meetings by sharing useful coaching tools and resources to help them improve their organization, effectiveness, and efficiency. All three coaches agreed, and this profile highlights several of the most useful coaching tools they shared from their own practices.

Beth shared a daily coaching log she recently had started using to record her coaching activities, follow-up plans, and coaching outcomes. She keeps a paper copy of her coaching log in a three-ring binder so she can write down information throughout the day as it happens. Since she started keeping a coaching log, Beth reports that she is more strategic about how she spends her time. For example, Beth had previously worked with a group of science teachers to develop lessons on reading and interpreting graphs and tables. However, when she looked at her recent coaching logs, it surprised her to see that she had not had a single interaction with a science teacher for 2 weeks. Once she realized this, Beth scheduled a follow-up meeting to talk with the teachers to see how the lessons were going and whether there was anything she could do to support their work. Beth also uses her log to make sure she is serving all of the teachers she is assigned to coach, which includes all of the ELA, social studies, and science teachers at her school. A blank coaching log is provided in Form 1.

Beth also has created a list of "go to" questions and prompts to guide her coaching, especially when conversations feel like they are getting stuck (see Figure 1). She keeps these prompts in her coaching binder, as well as on the desktop of her laptop computer. She also relies on a variation of Cathy Toll's "the Question" (2005, 2014) to get conversations going. "The Question" asks, "When you think about the kind of learning you want your students to do, what gets in the way?" Beth then uses the obstacles, challenges, and hurdles that teachers identify as the catalyst for their coaching work. She explains, "When we are working to solve real problems the teachers are facing, they are very motivated and committed to coaching. They see the value of coaching to help them resolve these problems."

Beth often jokes that she is a sprinter—running from one end of the building to the other and then back again. Because she rarely has a spare moment, Beth finds that being highly organized is essential. Some of her favorite organizational tips are summarized in Figure 2.

Beth is often asked to facilitate professional development (PD) sessions for teams or other groups at her school. In her first year as a coach, she started planning each PD session from scratch and found that this involved countless hours of work. Beth realized that having a small collection of easy-to-implement professional development activities and formats allowed her to focus on the content and processes of the PD sessions (see Figure 3). Beth explains, "These ideas are surefire successes. They get teachers involved, talking, thinking, and working together."

Beth points out, "These tips and tools have worked well for me and the other coaches in my district, but I'm always on the lookout for useful ideas that can make my coaching more efficient and effective. By connecting with my coaching colleagues on a regular basis to share these effective ideas, we pool our ideas and we all benefit!"

To get the conversation started
- "What would you like to see the students do better?"
- "What do the students find most challenging?"
- "What do you want to work on?"
- "What concerns you?"
- "What's going well?"
- "What can I do to help?"

To keep the conversation going
- "Say more about that. . . ."
- "What do you think?"
- "I wonder. . . ."

FIGURE 1. Coaching prompts for any situation.

- Color coding saves time and ensures you can find what you need when you need it. Color code files and resources by department, discipline, or teacher.
- Take 10–15 minutes at the end of each day to get organized. Record notes, double-check your to-do list, and get things ready for the next morning.
- Go digital! Use your laptop or iPad for all of your coaching work. This will allow you to have everything you need right at your fingertips.
- Your calendar is your best friend. Review your calendar at the end of each day so you can plan for the next day's coaching activities (or to make sure you are ready for the next day's coaching activities). Review your calendar at the beginning of each day so you know where you need to be, when you need to be there, and what you need to bring with you.
- Wear a watch or use the clock on your phone, laptop, or iPad to keep track of time. If you get off schedule with one coaching activity, the rest of your day can quickly get derailed.
- Create a checkout system for your books and instructional materials to keep track of which items teachers have borrowed.
- Organize electronic files that contain graphic organizers, sample lesson and unit plans, and other relevant resources on the school's shared computer drive so teachers can access them when they need them.

FIGURE 2. Organizational tips for coaching.

Format	Description
What would you do?	Present one or more scenarios that describe a teaching problem or decision that needs to be made. You can focus the scenarios on department or course-specific goals or learning standards to make them directly relevant to the teachers' work. Teachers work in small groups to discuss how to address the situation, and, if time permits, they present their ideas to the whole group.
Strategy demonstrations	Demonstrate an instructional strategy with the teachers participating as students. Use the "push 'pause'" technique periodically to explain what you are doing and why, so that teachers understand the instructional decisions involved with the strategy. Conclude the session by asking teachers to discuss how they could apply ideas from the strategy demonstrations into their classrooms.
Feedback carousel	Get feedback from a large group of teachers in a relatively short period of time. This strategy works well in such situations as a department creating a plan for a complex learning task, such as how they will teach students to write arguments or to synthesize comprehension of multiple texts. Put the key components of the plan on sheets of chart paper and post them on the walls around the meeting room. Explain that each quadrant of the paper has a specific purpose: the top left is for clarifying questions to ensure that the ideas are clear and complete, the top right is for probing questions to promote deeper thinking or encourage considering other perspectives, the bottom left is for recommendations of how to modify the plan, and the bottom right is for resources that will be needed. Give the teachers small sticky notes and ask them to rotate to each sheet of chart paper, write their feedback on a sticky note, and place it in the appropriate quadrant. Reserve several minutes to debrief the process and determine next steps.

FIGURE 3. Easy and effective formats for professional development sessions. Adapted from *www.nsrfharmony.org/system/files/protocols/consult_stud_work_0.pdf.* Copyright 2014 by the National School Reform Faculty® (NSRF). Reprinted by permission. NSRF® emphasizes that the protocols are most powerful and effective when facilitated by a trained coach.

Coaching Log

Day and time	Coaching activity	Teachers and disciplines	Disciplinary literacy focus	Outcomes	Coach follow-up
Monday					
Tuesday					
Wednesday					
Thursday					
Friday					

Weekly Coaching Summary and Reflection: What went well, what was challenging, what did I learn, and what do I need to do next?

From *Collaborative Coaching for Disciplinary Literacy: Strategies to Support Teachers in Grades 6–12* by Laurie Elish-Piper, Susan K. L'Allier, Michael Manderino, and Paula Di Domenico. Copyright © 2016 The Guilford Press. Permission to photocopy this form is granted to purchasers of this book for personal use only (see copyright page for details). Purchasers can download additional copies of this form (see the box at the end of the table of contents).

Developing a Support System

Marilyn Porter was a high school English teacher for 25 years at Central High School before she decided to "take a leap" and accept a position as a disciplinary literacy coach at the same school. Because all of the teachers and administrators already knew her and she already knew them, the curriculum, and the community, Marilyn expected she'd have an easy transition from teacher to coach. Although this was true in some respects, she often found herself feeling lonely, isolated, and "out of the loop."

Marilyn soon realized that the work she was doing as a disciplinary literacy coach was very different from what she had done as a teacher. She craved opportunities to talk to others about coaching, but she was the only coach at Central High School. Marilyn decided that she needed to look beyond her own school and create her own system of support. The first thing she did was reach out to the coaches at her district's four middle schools and the other high school. She asked them if they would like to meet informally to share ideas, challenges, and resources. All of the coaches agreed, and they scheduled a time to meet at a local coffee shop one day after school. Their initial conversation lasted almost 2 hours, and they decided to get together each month. Marilyn was pleased to have others to talk to about her coaching experiences, challenges, and questions.

While Marilyn valued the camaraderie of the other coaches, she also thirsted for professional development and guidance in her coaching work. Marilyn asked the other coaches if they felt the same way, and they all agreed that they did. On behalf of the group, Marilyn contacted the district literacy coordinator, Ms. Nadiya Shah, about having regular meetings that focused on professional development in coaching. Ms. Shah agreed and now meets with the coaches once per month. They have read and discussed articles and books about literacy coaching, including the book *Student-Centered Coaching at the Secondary Level* (Sweeney, 2013). Ms. Shah also suggested that each coach bring a "rose" and a "thorn" to each meeting. The "rose" was to focus on the best thing that had happened in their coaching since the previous meeting, and the "thorn" was to be the most difficult thing they had experienced in their coaching during the month. This part of the meeting soon became Marilyn's favorite because it provided an opportunity for the group to discuss the "thorns" and come up with possible solutions or next steps.

Marilyn spent a great deal of time online researching information about coaching. She learned about professional conferences, webinars, and Twitter chats related to literacy coaching, and she participated as often as she could. She also made sure to share her "finds" with the other coaches in her district, and they in turn shared their resources with her. Marilyn also joined Learning Forward, the professional learning association. Through this membership she was able to receive their journal, attend their conference, and access online professional development resources. Marilyn explained, "I am motivated to learn as much as I can about coaching. I have even been able to find helpful resources online at sites like Pinterest, Facebook, and Twitter."

Marilyn and the other coaches in her school district have started to extend their network to other nearby school districts. They recently organized a Saturday-morning secondary coaches meeting at a public library. They invited instructional coaches, literacy coaches, and disciplinary literacy coaches from nearby middle and high schools. Marilyn and her colleagues facilitated the meeting using a similar format to what they had been using at their monthly meetings with Ms. Shah, including sharing "roses" and "thorns." Marilyn recently reported, "It's amazing how much I'm learning from other coaches. It's great to have a group of people who understand what I face as a disciplinary literacy coach. I highly recommend that all coaches build a network of support as they take on coaching duties."

Final Thoughts

As you engage in your work as a disciplinary literacy coach, you will face many challenges and opportunities. Throughout this book, we have provided effective strategies for coaching large groups of teachers, small groups of teachers, and individual teachers. We have also provided useful tools and tips to make your coaching more productive and effective. In closing, we want to share several ideas that we hope will be your biggest "take-aways" from this book. First, coaching adults is different from teaching students. Coaching requires that you understand how adults learn. By keeping adult learning principles in mind, you will be able to support the teachers' professional learning and growth. Second, adoption of new standards that address disciplinary literacy presents a major change for teachers. Learning about disciplinary literacy and updating their teaching will take time and effort. By understanding the change process and using CBAM to guide your coaching, you will be able to provide the types of support that teachers need. Third, by using the three layers of coaching—large group, small group, and individual—you can use your time efficiently and make sure that teachers understand "the big picture" as well as how to incorporate disciplinary literacy instruction into their classrooms.

As you work with the teachers at your school to address disciplinary literacy, we offer some compelling advice from a skilled high school coach, Brandy Hughes. She shares her coaching philosophy in the following statements: "As a teacher, I put my students first. As a coach, I put the teachers first. I'm here to be a guide, supporter, cheerleader, sounding board, and resource so that teachers can help their students become successful learners who meet challenging new standards. It's hard work because teachers are stressed, the stakes are high, and everyone is super busy. I try to be a calming influence by encouraging teachers, celebrating their accomplishments, and assuring them that we can make these changes—together as a team."

As you engage in your work as a disciplinary literacy coach, we offer these parting words of advice:

- Coaching is a relationship. Take time to get to know teachers so they are comfortable and confident in their work with you.
- Positioning matters. The teacher is an expert in the discipline. Position yourself as a helpful, supportive peer who can assist teachers with meeting their goals and addressing their challenges.
- It's all about the students. All coaching needs to focus on the end goal—helping students learn and succeed.

References

Allen, J. (2006). *Becoming a literacy leader: Supporting learning and change*. Portland, ME: Stenhouse.

Allen, J. (2007). *Layered coaching* [DVD]. Portland, ME: Stenhouse.

Alvermann, D. E. (1991). The discussion web: A graphic aid for learning across the curriculum. *Reading Teacher, 45*(2), 92–99.

American College Testing. (2006). Reading between the lines: What the ACT reveals about college readiness for reading. Retrieved from *http://act.org/path/policy/reports/reading.html*.

American Education Research Association. (2005). Research point: Teaching teachers: Professional development to improve student achievement (Vol. 3, Issue 1) [Brochure]. Washington, DC: Author. Retrieved from *www.aera.net*.

Bain, R. B. (2008). Into the breach: Using research and theory to shape history instruction. *Journal of Education, 198*(1/2), 159–167.

Bazerman, C. (1985). Physicists reading physics: Schema-laden purposes and purpose-laden schema. *Written Communication, 2*(1), 3–23.

Bean, R., & DeFord, D. (2012). Do's and don'ts for literacy coaches: Advice from the field [Literacy Coaching Clearinghouse Brief]. Retrieved from *www.literacycoachingonline.org/briefs/DosandDontsFinal.pdf*.

Bean, R. M. (2009). *The reading specialist: Leadership for the classroom, school, and community* (2nd ed.). New York: Guilford Press.

Bean, R. M., & Eisenberg, E. (2009). Literacy coaching in middle and high schools. In K. D. Wood & W. E. Blanton (Eds.), *Literacy instruction for adolescents: Research-based practice* (pp. 107–124). New York: Guilford Press.

Bean, R. M., Kern, D., Goatley, V., Ortlieb, E., Shettel, J., Calo, K., et al. (2015). Specialized literacy professionals as literacy leaders: Results of a national survey. *Literacy Research and Instruction, 54*(2), 83–114.

Biancarosa, G., Bryk, A. S., & Dexter, E. R. (2010). Assessing the value-added effects of Literacy Collaborative professional development on student learning. *Elementary School Journal, 111*(1), 7–34.

Blachowicz, C. L. Z. (1986). Making connections: Alternatives to the vocabulary notebook. *Journal of Reading, 29*(7), 643–649.

Bredeson, P., & Johansson, O. (2000). The school principal's role in teacher professional development. *Journal of In-Service Education, 26*(2), 385–401.

Brozo, W. G., Moorman, G., Meyer, C., & Stewart, T. (2013). Content-area reading and disciplinary literacy: A case for the radical center. *Journal of Adolescent and Adult Literacy, 56*(5), 353–357.

Bryk, A. S., Sebring, P. B., Allensworth, E., Luppescu, S., & Easton, J. Q. (2010). *Organizing schools for improvement.* Chicago: University of Chicago Press.

Buehl, D. (2011). *Developing readers in the academic disciplines.* Newark, DE: International Reading Association.

Burbank, M. D., Kauchak, D., & Bates, A. J. (2010). Book clubs as professional development opportunities for preservice teacher candidates and practicing teachers: An exploratory study. *New Educator, 6*(1), 56–73.

Casey, K. (2006). *Literacy coaching: The essentials.* Portsmouth, NH: Heinemann.

Chall, J. S. (1983). *Stages of reading development.* New York: McGraw-Hill.

Chappuis, J., Stiggins, R. J., Chappuis, S., & Arter, J. A. (2011). *Classroom assessment for student learning: Doing it right—using it well* (2nd ed.). Portland, OR: ETS Assessment Training Institute.

Christenbury, L., & Kelly, P. P. (1983). *Questioning: A path to critical thinking.* Urbana, IL: National Council of Teachers of English.

Cisneros, S. (1991). *The house on Mango Street.* New York: Vintage Books.

Commeyras, M., Bisplinghoff, B. S., & Olson, J. (Eds.). (2003). *Teachers as readers: Perspectives on the importance of reading in teachers' classrooms and lives.* Newark, DE: International Reading Association.

Conley, M. W. (2008). Cognitive strategy instruction for adolescents: What we know about the promise, what we don't know about the potential. *Harvard Educational Review, 78*(1), 84–106.

Cunningham, J. W. (2013). Research on text complexity: The Common Core State Standards as catalyst. In S. B. Neuman & L. B. Gambrell (Eds.), *Quality reading instruction in the age of Common Core Standards* (pp. 136–148). Newark, DE: International Reading Association.

Damico, J., Baildon, M., Exter, M., & Guo, S. (2009/2010). Where we read from matters: Disciplinary literacy in a ninth-grade social studies classroom. *Journal of Adolescent and Adult Literacy, 53*(4), 325–335.

Davey, B. (1983). Think aloud: Modeling the cognitive processes of reading comprehension. *Journal of Reading, 27*(1), 44–47.

Desimone, L. M. (2009). Improving impact studies of teachers' professional development: Toward better conceptualizations and measures. *Educational Researcher 38*(3), 181–189.

Di Domenico, P. M. (2014). *High school teachers' disciplinary literacy knowledge: A mixed-method study* (Doctoral dissertation). Available from ProQuest Dissertations and Theses database (UMI No. 3681928).

DuFour, R., DuFour, R., Eaker, R., & Many, T. (2010). *Learning by doing: A handbook for professional learning communities at work* (2nd ed.). Bloomington, IN: Solution Tree Press.

Elish-Piper, L., & L'Allier, S. K. (2014). *The Common Core coaching book: Strategies to help teachers address the K–5 ELA standards.* New York: Guilford Press.

Elish-Piper, L., L'Allier, S. K., Di Domenico, P., Manderino, M., Hyink, J., & Henry, M. (2012, April). *Literacy coaching at the secondary level: Promising practices for success.* Paper presented at the annual convention of the International Reading Association, Chicago, IL.

Elish-Piper, L., Manderino, M., Di Domenico, P., & L'Allier, S. K. (2014, November). *Disciplinary literacy coaching in high schools: Guiding principles for effective practice.* Paper presented at the annual conference of the Association of Literacy Educators and Researchers, Delray Beach, FL.

Elish-Piper, L. A., L'Allier, S. K., & Zwart, M. (2009). Literacy coaching: Challenges and promising practices for success. *Illinois Reading Council Journal, 37*(1), 10–21.

Faggella-Luby, M. N., Graner, P. S., Deshler, D. D., & Drew, S. V. (2012). Building a house on sand: Why disciplinary literacy is not sufficient to replace general strategies for adolescent learners who struggle. *Topics in Language Disorders, 32*(1), 69–84.

Fang, Z. (2012). Language correlates of disciplinary literacy. *Topics in Language Disorders, 32*, 19–34.

Fang, Z., & Coatoam, S. (2013). Disciplinary literacy: What you want to know about it. *Journal of Adolescent and Adult Literacy, 56*(8), 627–632.

Fisher, D., Brozo, W. G., Frey, N., & Ivey, G. (2014). *50 instructional routines to develop content literacy* (3rd ed.). New York: Pearson.

Fisher, D., & Frey, N. (2012, January). *ILA E-ssentials: Engaging the adolescent learner: Text complexity and close readings.* Newark, DE: International Literacy Association.

Flanigan, K., & Greenwood, S. (2007). Effective content vocabulary instruction in the middle: Matching students, purposes, words, and strategies. *Journal of Adolescent and Adult Literacy, 51*(3), 226–238.

Frey, N., & Fisher, D. (2011). *The formative assessment action plan: Practical steps to more successful teaching and learning.* Alexandria, VA: ASCD.

Frost, S. (n.d.). Eight tips for building relationships: A tale of two literacy coaches. Choice Literacy. Retrieved from *www.choiceliteracy.com/articles-detail-view.php?id=456.*

Geisler, C. (1994). Literacy and expertise in the academy. *Language and Learning across the Disciplines, 1*(1), 35–57.

Gillis, V. (2014a). Disciplinary literacy. *Journal of Adolescent and Adult Literacy, 57*(8), 614–623.

Gillis, V. (2014b). Talking the talk: Vocabulary instruction across the disciplines (or what to do instead). *Journal of Adolescent and Adult Literacy, 58*(4), 281–287.

Grant, M., Lapp, D., Fisher, D., Johnson, K., & Frey, N. (2012). Purposeful instruction: Mixing up the "I," "we," and "you." *Journal of Adolescent and Adult Literacy, 56*(4), 45–55.

Gross, P. A. (2010). Not another trend: Secondary-level literacy coaching. *Clearing House, 83*, 133–137.

Hall, G. E., & Hord, S. M. (1987). *Change in schools: Facilitating the process.* Albany: State University of New York Press.

Hall, G. E., & Hord, S. M. (2006). *Implementing change: Patterns, principles, and potholes* (2nd ed.). Boston: Allyn & Bacon.

Hoffman, J. V. (1979). The Intra-Act Procedure for critical reading. *Journal of Reading, 22*(7), 605–608.

Hoffman, J. (1992). Critical reading/thinking across the curriculum: Using I-charts to support learning. *Language Arts, 69*(2), 121–127.

Hord, S. M., & Tobia, E. F. (2012). *Reclaiming our teaching profession: The power of educators learning in community.* New York: Teachers College Press.

International Reading Association. (2006). *Standards for middle and high school literacy coaches.* Newark, DE: Author.

Ippolito, J., & Lieberman, J. (2012). Reading specialists and literacy coaches in secondary schools. In R. M. Bean & A. S. Dagen (Eds.), *Best practices of literacy leaders: Keys to school improvement* (pp. 63–85). New York: Guilford Press.

Keene, E. O., & Zimmermann, S. (2007). *Mosaic of thought: The power of comprehension strategy instruction* (2nd ed.). Portsmouth, NH: Heinemann.

Kerr, L. A. N. (1999). The Mexicans in Chicago. *Illinois History Teacher, 6*(2), 62–75.

Killion, J. (2009). Coaches' roles, responsibilities, and reach. In J. Knight (Ed.), *Coaching: Approaches and perspectives* (pp. 7–28). Thousand Oaks, CA: Corwin Press.

Killion, J. (2010, December). Reprising coaching heavy and coaching light. *Learning Forward*, pp. 8–9.

Kirmes, J. (2009). Independence is the greatest gift I can give: Using the gradual release of responsibility framework. In S. Plaut (Ed.), *The right to literacy in secondary schools: Creating a culture of thinking* (pp. 152–164). New York: Teachers' College Press.

Knight, J. (2009). What can we do about teacher resistance? *Phi Delta Kappan, 90*(7), 508–513.

Knowles, M. S. (1970). *The modern practice of adult education: Andragogy versus pedagogy.* New York: Association Press.

Knowles, M. S., Holton, E. F., & Swanson, R. A. (2005). *The adult learner* (6th ed.). Burlington, MA: Elsevier.

Kral, C. (2007). Principal support for literacy coaches [Literacy Coaching Clearinghouse Brief]. Retrieved from *www.literacycoachingonline.org/briefs/PrincipalSupportFinal3-22-07.pdf.*

L'Allier, S., Elish-Piper, L., & Bean, R. M. (2010). What matters for elementary literacy coaching? Guiding principles for instructional improvement and student achievement. *Reading Teacher, 63*(7), 544–554.

L'Allier, S. K., & Elish-Piper, L. (2012a). Literacy coaches in elementary schools. In R. M. Bean & A. S. Dagen (Eds.), *Best practices of literacy leaders: Keys for school improvement* (pp. 43–62). New York: Guilford Press.

L'Allier, S. K., & Elish-Piper, L. (2012b). *The literacy coaching series* [DVD]. Elburn, IL: LearnSure.

Lassonde, C. A., & Tucker, K. C. (2014). *Literacy leadership handbook: Best practices for developing literacy communities.* Boston: Pearson.

Learning Forward. (2010, December). Key points in Learning Forward's definition of professional development. *Journal of Staff Development, 31*(6), 16–17.

Lee, C. D., & Spratley, A. (2010). *Reading in the disciplines: The challenges of adolescent literacy.* New York: Carnegie Corporation of New York.

Leithwood, K., Seashore-Louis, K. S., Anderson, S., & Wahlstrom, K. (2004). *How leadership influences student learning.* Minneapolis: University of Minnesota, Center for Applied Research and Educational Improvement.

Lipton, L., & Wellman, B. (2007). How to talk so teachers listen. *Educational Leadership, 65*(1), 30–34.

Little, M. E., & Dieker, L. (2009). Co-teaching: Two are better than one. *Principal Leadership, 9*(8), 42–46.

Manderino, M. (2012). Disciplinary literacy in new literacies environments: Expanding the intersections of literate practice for adolescents. In P. J. Dunston, S. King Fullerton, C. C. Bates, K. Headley, & P. M. Stecker (Eds.), *61st yearbook of the Literacy Research Association* (pp. 69–83). Oak Creek, WI: Literacy Research Association.

Manderino, M., Johns, J. L., & Berglund, R. L. (2014). *Content area learning: Bridges to disciplinary literacy.* Dubuque, IA: Kendall Hunt.

Manderino, M., & Wickens, C. M. (2014). Addressing disciplinary literacy in the Common Core State Standards. *Illinois Reading Council Journal, 42*(2), 28–39.

Martin-Hansen, L. (2002). Defining inquiry: Exploring the many types of inquiry in the science classroom. *Science Teacher, 69*(2), 34–37.

Matsumura, L. C., Sartoris, M., Bickel, D. D., & Garnier, H. E. (2009). Leadership for literacy coaching: The principal's role in launching a new coaching program. *Educational Administration Quarterly, 45*(5), 655–693.

McConachie, S., Hall, M., Resnick, L., Ravi, A. K., Bill, V. L., Bintz, J., et al. (2006). Task, text, and talk: Literacy for all subjects. *Educational Leadership, 64*(2), 8–14.

McConachie, S. M., & Petrosky, A. R. (Eds.). (2010). *Content matters.* San Francisco: Jossey-Bass.

McKenna, M. C., & Walpole, S. (2008). *The literacy coaching challenge: Models and methods for grades K–8.* New York: Guilford Press.

McTighe, J., & Wiggins, G. (2013). *Essential questions: Opening doors to student understanding.* Alexandria, VA: ASCD.

Moje, E. B. (2007). Developing socially just subject-matter instruction: A review of the literature on disciplinary literacy teaching. *Review of Research in Education, 31*, 1–44.

Moje, E. B. (2008). Foregrounding the disciplines in high school literacy teaching and learning: A call for change. *Journal of Adolescent and Adult Literacy, 52*, 96–107.

Moje, E. B. (2009). Standpoints: A call for new research on new and multi-literacies. *Research in the Teaching of English, 43*(4), 348–352.

Monte-Sano, C., & De La Paz, S. (2012). Using writing tasks to elicit adolescents' historical reasoning. *Journal of Literacy Research, 44*(3), 273–299.

Moran, M. C. (2007). *Differentiated literacy coaching: Scaffolding for student and teacher success.* Alexandria, VA: ASCD.

Morris, E. (2003). The fog of war: Eleven lessons from the life of Robert S. McNamara. New York: Sony Pictures Classics. (Clips available for viewing at *www. sonyclassics. com/fogofwar.*)

National Center for Education Statistics. (2010). *The nation's report card: Grade 12 reading and mathematics 2009 national and pilot state results* (NCES 2011–455). Washington, DC: U.S. Department of Education Institute of Education Sciences.

National Council for the Social Studies. (2013). *The College, Career, and Civic Life (C3) Framework for Social Studies State Standards: Guidance for enhancing the rigor of K–12 civics, economics, geography, and history.* Silver Spring, MD: Author.

National Governors Association Center for Best Practices and Council of Chief State School Officers. (2010). *Common Core State Standards for English language arts and literacy in history/social studies, science, and technical subjects.* Washington, DC: Author.

NGSS Lead States. (2013). *Next Generation Science Standards: For states, by states.* Washington, DC: National Academies Press.

Nokes, J. D. (2008). The Observation/Inference Chart: Improving students' abilities to make inferences while reading nontraditional texts. *Journal of Adolescent and Adult Literacy, 51*(7), 538–546.

Pearson, P. D., & Gallagher, M. C. (1983). The instruction of reading comprehension. *Contemporary Educational Psychology, 8,* 317–344.

RAND Reading Study Group. (2002). *Reading for understanding: Toward a research and development program in reading comprehension.* Santa Monica, CA: Office of Education Research and Improvement.

Reeves, A. (2011). *Where great teaching begins: Planning for thinking and student learning.* Alexandria, VA: ASCD.

Reeves, D. B. (Ed.). (2007). *Ahead of the curve: The power of assessment to transform teaching and learning.* Bloomington, IN: Solution Tree Press.

Reisman, A. (2012a). The "document-based lesson": Bringing disciplinary inquiry into high school history classrooms with adolescent struggling readers. *Journal of Curriculum Studies, 44*(2), 233–264.

Reisman, A. (2012b). Reading like a historian: A document-based history curriculum intervention in urban high schools. *Cognition and Instruction, 33*(1), 86–112.

Schmidt, B., & Buckley, M. (1991). Plot relationships chart. In J. M. Macon, D. Bewell, & M. Vogt (Eds.), *Responses to literature: Grades K–8* (pp. 7–8). Newark, DE: International Reading Association.

Shanahan, C. (2009). Disciplinary comprehension. In S. E. Israel & G. G. Duffy (Eds.), *Handbook of research on reading comprehension* (pp. 240–260). New York: Routledge.

Shanahan, C. (2015). *ILA E-ssentials: Literacy practices that adolescents deserve: Disciplinary literacy strategies in content area classrooms.* Newark, DE: International Literacy Association.

Shanahan, C., Shanahan, T., & Misischia, C. (2011). Analysis of expert readers in three disciplines: History, mathematics, and chemistry. *Journal of Literacy Research, 43*(4), 393–429.

Shanahan, T., & Shanahan, C. (2008). Teaching disciplinary literacy to adolescents: Rethinking content-area literacy. *Harvard Educational Review, 78,* 40–59.

Shanahan, T., & Shanahan, C. (2012). What is disciplinary literacy and why does it matter? *Topics in Language Disorders, 32*(1), 7–18.

Short, K. G., Harste, J. C., & Burke, C. (1996). *Creating classrooms for authors and inquirers* (2nd ed.). Portsmouth, NH: Heinemann.

Shulman, L. S. (1986). Those who understand: Knowledge growth in teaching. *Educational Researcher, 15*(2), 4–14.

Snow, C., Ippolito, J., & Schwartz, R. (2006). What we know and what we need to know about literacy coaches in middle and high schools: A research synthesis and proposed research agenda. In International Reading Association, *Standards for middle and high school literacy coaches* (pp. 35–49). Newark, DE: International Reading Association.

Sturtevant, E. G. (2003). *The literacy coach: A key to improving teaching and learning in secondary schools.* Washington, DC: Alliance for Excellent Education.

Sweeney, D. (2013). *Student-centered coaching at the secondary level.* Thousand Oaks, CA: Corwin.

Templeton, S., Johnston, F., Bear, D. R., & Invernizzi, M. (2010). *Vocabulary their way: Word study with middle and secondary students*. New York: Pearson.

Tierney, R. J., & Readence, J. E. (2005). *Reading strategies and practices: A compendium* (6th ed.). Boston: Pearson.

Tofade, T., Elsner, J., & Haines, S. T. (2013). Best practice strategies for effective use of questions as a teaching tool. *American Journal of Pharmaceutical Education, 77*(7), 155.

Toll, C. A. (2004). Separating coaching from supervising. *English Leadership Quarterly, 27*(2), 5–7.

Toll, C. A. (2005). *The literacy coach's survival guide: Essential questions and practical answers*. Newark, DE: International Reading Association.

Toll, C. A. (2014). *The literacy coach's survival guide* (2nd ed.). Newark, DE: International Reading Association.

Townsend, D. (2015). Who's using the language? Supporting middle school students with content-area academic language. *Journal of Adolescent and Adult Literacy, 58*(5), 376–387.

Vacca, R. T., Vacca, J. A. L., & Mraz, M. E. (2005). *Content area reading: Literacy and learning across the curriculum*. Boston: Allyn & Bacon.

Vogt, M., & Shearer, B. A. (2011). *Reading specialists and literacy coaches in the real world* (3rd ed.). Boston: Pearson.

Wiggins, G. P., & McTighe, J. (2005). *Understanding by design*. Alexandria, VA: ASCD.

Wilson, A. A. (2011). A social semiotics framework for conceptualizing content area literacies. *Journal of Adolescent and Adult Literacy, 54*(6), 435–444.

Wineburg, S. S. (1991). Historical problem solving: A study of the cognitive processes used in evaluation of documentary and pictorial evidence. *Journal of Educational Psychology, 83*(1), 73–87.

Zygouris-Coe, V. (2012). Disciplinary literacy and the Common Core State Standards. *Topics in Language Disorders, 32*(1), 35–50.

Index